COLLOQUIAL
JAPANESE

THE COLLOQUIAL SERIES

*Accompanying cassette available

COLLOQUIAL
JAPANESE

H. D. B. Clarke
and
Motoko Hamamura

R
Routledge
London and New York

First published in 1981
Reprinted in 1987
Reprinted (with corrections and index) 1989
by Routledge
11 New Fetter Lane, London EC4P 4EE
29 West 35th Street, New York, NY 10001

British Library Cataloguing in Publication Data

Clarke, H D B

Colloquial Japanese.
1. Japanese language – Grammar
I. Title   II. Hamamura, Motoko
495.6'8'2421   PL535   80-41562
ISBN 0-415-04544-4
ISBN 0-415-04740-4 (cassette)
ISBN 0-415-04741-2 (book and cassette course)

CONTENTS

PREFACE

There are some excellent Japanese courses now available. Most of these, however, are designed for intensive instruction with trained teachers over several years of study. Consequently they introduce grammatical features at a relatively slow rate. It is hoped this entirely new edition of *Colloquial Japanese* will meet the need of students, whether self-taught or taking formal courses in the language, who require an overall understanding of spoken Japanese within a relatively short period. The book is based on the assumption that fluency in a language can be achieved only through the acquisition of the basic grammatical framework. This does not necessarily mean the rote learning of grammatical tables. Here the grammatical points are introduced in simple dialogues and are reinforced and tested in the exercises. The student with little interest in grammar should be able to acquire the basic grammar of the language by memorizing the dialogues. On the other hand, it is hoped the book might also be useful as a handy practical reference grammar, even for students who have achieved a degree of fluency in Japanese.

The treatment of grammar incorporates a number of new ideas, which should make the learning of the language easier.

I hope in some small way this book might help to spread a knowledge of one of the world's major languages and lead to a better understanding of Japan and the Japanese.

Hugh Clarke

INTRODUCTION

Japanese has the reputation of being a difficult language. Much of this difficulty stems from the cumbersome writing system which combines well over 2,000 Chinese characters with two separate native Japanese syllabaries. (The syllabaries, *hiragana* and *katakana*, can be learnt with little effort and are included in a chart at the back of this book.) In other respects Japanese is not particularly difficult to learn. The relatively simple pronunciation makes it possible to produce perfectly understandable sentences after the first few hours' study.

There is no need to worry about gender and number and the inflections of the verb are far fewer than in most European languages. With sustained application you can achieve a surprising degree of fluency in basic conversation in a short time.

The aim of this book is to give the reader studying by himself or with a teacher a good grounding in spoken Japanese and to enable him to communicate in most simple everyday situations.

HOW TO USE THIS BOOK

Always bear in mind that this book does not enable you to read or write Japanese. For that reason the romanized text should be regarded as a memory aid to help you to pronounce Japanese sentences correctly and to recognize them when you hear them spoken. As far as possible you should adopt the oral method, reading the dialogues and exercises aloud, then trying to reproduce them from memory. After you have done the exercises orally you may write down your answers to check them with the key at the back of the book.

Each lesson consists of four sections: the Japanese text, explanation of points of grammar, vocabulary and exercises. The text is in turn divided into a section on greetings and other useful expressions, six sentences illustrating the most important grammatical patterns introduced in the lesson and, finally, a number of short dialogues based on these sentence patterns. The 'useful expressions' should be learnt by heart without paying too much attention to their grammatical structure. Before proceeding to the grammar you should read through the sentence patterns and dialogues, aloud if your surroundings permit it, and, by comparing the Japanese with the English translation, see what you can deduce yourself about the points of grammar they contain. Then read the grammar notes carefully. Now return to the text and try to commit the questions and responses of the dialogues to memory. To help you test yourself the Japanese and English are arranged on facing pages and the dialogues are arranged with A on one side of the page and B on the other. First test whether you can put the Japanese into English. Then cover the Japanese equivalents for the English sentences. Next cover the 'B' side of the page to see if you can give correct Japanese responses to A's questions, and finally cover A and see if you can provide the questions which result in B's replies. By repeating these steps several times you should be able to remember most of the dialogues and internalize the grammatical patterns they contain. Now re-read the grammar and study the vocabulary list before going on to the exercises. You will probably find it more useful to learn the new words in sentences than as items in a list. With the transformation and substitution exercises make sure you also understand the meaning of each sentence before going on to the next. The vocabularies at the end of each lesson are intended to help you learn the new words introduced in the lesson. Where possible they have been arranged into rough sequence based on their meanings and grammatical function (nouns, adjectives, verbs, adverbs, particles and so on). When learning new vocabulary you may find it helpful to combine two or three words at a time into a simple sentence. To find the meaning of Japanese words used in this book it is quicker to use the alphabetically arranged vocabulary at the back of the book. As it is impossible to predict what words you will need in actual conversation, you will also need to provide yourself with a good romanized dictionary. Make sure that not only the main entries, but also the example sentences are fully romanized. It is worth paying a little extra to get a dictionary which gives examples in both romanization and Japanese script, such as Takahashi's *Romanized English–Japanese, Japanese–English Dictionary*.

A cassette has been produced to accompany this book so that you can hear Japanese spoken by native speakers. All material on the cassette is marked by a ■ in the text.

■ PRONUNCIATION

This book uses a modification of the Hepburn system of romanization, which, having roughly 'consonants as in English and vowels as in Italian', is the most practical for English speakers. In addition two diacritics, explained below, have been added to indicate the Japanese pitch accent and the devoicing of certain vowels. As the diacritics are to help you achieve a correct pronunciation and would not normally be used in writing romanized Japanese, they are not used in the exercises or the key to the exercises. The following descriptions are based on British English.

The vowels

Short vowels

a   Somewhere between the 'a' in cat and the 'u' in cut.
    Like the vowel in French *chat*.
e   As in English 'get'.
i   Like the 'ee' in 'see', but shorter like the vowel in 'sit'.
o   Like the 'au' in 'taught' but shorter like the vowel in 'hot'.
u   The tongue position is close to that for the vowel in 'put' but the lips are spread not rounded. Pull the corners of the mouth back slightly when pronouncing this vowel.

The long vowels

In addition to the simple vowels above Japanese also has long vowels, indicated by double letters in this romanization. The long vowels are pronounced as a single unbroken sound twice the length of the short vowels. Failure to distinguish between long and short vowels is one of the most common faults made by foreign students of Japanese. At times it can have disastrous effects. Consider the difference between *komon*, 'advisor', and *koomon*, 'anus'.

When two or more vowels come together in sequence each retains its original pronunciation. The diphthongs are pronounced without a break in the middle, as a single sound, but they are longer than the simple short vowels. The following English equivalents provide a rough guide only.

ai Something like '*eye*' (in Scottish English)

oi Something like '*oy*' in b*oy*.

ei This combination is usually pronounced in the same way as the long vowel *ee*. It is like northern English pronunciation in words like 'great', 'mate', etc.

ui A combination of *u* and *i* which has no equivalent in English. A bit like the diphthong in the French pronunciation of the Christian name, Louis, but without the lip-rounding.

au Something like the '*ow*' in c*ow*.

ou Similar to the vowel in *owe*.

ae This combination does not occur in English. It is simply a sequence of *a* and *e*. In rapid speech it is often pronounced the same as *ai*.

oe No English equivalent, *o* plus *e* each given its full original value.

ue *u* and *e*. In rapid speech something like *we* in *we*nt.

uo *u* plus *o*. In rapid speech something like *wa* in *wa*lk.

The consonants

p As in English *p*at.

b As in English *b*at.

t As in English *t*op.

d As in English *d*ay.

k As in English *c*at.

g At the beginning of a word, as in *g*ot; in the middle of a word, like the *ng* in si*ng*er, but many speakers pronounce it like the *g* in '*g*ot' in all positions.

ch As in English *ch*urch, but for many speakers with the tip of the tongue down behind the lower front teeth.

j As in English *j*u*dg*e, but for many speakers with the tip of the tongue against the lower front teeth.

ts As in English ca*ts*. This sound often occurs at the beginning of a word in Japanese and requires practice.

s As in English *s*ee.

z As in English *z*oo. Many people pronounce this sound like the *ds* in English car*ds* at the beginning of a word and like z in zoo elsewhere.

f This differs slightly from English *f*. Instead of the lower lip touching the upper teeth as in English the sound is made by the air escaping between the narrow slit between the lips. It is like the sound we make when blowing out a candle. In Japanese *f* occurs only before *u* (except that in certain loanwords from English some speakers manage to pronounce it before other vowels, e.g. *fa*n or *fua*n).

h Before *a*, *e* and *o*, like the *h* in English '*h*at'; before *i*, like the *ch* in German *Ich*.

n This sound has a number of pronunciations in Japanese depending on its position in the word. Before a vowel, as in English *no*; at the end of a word (note this is the only consonant in Japanese which can occur at the end of a word or syllable) it is usually pronounced somewhere between the final '*n*' in 'ma*n*' and the '*ng*' in 'sa*ng*'. Try pronouncing 'man' without touching the tip of the tongue against the roof of the mouth. It is a 'syllabic consonant', which means it constitutes a syllable on its own and is longer than the other consonant sounds. In English we often pronounce words like 'dozen' with a syllabic 'n' at the end. Some Japanese hardly pronounce the n at the end of a word at all. They simply nasalize and lengthen the preceding vowel. At the end of a syllable: *n* is pronounced as in *n* when it is followed by *n*, *t*, *d*, *s*, *z*, *r*, *w*; *n* is pronounced like *ng* in si*ng*er or the *n* in si*n*k when it is followed by *k* or *g* (remember in this case *g* would probably also be pronounced like *ng* in si*ng*er); *n* is pronounced like *m* when it is followed by *p*, *b* or *m*.

m   As in English *m*an.

y   As in English *y*ou. This sound combines with other consonants:

    ky is as in English *cue* or *queue*;

    py as in *pew*ter, *my* as in *mu*se, etc.

r   This sound does not occur in English. In fact the Japanese themselves pronounce the sound in several different ways. To our ears the Japanese r sometimes sounds like an *l* or even a *d*. The sound is made by tapping the tip of the tongue against the gum ridge behind the upper front teeth. The tip of the tongue is curled up slightly and is flapped forward as it comes into contact with the gum ridge. You can achieve something of the effect by trying to pronounce an English '*r*' as in '*r*at' at the same time putting the tip of your tongue in the position for pronouncing 'd'.

w   Like the *w* in *w*alk but with the corners of the mouth pulled back.

Double consonants

The double consonants *pp*, *tt*, *tts*, *tch*, *ss*, *ssh*, *kk*, *nn* and *nm* (pronounced '*mm*') have twice the duration of their single counterparts. When the first element is a stop, *p*, *t* or *k*, the articulation is begun, then held for a syllable beat, before being released as the second element of the double (or long) consonant. Double consonants occur in Italian and can be heard in English at word boundaries as in 'about time', 'take care'. Failure to distinguish between single and double (or short and long) consonants is a common mistake among foreign speakers of Japanese. Contrast *kata*, 'shoulder'; *katta*, 'won'; *bata*, 'butter'; *batta*, 'grasshopper'; *kakoo*, 'let's write'; *kakkoo*, 'shape, appearance'.

Devoicing of vowels

The close vowels *i* and *u* are often devoiced, that is whispered, when they occur between voiceless consonants or after a voiceless consonant and before a pause. The voiceless consonants are *p*, *f*, *t*, *ts*, *ch*, *s*, *sh*, *k* and *h*. In this book, except in the exercises, this devoicing is indicated by an oblique through the devoiced vowel, e.g. *kɩ̸kimasɩ̸*, 'to hear'; *desɩ̸*, 'is'; *kakɩ̸ to*, 'whenever I write'. The *ɩ̸* in *desɩ̸* and the ending *-masɩ̸* tends to be replaced by a slight lengthening of the preceding *-s-* not only before a pause but also before the sentence final particle *ne*, 'isn't it so that . . . ?'

The apostrophe

In the romanization used here an apostrophe is used to separate a syllabic *n* from a following vowel. This is to avoid confusion with syllable-initial *n* which is pronounced differently. Compare *tán'i*, 'a unit', and *taní*, 'valley'. The former has three syllables, the latter two. In *tán'i* the *n* is held for the duration of one syllable beat and the *i* is pronounced as a separate syllable, often preceded by a slight *y* glide-sound, something like *tánn*^{y}*i*. This *y* glide is heard often between a syllabic *n* and a following *e* and less commonly between syllabic *n* and *i*; *san'en*, 'three yen', is pronounced *sann*^{y}*en*; *kin'en*, 'no smoking', is *kinn*^{y}*en* and so on. Where the following vowel is *o* the glide-sound is *w*; *san'oku*, 'three hundred million', is something like *sann*^{w}*oku* and *hón o yómu*, 'read a book', is *hónn*^{w}*o yómu*. The glides have been written above the line to indicate they are not given the full, definite pronunciation of the consonants *y* and *w*. The apostrophe is also used to mark the syllable boundary between long and short varieties of the same vowel when they occur in sequence, e.g. *soo'on*, 'noise'.

Pitch

Japanese employs high and low pitch to group syllables into words and phrases much as English uses stress. In this book the pitch accent is indicated by the acute accent ´. A word and the following particles or suffixes together form an accent-phrase. The accent-phrase may be unaccented (i.e. may have no syllable with an acute accent) or may have one accented syllable. The first syllable of the accent-phrase is pronounced on a low pitch unless it carries the accent mark. In an accent-phrase the syllable bearing the accent mark carries a high pitch, all syllables preceding it, except the first, are also high-pitched and all syllables after the accented syllable are low-pitched. The following examples should make the situation clearer.

1 Unaccented phrase: *kodomo ga*, 'the child' (as subject), is pronounced *ko^{domoga}* (low, high, high, high).

2 Accented phrase (a) Initial accent: *áni ga*, 'elder brother' (as subject), is pronounced *^{a}niga* (high, low, low); (b) Medial accent: *otokónoko ga*, 'the boy' (as subject), is pronounced *o^{toko}nokoga* (low, high, high, low, low, low).

Sometimes words which are pronounced the same in isolation have a different pronunciation within an accent-phrase. This difference is marked in the vocabularies by an acute accent on the final syllable. For example, *hana*, 'nose', and *haná*, 'flower', are both pronounced *ha^{na}* when no particle follows, but within the longer accent phrases, *hana ga* and *haná ga*, the distinction between 'nose' and 'flower' is clear: *ha$^{naga\ akai}$* ('his nose is red') contrasts with *ha^{na}ga akai* ('the flower is red'). The behaviour of the pitch-accent in sentences is too complicated to introduce in detail at this stage. Some of the rules governing the pitch-accent will be given at the relevant points in the following lessons. Here it should be sufficient to say that many sentences have more than one possible pitch-accent. In slow, deliberate speech each accent-phrase may be given its full pitch value, but in rapid speech accent-phrases are often run together, with only the first receiving its full value. For example, the *haná ga akai* introduced above consists of two accent-phrases, *haná ga*, 'the flower' (as subject), and *akai*, 'is red'. In extremely slow speech this might be pronounced *ha^{na}ga a^{kai}* with each accent-phrase being assigned its full pitch value. In natural speech, however, it is more likely to be pronounced *ha^{na} ga akai* as a single-accent phrase dominated by the first accented syllable.

In the dialogues in this book the aim has been to indicate clear yet natural Japanese pronunciation. If you find it difficult to hear or reproduce pitch distinctions you may disregard the accent marks altogether. There is much regional variation in the pitch patterns of Japanese and context will usually make your meaning clear. You should try, however, to avoid the strong stress, particularly on the first syllable, so common in English and keep your Japanese on a level pitch giving the same emphasis to each syllable.

Practise pronouncing the following Japanese words.

Short vowels

Yokohama, *Nagásaki*, *Hiroshima*, *Tanaka*, *Tóyota*, *Suzuki*, *Yamaha*, *karate*, *ikébana* ('flower arrangement'), *tsunami* ('tidal wave'), *sakura* ('cherry blossom'), *sashimí* ('raw fish'), *orígami* ('paper-folding')

Long vowels

Tookyoo, *Oosaka*, *Kyóoto*, *Kyúushuu*, *Kátoo*, *Sátoo*, *Oohira*, *Tooshiba*, *júudoo* ('judo'), *su̧moo* ('Japanese wrestling'), *noo* ('Noh theatre')

Devoiced vowels

su̧kiyaki (a beef dish), *su̧shí* ('vinegared rice with fish'), *ki̧kú* ('chrysanthemum'), *shi̧ka* ('deer'), *désu̧* ('is'), *Tsu̧chida*, *Chi̧kámatsu*

Vowel sequences

aikídoo ('a martial art'), *taifúu* ('typhoon'), *samurai* ('warrior'), *kói* ('carp'), *oishii* ('delicious'), *kírei* ('beautiful'), *atsúi* ('hot')

Syllabic n

én ('yen'), *Nihón* ('Japan'), *kéndoo* ('Japanese fencing'), *bonsai* ('miniature trees'), *banzái* ('long live!'); in the following *n* is pronounced *ng*: *ringo* ('apple'), *bonkei* ('tray landscape'), *Nihón kara* ('from Japan'); in the following *n* is pronouned *m*: *shinbun* ('newspaper'), *kanpai* ('cheers!'), *konban wa* ('good evening') (only the first *n* pronounced *m*), *Nihón mo* ('Japan too')

Double consonants

Nippón ('Japan') (more formal pronunciation), *Hokkáidoo*, *Níkkoo*, *Sapporo*, *seppu̧ku* (ritual suicide – 'harakiri'), *Hattori*, *kappa* ('river goblin')

Consonants followed by y

kyúuri ('cucumber'), *kyóo* ('today'), *kyaku* ('guest'), *ikkyuu* ('first class'), *ryokan* (Japanese inn), *Ryuukyúu*, *kairyoo* ('improvement')

Pronunciation of words of foreign origin

Japanese has borrowed a large number of foreign words, mostly from English, and has incorporated them into its sound system. It is important to pronounce these words of foreign origin as if they were Japanese words, closely following the romanization. Pronouncing these words as they are in English is one of the most common mistakes English-speakers make when speaking Japanese. Due to the phonetic structure of Japanese and the syllabic nature of the writing system it is not possible to produce consonant sequences (except where the first consonant is *n*, or the sequence is a double consonant). For this reason foreign words taken into Japanese often have more syllables than the originals. Practise the following:

náifu ('knife'), *fóoku* ('fork'), *supúun* ('spoon'), *sooséeji* ('sausage'), *garasu* ('glass' – the substance; window glass etc.), *gúrasu* (a drinking glass), *bíiru* ('beer'), *uísukii* ('whisky'), *teeburu* ('table').

DÁI ÍKKA

■ **BÉNRI NA HYOOGEN**

Ohayoo gozaimásу̣.   Oyasumi nasái.
Konnichi wa.   (Dóomo) arígatoo gozaimasу̣.

Konban wa.   Dóo itashimashị̣te.

BUNKEI

Ikimásу̣.   Ikimasén.
Kinoo ikimáshị̣ta.   Ikimasén deshị̣ta.
Ashị̣ta ikimásу̣ ka.   Ikimashóo.

■ **KAIWA**

1 A: Tanaka san.   B: Hái.
   A: Owarimáshị̣ta ka.   B: Hái, owarimáshị̣ta.
   A: Jáa, kaerimashóo ka.   B: Ée, soo shimashóo.

2 A: Wakarimáshị̣ta   B: Iie, wakarimasén deshị̣ta.
      ka.
   A: Déwa, yukkúri hana-   B: Ée, wakarimásу̣.
      shimasу̣.
      Íma wakarimásу̣ ka.   Arígatoo gozaimashị̣ta.

3 A: Ashị̣ta irasshaimásу̣ ka.   B: Iie, ikimasén.
   A: Déwa mata asátte   B: Sayonara.
      aimashoo. Sayoonara.

4 A: Tabemáshị̣ta ka.   B: Ie, máda tabemasen.
   A: Jáa, issho ni tabemasén   B: Hái, issho ni tabemashóo.
      ka.

5 A: Dóomo arígatoo   B: Dóo itashimashị̣te.
      gozaimashị̣ta.
   A: Sayonara.   B: Mata ashị̣ta.

6 A: Íma shimasу̣ ka.   B: Shimasén. Áto de shimasу̣.

12

LESSON ONE

USEFUL EXPRESSIONS

Good morning.
Hello, good day, good
  afternoon.
Good evening.

Good night (before retiring).
Thank you [very much].

Not at all, Don't mention it.

SENTENCE PATTERNS

[I] go.
[I] went yesterday.
[Am I, is he, etc.] going
  tomorrow?

[I] don't go.
[I] did not go.
Let's go.

CONVERSATIONS

1 A: Mr Tanaka!   B: Yes.
   A: Have you finished?   B: Yes, I have.
   A: Well then, shall we go   B: Yes, let's do that.
         home?

2 A: Did you understand?   B: No, I didn't.
   A: Then I'll speak slowly.   B: Yes, I do. Thank you.
         Do you understand now?

3 A: Are you going   B: No, I'm not.
         tomorrow?
   A: Then I'll see you again   B: Goodbye.
         the day after
         tomorrow. Goodbye.

4 A: Have you eaten?   B: No, I haven't eaten yet.
   A: Won't you eat with me   B: Yes, let's eat together.
         then?

5 A: Thank you very much.   B: Don't mention it.
   A: Goodbye.   B: I'll see you again tomorrow.

6 A: Will you do it now?   B: No, I'll do it later.

7   A: Ítsu irasshaimashịta ka.   B: Kinoo kimáshịta.
    A: Ítsu kaerimasɥ ka.   B: Raishuu kaerimásɥ.

    A: Jáa, mata ashịta   B: Ée, ashịta aimashóo.
       aimashóo   Sayonara.

7   A: When did you come?   B: I came yesterday.
    A: When are you returning   B: I'm going back next week.
       home?
    A: Then let's meet again   B: Yes, let's meet tomorrow.
       tomorrow.   Goodbye.

THE SIMPLE SENTENCE – VERB AND ADVERB

Adverb	Verb stem	Polite-address suffix	Tense, etc.: present + present − past + past − propositive	Question marker
kinoo	ai-		-u	
kyóo	hanashi-		-én	
ashɟta	iki-		-(hɟ)ta	
íma	irasshai-	-mas-	-én deshɟta	ka
áto de	ki-		-(h)óo*	
	shi-			
	tabe-			

+ indicates affirmative, − negative. *not used with irasshai-

This chart summarizes the sentence pattern introduced in this lesson. The adverb and question-marker categories are optional, but virtually all Japanese sentences contain at least one verb and verbs carry inflections which indicate the degree of politeness and the tense.

In English we use sentences like, Coming?, Hurry!, Stop! etc., but in Japanese, because it is usual to dispense with pronouns, there is much greater scope for sentences consisting of only a verb, or a verb preceded by an adverb or adverbial phrase. The verb is the kernel of the Japanese sentence. It occurs at the end of the sentence where it may be followed by a sentence-final particle like the question marker *ka* introduced in this lesson.

The Japanese verb carries no indication of number or person. *Hanashimásɟ*, for example, means 'I speak', 'you speak', 'he [or she] speaks', 'we speak' and 'they speak'. For this reason the English translation of a particular Japanese sentence depends largely on the context. The English glosses for the phrases and sentences given above are meant to be colloquial English equivalents in the given context and not necessarily literal translations of the Japanese.

The present tense, -más‍ɰ

In Japanese the present tense covers present and future action. *Ikimás‍ɰ* means 'go[es]' or 'will go'; *tabemás‍ɰ* means 'eat[s]' or 'will eat', and so on. For most Japanese verbs the *-más‍ɰ* ending refers to general truths and habitual actions, e.g. 'the sun sets in the west', 'I like bananas', 'I go to the office every day', etc., and to future actions, e.g. 'I shall meet you at two o'clock', 'he is going to Japan tomorrow', etc. With some verbs which describe a state rather than an action, the *-más‍ɰ* ending can refer to a single point of present time, as in conversation 2: *íma wakarimás‍ɰ ka*, 'do you understand now?' But with action verbs the *-más‍ɰ* ending cannot be used to describe actions actually in progress. *Íma hanashimas‍ɰ* does not mean 'I *am* speaking now', but 'I *shall* speak now'.

The polite style, -más-

The use of different styles of speech indicating varying degrees of politeness or respect towards persons addressed or referred to is a characteristic of the Japanese language which will be treated in some detail in a later chapter. The suffix *-más-* is used to indicate politeness to the person addressed. In general, this is the form used for all communication outside one's immediate family and circle of close friends. Foreigners are advised to stick to this form until they fully understand the social implications of the other speech styles.

Note that the verb *irasshaimás‍ɰ* (verbs are referred to in their present tense form) is an honorific verb indicating respect for the subject of the action, so it cannot be used for one's own actions. Its use often indicates a second person subject, e.g. *irasshaimás‍ɰ*, 'you go' or 'you come', but *ikimás‍ɰ*, 'I go'.

The past tense, -máshɿta

The suffix *-ta* is the marker of the past tense in Japanese. It combines with the polite suffix *-mas-* to form the polite past *-máshɿta* ending. *Ikimáshita*, 'I went'.

The present negative, -masén

The suffix -*más*- combines with the suffix -*n*, one of the ways of forming the negative in Japanese; to give the polite present negative ending -*masén. Ikimasén*, 'I do not go', 'I shall not go', etc.

The past negative, -masén deshịta

The past negative of the polite style is formed with the present negative and *déshịta*, the past tense of *désụ*, a verb introduced in Lesson Three. *Ikimasén deshịta*, 'I did not go'.

The propositive ending, -mashóo

This ending is used in making a suggestion of the type, 'let's . . .'; e.g., *ikimashóo*, 'let's go', *tabemashóo ka*, 'shall we eat?'. Note that as this construction always implies a first person subject it cannot be used with the honorific verb, *irasshaimásụ*.

The question marker, -ka

Statements are turned into questions simply by adding the sentence-final particle -*ka*, e.g. *aimáshịta ka*, 'did [you] meet [him]?' This particle may be pronounced with a low-level or high-level intonation, but this does not affect the intonation of the rest of the sentence. Be careful to avoid the rising and falling intonation of English questions.

It is also possible, though slightly more familiar in style, to indicate a question by a sharp rise in pitch on the final syllable of the verb, in which case the particle -*ka* is dropped, and the final -*u* of -*másu* is clearly pronounced. This kind of question is indicated in this book by the addition of the question mark.

NOTES

Ohayoo gozaimásụ is used until around 10.00 a.m., after which *konnichi wa* is used until dark, when *konban wa* (remember to pronounce it *komban* wa) is the usual greeting. *Oyasumi nasái* is used in the sense of 'good night', said before going to bed or saying goodbye late at night. It is not usual to attach a name to a greeting in

Japanese as we do in English – 'good morning, Mr Smith', etc.

(Dóomo) arígatoo gozaimasụ̀ is, in form, a verb and also often occurs in its past tense form *arígatoo gozaimashịta*. In the familiar style *arígatoo* 'thanks' or simply *dóomo* 'thanks' are often heard.

Conversation 1 San is a title of respect used after a Japanese name. It may occur after the family name or the given name. When the full Japanese name is used, the family name is placed first, and *san* follows the given name; e.g., *Tanaka san*, 'Mr/ Mrs/ Miss Tanaka'; *Taroo san* (given name), 'Taroo'; *Tanaka Taroo san*, 'Mr Taroo Tanaka'. As *san* is an honorific term it is never used with one's own name. It is rude when speaking Japanese to refer to someone without using *san* or some other title after his name. *Chan* is used instead of *san* after the names of children.

Conversation 4 The simple present-negative ending -*masén* is often used where we would say 'have not yet . . .' in English. There is, however, also a tendency to use another construction more closely resembling the English usage. This is introduced on p. 112.

VOCABULARY

aimásụ̀	to meet	*máda*	(not) yet
hanashimásụ̀	to talk	*ototoi*	day before
ikimásụ̀	to go		yesterday
irasshaimásụ̀	to go, to come	*kinoo*	yesterday
	(not first	*kyóọ*	today
	person)	*ashịta*	tomorrow
kaerimásụ̀	to return (home)	*asátte*	day after
kimásụ̀	to come		tomorrow
owarimásụ̀	to finish	*senshuu*	last week
shimásụ̀	to do	*konshuu*	this week
tabemásụ̀	to eat	*raishuu*	next week
wakarimásụ̀	to understand	*kyónen*	last year
íma	now	*kotoshi*	this year
áto de	later	*rainen*	next year
issho ni	together	*mata*	again
jáa, déwa	well then	*ítsu*	when
hái, ée	yes	*san*	Mr, Mrs, Miss
iie, ie*	no	*soo*	so, thus, like that

*The shorter form is slightly less formal.

*sayo(o)nará**	goodbye	*-máshįta*	*see* p. 17
-másų	*see* p. 17	*-masén deshįta*	*see* p. 18
-masén	*see* p. 18	*-mashóo*	*see* p. 18

EXERCISE 1

A Change as indicated in brackets:
1 Wakarimasu. (negative) 2 Ikimasen. (past) 3 Itsu irasshaimasu ka.
(past) 4 Kimasu. (negative) 5 Hanashimasen deshita. (present). 6
Shimasen. (affirmative) 7 Aimashita. (present) 8 Ikimashita. (hortative) 9 Kaerimasen. (affirmative) 10 Shimashita. (negative question)

B Substitute the word in brackets for the word in italics and make
other changes as the sense demands:
1 *Ashita* irasshaimasu ka (kinoo). 2 *Kinoo* shimashita (ato de). 3 *Ima*
kimashita (kyoo). 4 *Ato de* hanashimasu (kinoo). 5 *Kinoo* owarimashita (itsu). 6 *Ee*, wakarimasu (iie). 7 *Hai*, ikimashita (iie). 8 *Ima*
tabemasu (mada). 9 *Senshuu* kaerimashita (raishuu). 10 *Asatte*,
aimashoo (ototoi).

C Translate into English:
1 Ashita aimasu ka. 2 Ohayoo gozaimasu. 3 Itsu irasshaimasu ka. 4
Kinoo hanashimasen deshita. 5 Wakarimasen. 6 Konban wa. 7 Kyoo
kimasu. 8 Ikimasen deshita. 9 Konnichi wa. 10 Doomo arigatoo
gozaimashita.

D Translate into Japanese:
1 He is coming tomorrow. 2 I didn't see him yesterday. 3 Good
evening. 4 He did not talk about it. 5 Are you going tomorrow? 6 I did
not understand. 7 In that case I shall do it now. 8 We didn't finish
yesterday. 9 I shall be meeting him later. 10 I haven't eaten yet.

*The shorter form is slightly less formal.

DÁI NÍKA

■ **BÉNRI NA HYOOGEN**

Ikága desu̶ ka.
O-génki desu̶ ka.
O-kagesama de. Génki desu̶.

Sumimasén.
Dóozo.
Shi̶tsúrei shimasu̶.

BUNKEI

Ashi̶ta Tookyoo e ikimásu̶.
Bíiru o nomimashi̶ta.
Suzuki san ni hón o agemasu̶.

Tanaka san ni aimáshi̶ta ka.
Dóko de o-sake o kaimásu̶ ka.
Zasshi mo kaimáshi̶ta.

■ **KAIWA**

1 A: Shinbun o dóko de
yomimasu̶ ka.

   A: Kinoo kaisha e
irasshaimáshi̶ta ka.

   B: Máinichi kaisha de
yomimásu̶.

   B: Ée, kinoo mo ototói mo
ikimáshi̶ta.

2 A: Ashi̶ta kooen ni
ikimashóo ka.

   A: Jáa, éiga ni ikimashóo
ka.

   B: Ítsumo kooen ni ikimásu̶.

   B: Ée, sóo shimashóo.

3 A: Konogoro Abe san ni
aimasén né.

   A: Iie, máda kaerimasén
yo.

   B: Ée, móo Nihón e
kaerimashi̶ta ka.

4 A: Issho ni báa e
irasshaimasén ka.

   A: Náni o nomimashóo ka.

   B: Ée, kónban ikimashóo.

   B: Uísu̶kii o nomimashóo.

5 A: Shachoo ni tegami o
kakimáshi̶ta ka.

   A: Móo dashimáshi̶ta ka.

   B: Hái, kakimáshi̶ta.

   B: Hái, yuubínkyoku de
dashimáshi̶ta.

LESSON TWO

USEFUL EXPRESSIONS

How are you?

Are you well? How are you?

I'm very well, thank you.

I'm sorry.

Please.

Excuse me. I'm sorry. Goodbye.

SENTENCE PATTERNS

I'm going to Tokyo tomorrow.

I drank beer.

I'll give the book to Mr Suzuki.

Did you meet Mr Tanaka?

Where do you buy the sake?

I bought a magazine too.

CONVERSATIONS

1 A: Where do you read the newspaper?

   B: I read it at the company every day.

   A: Did you go to the office yesterday?

   B: Yes I went yesterday and the day before that too.

2 A: Shall we go to the park tomorrow?

   B: We always go to the park.

   A: Shall we go to a movie, then?

   B: Yes, let's do that.

3 A: We don't see Mr Abe these days, do we?

   B: You're right. Has he gone back to Japan already?

   A: No, he has not gone back yet.

4 A: Won't you come to a bar with me?

   B: Yes, let's go tonight.

   A: What shall we drink?

   B: Let's drink whisky.

5 A: Did you write a letter to the boss?

   B: Yes, I did.

   A: Have you posted it yet?

   B: Yes, I sent it at the post office.

6 A: Sh/tsúrei shimasψ.   B: Dóko e irasshaimasψ ka.
    A: Oosaka e ikimásψ.   B: Sayonara.

7 A: Dáre ni hón o agemasψ   B: Tanaka san ni agemásψ.
       ka.
    A: Kinoo ginkoo de Tanaka
       san ni aimásh/ta yo.

8 A: Nihongo o hanashimásψ   B: Iie, hanashimasén.
       ka.
    A: Wakarimásψ ka.   B: Sψkóshi wakarimásψ.

6 A: Excuse me, I must be   B: Where are you off to?
       going.

   A: I'm going to Osaka.   B: Goodbye.

7 A: Who will you give the   B: I'm giving it to Mr Tanaka.
       book to?

   A: I met Mr Tanaka in the
       bank yesterday, you
       know.

8 A: Do you speak Japanese?   B: No, I don't.

   A: Do you understand it?   B: A little.

1	2	3	4	5	6
					ka
				dashimáshịta	ka
			tegami o	dashimáshịta	ka
		shachoo ni	tegami o	dashimáshịta	ka
	yuubínkyoku de	shachoo ni	tegami o	dashimáshịta	ka
kinoo	yuubínkyoku de	shachoo ni	tegami o	dashimáshịta	ka
Time phrase	Place of action	Indirect object	Object	Verb	Part-icle
yesterday	post office at	director to	letter (obj.)	sent	?

This diagram represents a further expansion of the simple sentence introduced in Lesson One. The verb occupies column 5. Of course, the verb itself is made up of the stem, a polite address suffix and a tense suffix, but as this was dealt with in detail in the last lesson there is no need for further mention of it here. We also met columns 1 and 6 in Lesson One.

The verb in column 5 makes a perfectly good Japanese sentence by itself. It can occur in combination with any number of the categories represented in the other columns. The order of the elements preceding the verb is rather flexible, though the one given here is perhaps the most natural, neutral arrangement. The adverb is usually either first word in the sentence or in the position immediately preceding the verb. Words towards the beginning of the sentence tend to carry more emphasis. *Tegami o shachoo ni yuubínkyoku de kinoo dashimáshịta*, although a little unusual, is correct Japanese, emphasizing *tegami* and *shachoo* rather than *yuubínkyoku* and *kinoo*, 'I sent *the letter* to the *director* yesterday.'

You will notice that columns 2, 3 and 4 of the diagram consist of a noun followed by a particle showing the grammatical relationship of the noun to the rest of the sentence. These particles are similar in function to the prepositions like 'on', 'by', 'to', etc., used in English, but differ from prepositions inasmuch as they follow the nouns to which they refer. For this reason they are sometimes called 'postpositions'. They are pronounced with the preceding noun without a break in between. Any pause in the sentence will come after a particle, never before.

Before discussing the particles introduced in this lesson, a word about nouns. The Japanese noun presents the learner with none of the difficulties of number and gender found in European languages. *Tegami* means 'a letter', 'letters', 'the letter', 'the letters'.

THE PARTICLES

o   The object marker
This particle indicates that the noun preceding it is the direct object of the verb. That is, it tells us who or what the action of the verb is aimed against; e.g., *Sakana o tabemásu*, 'I eat fish.'

ni   The indirect object marker; 'to'
Ni is used after the person or thing to or for which the action of the verb is directed: *Tanaka san ni agemáshʃta*, 'I gave it to Mr Tanaka.'
Note, in Japanese the verb 'to meet', *aimásu*, takes an indirect object; e.g., *Shachoo ni aimáshʃta*, 'I met the director.'

de   The marker of the place where an action occurs; 'in', 'at'
When this particle occurs after a noun denoting a place it is equivalent to the English prepositions 'in' or 'at'. It indicates the place where an action occurs, but as we shall see later, it is not used with verbs which indicate existence or state. *Misé de zasshi o kaimáshʃta*, 'I bought the magazine in the shop.'

e   The marker of movement to or towards a place; 'to', 'towards'
This particle is used in conjunction with verbs of motion, such as *ikimásu*, *kimásu* and *irasshaimásu*; e.g., *Tookyoo e ikimásu*, 'I go to Tokyo.'
Note that *ni* is very often used in the same way as *e*: *Ítsu Nihón ni irasshaimáshʃta ka*, 'When did you come to Japan?'

mo   'Also', 'too', 'even'
This particle is used after nouns, including time phrases, and is equivalent to English 'too', 'also', 'even' etc. *O-sake mo nomimásu*, '[He] drinks sake, too.' *Kinóo mo ikimáshʃta*, 'I went yesterday too.'
Notice that *mo* replaces the object marker *o*, but follows the particles *de*, *e* and *ni*. *Tookyoo démo aimáshʃta*, '[I] met [him] in

Tokyo, too.' *Amerika émo irasshaimáshḷta ka*, 'Did you go to America too?' When *mo* combines with another particle it forms a kind of compound particle with an accented first syllable. For this reason they are written together in this book.

With a negative verb *mo* corresponds to English '[not] . . . either': *Tegami mo kakimasén*, '[I] don't write letters either.'

A mo B mo with an affirmative verb means 'both A and B' and with a negative verb, 'neither A nor B': *Tookyoo émo Yokohama émo ikimasén deshḷta*, 'I went to neither Tokyo nor Yokohama.'

né Sentence final particle, 'isn't it true that'

This particle, like the particle *ka* introduced in Lesson One, follows the main verb at the end of the sentence, unlike the particles above, which may be called case particles or phrase-final particles, because they form a phráse with the preceding noun.

Né is used when the speaker expects the person addressed to agree with him. It is very like the English, 'isn't he', 'don't you', 'didn't we', etc. which we so often tack on to our sentences. *Ototói irasshaimashḷta ne*, 'You arrived the day before yesterday, didn't you?'

yo Emphatic sentence-final particle

Yo is used to make an assertive, emphatic or exclamatory statement. It is sometimes equivalent to English, 'you know', or 'I'm sure' or simply an emphatic tone of voice. *Yo* can be pronounced either on a low pitch or with a rising pitch. *Moo owarimáshḷta yo*, 'It's already finished!' or 'It *has* finished'. As this is a rather assertive form, it should be used sparingly with superiors or people one does not know well.

NOTES

Useful expressions *O-kágesama de* really means something like 'thank you for asking' and can be used alone or with *génki desṳ* (which can also be used alone) in reply to either of the questions above. Notice that one cannot use the respectful prefix *o-* to refer to oneself. This prefix is used with a number of terms referring to food and drink as in *o-cha*, 'tea', and *o-sake*, 'sake', in this lesson. This latter usage has become conventionalized and the forms given with the *o-* prefix in the vocabularies should always be used with the prefix.

Sumimasén is also often used for 'thank you', particularly when giving thanks for a favour, hospitality, etc.

Dóozo is used when offering something or asking someone to go first.

Shitsúrei shimas̩, literally 'I am going to commit an incivility', is used in the sense of 'excuse me' when pushing past someone on a crowded train, or 'sorry to bother you' when interrupting a conversation, etc., or simply 'goodbye'. The past tense form means 'sorry to have bothered you'.

Conversation 3 Notice that Japanese uses *ée* where English would use 'no' to answer a negative question. This is because the basic meaning of *hái* and *ée* is 'what you said is true.' However, where the negative question is really a form of request or proposition as in Conversation 4, the Japanese usage follows the English.

VOCABULARY

agemás̩	to give (a re-spected person)	*yuubínkyoku*	post office
		éki	station
dashimás̩	to post; to put out	*kooen*	park
		báa	bar
kaimás̩	to buy	*éiga*	film; movie
kakimás̩	to write	*ítsumo*	always
nomimás̩	to drink	*kónban*	tonight
yomimás̩	to read	*konogoro*	these days; lately
Tookyoo	Tokyo	*máinichi*	every day
Yokohama	Yokohama	*móo*	already
Oosaka	Osaka	*s̩kóshi*	a little
Amerika	America	*dáre*	who?
Igiris̩	England	*dóko*	where?
Nihón	Japan	*náni*	what?
Nihongo	Japanese language	*hón*	book
		shinbun	newspaper
misé	shop	*zasshi*	magazine
kaisha	company; firm; office	*tegami*	letter
		shachoo	company director; boss
ginkoo	bank		

bíiru	beer	*e*	to (not indirect object)
o-cha	Japanese tea		
o-sake	sake, rice wine	*o*	object marker
uisuikii	whisky	*ni*	to (indirect object)
sakana	fish		
suikiyaki	beef and vegetable dish	*de*	in, at
		mo	too, also, even
		né	'isn't it true that . . . ?'
		yo	emphatic particle

EXERCISE 2

A Change as indicated in brackets:
1 Zasshi o yomimasu. (negative) 2 Kinoo kaimashita. (present) 3 Tegami o dashimashita. (negative) 4 Eiga e ikimasu. (negative past) 5 Shachoo ni agemasen deshita. (affirmative) 6 Nani o tabemasu ka. (past) 7 Dare ni agemasu ka. (hortative) 8 Hon o kakimasu. (negative question) 9 Mada wakarimasen. (affirmative) 10 Sukiyaki o tabemasu. (negative question)

B Substitute the word in brackets for the word in italics and make any changes the sense demands:
1 Kinoo zasshi *o* dashimashita (mo). 2 *Konogoro kooen* e ikimasu (senshuu, ginkoo). 3 Shachoo ni *uisukii* o agemashita (nani). 4 *Ashita* shinbun o kaimasu ka (kinoo). 5 Issho ni *baa* e ikimasu (doko). 6 *Ashita* dare ni aimasu ka (asatte). 7 *Raishuu tegami* o kakimasu (senshuu, nani). 8 *Kooen* de issho ni *tabemasu* (kaisha, hanashimasu). 9 Eki de *shinbun* o *kaimashita* (Suzuki san, aimashita). 10 *Konshuu* irasshaimasu (itsu).

C Translate into English:
1 Sumimasen. 2 Shitsurei shimasu. 3 Kotoshi mo issho ni Nihon e ikimasu. 4 Kinoo shinbun o yomimasen deshita. 5 Doko ni tegami o dashimashita ka. 6 Suzuki san ni nani o agemashoo ka. 7 Kooen de dare ni aimashita ka. 8 Itsu kaerimashita ka. 9 Konogoro baa de uisukii o nomimasen ne. 10 Mise de nani o kaimashoo ka.

D Translate into Japanese:

1 Please. 2 How are you? 3 I'm very well, thank you. 4 Have you finished your letter? 5 Has he come yet? 6 Where are you off to? 7 I spoke a little Japanese in Japan. 8 I don't understand. 9 I always met Mr Suzuki at the station. 10 Is Mr Abe coming too?

DÁI SÁNKA

■ BÉNRI NA HYOOGEN

Tanaka san o go-shookai
  shimásu.
Hajimemáshite.
Dóozo yoroshiku.

Kochira kóso.

Okusan ni yoroshiku.
O-jama shimáshita.

BUNKEI

Kore wa hón desu.
Sore wa dáre no hon desu ka.
Yuubínkyoku wa dóko desu ka.

Are wa nán desu ka.
Ríi san wa Nihonjín ja arimasen.
Amerika kara hikóoki de
  kimasu.

■ KAIWA

1 A: Áa, Buráun san.
    A: Konoaida wa dóomo
       arígatoo gozaimáshita.
    A: Minásan o-genki desu ka.

B: Konnichi wa.
B: Dóo itashimáshite.

B: Ée, o-kagesama de.

2 A: Tomodachi o go-shookai
       shimásu. Watanabe
       san désu.
    W: Dóozo yoroshiku.
    A: Watanabe san wa ashita
       Amerika e ikimásu.
    W: Nyuuyóoku desu.

B: Hajimemáshite.

B: Kochira kóso.
B: Áa, sóo desu ka. Amerika no
   dóko desu ka.
B: Watashi wa Nyuuyóoku kara
   desu yo.

3 A: Anokata wa dónata
      desu ka.
    A: Chuugokújin desu ka.

B: Ríi san desu.

B: Iie, sóo ja arimasen.
   Kankokújin desu.

LESSON THREE

USEFUL EXPRESSIONS

Let me introduce Mr Tanaka.

The pleasure is mine. (Me too.)

How do you do?
How do you do?/Pleased to meet
  you.

Give my regards to your wife.
Sorry to have bothered you.

SENTENCE PATTERNS

This is a book.
Whose book is that?
Where is the post office?

What is that?
Mr Lee is not Japanese.
They are coming from America
  by plane.

CONVERSATIONS

1 A: Ah, Mr Brown!
   A: Thanks very much for
      the other day.
   A: Is everyone [in your
      family] well?

   B: Good afternoon.
   B: Don't mention it!

   B: Yes, thank you.

2 A: Let me introduce my
      friend. This is Mrs
      Watanabe.
   W: Glad to meet you.
   A: Mrs Watanabe is going to
      America tomorrow.
   W: To New York.

   B: How do you do?

   B: The pleasure is mine.
   B: Really? What part of
      America?
   B: I am from New York, you
      know.

3 A: Who is that gentleman
      over there?
   A: Is he Chinese?

   B: It's Mr Lee.

   B: No he's not. He is Korean.

4 A: Sono hón o dóko de
        kaimásh/ta ka.

   A: Hái, sóo des/.

5 A: Are wa nán des/ ka.

   A: Nihongo no shinbun
        dés/ ka.

B: Kore dés/ ka.

B: Kore wa éki no hon'ya de
    kaimásh/ta.

B: Kinóo no shinbun dés/.

B: Iie, Eigo no shinbun dés/.

4   A: Where did you buy that book?   B: You mean this one?

     A: Yes, that's right.   B: I bought it at the bookshop in the station.

5   A: What is that?   B: It's yesterday's newspaper.

     A: Is it a Japanese paper?   B: No, it is in English.

A wa	*B*	dés*ų*
Kore	(nán)	
Sore	hón	
Are	h*į*kóoki	

	wa		dés*ų* (ka)
Watashi		Nihonjín	
Anáta		gak*ų*sei	
Anóhito		senséi	
Suzuki san		shachoo	

Yuubínkyoku	(dóko)	
Daigaku	koko	
Koojoo	soko	
O-teárai	asoko	

The words in brackets occur only in questions and never before *wa*

Here we are dealing with the Japanese equivalent of the verb 'to be' in the sense of 'A is B', 'A equals B' and so on.

*Dés*ų* differs in form and function from the verbs introduced so far and hence is usually called *the copula*. Note the changes for tense and negation:

	Present	Past
Affirmative	*dés*ų*	*désh*į*ta*
Negative	*ja arimasén*	*ja arimasén desh*į*ta*

The long negative and past forms are due to the fact that *dés*ų* is itself a contraction of *de arimás*ų*. *Ja arimasén* is a contraction of *dewa arimasén*, a form which is also in common use.

If we assume *dés*ų* is the equals sign in the equation A = B, then we can see that A is equivalent to a noun or pronoun followed by the particle *wa*.

THE PARTICLE WA

This particle is used to mark the topic of the sentence. It is used after a word to indicate that the speaker assumes the person addressed is acquainted with that word, either because it has been introduced earlier in the conversation or is common knowledge. It means something like, 'speaking of . . .' or 'as far as . . . is concerned' or 'as for . . .', but is, of course used far more frequently than such expressions are in English. Notice that question words like *dóko*, 'where', *dáre*, 'who', and *náni* (final *i* lost before *d* or *n*), 'what', never occur before the topic marker. In English we say, 'What is this?' but in Japanese you must say, 'This is what?' *Kore wa nán desu̱ ka*.

A rather peculiar use of this construction which helps to demonstrate the function of the particle *wa* is in sentences of the following type:

Watashi wa koohíi desu̱.	'Make mine coffee.'
	[As far as I'm concerned it is coffee.]
Shachoo wa jimúsho desu̱.	'The director is in his office.'

THE DEMONSTRATIVE PRONOUNS

Kore	'this'
Sore	'that'
Are	'that' (over there)

Japanese makes a distinction between that which is near the speaker, *kore*, that which is near the person addressed, *sore*, and that which is away from both the speaker and the addressee, *are*. Usually questions with *kore* imply answers with *sore* and vice versa. 'Which one?' is *dóre*.

Kore wa nán desu̱ ka.	'What is this?'
Sore wa enpi̱tsu désu̱.	'That is a pencil.'
Sore wa nán desu̱ ka.	'What is that?'
Kore wa hón desu̱.	'This is a book.'

But:

Are wa nán desu̱ ka.	'What is that?'
Are wa térebi no koojoo désu̱.	'That is a TV factory.'
Dóre o kaimasu̱ ka.	'Which one will you buy?'

The same applies to the pronouns indicating place:

Koko	'here' (by me)
Soko	'there' (by you)
Asoko	'there' (by him; over there)

PERSONAL PRONOUNS

As we have seen, many Japanese sentences do without a subject, particularly where we would use a pronoun in English. Sometimes, however, it is necessary to use a personal pronoun to avoid ambiguity. The personal pronouns function very much like other nouns in Japanese except that they have plural forms.

watashi	I	*watashĮtachi*	we
anáta	you	*anatagáta*	you (plural)
anóhito	he, she	*anóhitotachi*	they
anokáta	he, she (respectful)	*anokatágata*	they (respectful)
káre	he	*káretachi*	they (*kárera* – they (male))
kánojo	she	*kánojotachi*	they
anóko	he, she (child)	*anókotachi*	they (children)

Káre and *kánojo* are a little more familiar than the other third person pronouns, but are becoming popular, probably because it is sometimes useful to distinguish between 'he' and 'she'.

The plural forms have the suffix *-tachi* or *-gáta* added to the singular. *-gáta* is a respectful form and is hence not used with the first person. *Anátatachi* occurs, but is less respectful.

The second person singular pronoun is rarely used. It should not be used to superiors or persons of little acquaintance. Instead use the name followed by *san*:

Tanaka san mo irasshaimásĮ ka.   'Are you going too, Mr Tanaka?'

The suffixes *-tachi* and *-gáta* can be attached to other nouns denoting human beings: *gakĮséitachi*, 'the students'; *senseigáta*, 'the teachers' (respectful). *-tachi* is often used not to make the noun to which it is attached plural, but to indicate that the noun is one of a larger group: *Suzuki san-tachi*, 'Mr Suzuki and the others', 'Mr Suzuki's group' etc.

THE POSSESSIVE PARTICLE

The particle *no* links two nouns into a relationship in which the first possesses or somehow describes the second: *gakɯsei no hón*, 'the student's book'; *Tookyoo no hón'ya*, 'the bookshops of Tokyo'.

In Japanese, descriptive words always precede the words they describe. *No* occupies the same position as the apostrophe *s* in English. Japanese does have compound nouns like *Tookyoo-dáigaku* without a *no* in between, but these words are best learnt separately. As a general rule when a noun is used to describe another noun it will be followed by *no* and will precede the noun it describes.

Another use of *na*, which follows the rule of descriptive words preceding the words they describe, is when two nouns occur in apposition, e.g. *Gakɯsei no Tanaka san*, 'Mr Tanaka, the student' compared with *Tanaka san no gakɯsei*, 'Mr Tanaka's student'.

DE, 'BY MEANS OF'

We have met *de* as the particle denoting the place where an action occurs. Another common use of this particle is to show the instrument or means through which the action of the verb occurs.

Enpɪtsu de kakimáshɪta.	'He wrote it with a pencil/in pencil.'
Hɪkóoki de kaerimashɪta.	'I went home by plane.'
Nihongo de hanashimásɯ.	'I'll speak in Japanese.'
Kí de tsɯkurimashɪta.	'I made it out of wood.'
Tetsu de tsɯkurimasén.	'We don't make them from iron.'

KARA, 'FROM'

This particle indicates the point from which the action of the verb originates.

Daigaku kara básɯ de kimáshɪta.	'I came from the university by bus.'

NATIONALITY AND LANGUAGE

-jin added to the name of a country denotes a national of that country.

Índo	'India'	*Indójin*	'an Indian'
Amerika	'America'	*Amerikájin*	'an American'

Note that the vowel before *-jin* is accented regardless of the original accent, but the following is an exception:

Nihón	'Japan'	*Nihonjín*	'a Japanese'

-go added to the name of a country indicates language:

Furansu̥	'France'	*Furansugo*	'French'
Chúugoku	'China'	*Chuugokugo*	'Chinese'

The names of languages are unaccented. Note, too, that 'English' is *Eigo* but 'England' is *Igirisu̥* or *Eikoku*.

In English we use the same adjective in 'the Japanese book', 'my Japanese friend' and 'Japanese cars', but in Japanese these are clearly distinguished: *Nihongo no hón*, *Nihonjín no tomodachi* and *Nihón no kuruma* (or *Nihonsei no kuruma*, 'Japanese-made cars').

NOTES

Useful expressions Hajimemáshi̥te and dóozo yoroshi̥ku are not question and answer, but merely two common greetings used when meeting someone for the first time. You may use them in the reverse order or use the same word as the original greeting in your reply.

Oku̥san means 'your wife' or 'his wife', never 'my wife'. 'My wife' is *kánai*.

VOCABULARY

kore	this	*koko*	here
sore	that	*soko*	there
are	that (over there)	*asoko/*	over there
dóre	which?	*asu̥ko*	

watashi	I	*o-teárai*	lavatory, toilet
anáta	you		
anóhḻto	he, she	*jimúsho*	office
anókata	he, she (respectful)	*gakkoo*	school
		daigaku	university
anóko	he, she (child)	*koojoo*	factory
káre	he	*hḻkóoki*	aeroplane
kánojo	she	*fúne*	ship, boat
senséi	teacher	*básu*	bus
gakṵsei	student	*jidóosha/ kuruma*	car
okṵsan	your/his wife, Mrs . . .	*enpḻtsu*	pencil
kánai	my wife	*pén*	pen
Nihonjín	Japanese (person)	*térebi*	television
		rájio	radio
Nihonsei	made in Japan	*kí*	tree, wood
Eigo	English (language)	*tetsu*	iron
		kami	paper
Ájia	Asia	*tsṵkurimásṵ*	to make
Afurika	Africa	*désṵ*	is
Yooróppa	Europe	*ja arimasén*	is not
Oosṵtorária/ Góoshuu	Australia	*déshḻta*	was
		ja arimasén deshḻta	was not
Chúugoku	China		
Kánkoku	South Korea	*wa*	topic particle
Índo	India	*no*	(possessive particle)
Sóren	Soviet Union		
Dóitsṵ	Germany	*de*	by means of
Furansṵ	France	*kara*	from
Kánada	Canada	*-tachi*	(plural suffix)
Nyuuyóoku	New York	*-gáta*	(plural suffix)
hón' ya	bookshop, bookseller	*-jin*	person (in compounds)
koohíi	coffee	*-go*	language (in compounds)

EXERCISE 3

A Change as indicated in brackets:
1 Koko wa kooen desu. (question) 2 Anokata wa Suzuki san de wa arimasen. (affirmative) 3 Sensei wa Igirisujin desu. (negative) 4 Watashitachi wa basu de kimashita. (present) 5 Doko de tabemasu ka. (hortative) 6 Gakusei wa tegami o enpitsu de kakimasen. (past affirmative) 7 Kono tegami wa Doitsu kara kimashita. (negative question) 8 Gakkoo e nan de ikimasu ka. (hortative) 9 Afurika no hon o yomimasu. (past) 10 Eigo de tegami o kakimashita. (negative)

B Supply the missing particles:
1 Kyonen fune ( ) Nihon ( ) kimashita. 2 Mise ( ) zasshi ( ) kaimashita. 3 Abe san ( ) go-shookai shimasu. 4 Kore ( ) dare ( ) hon desu ka. 5 Ri san ( ) doko ( ) kimashita ka. 6 Ginkoo ( ) Suzuki san ( ) aimashita. 7 Nakamura san ( ) pen ( ) doko desu ka. 8 Are ( ) terebi ( ) koojoo desu. 9 Anokata ( ) Nihon ( ) shinbun ( ) agemashita. 10 Issho ( ) yuubinkyoku ( ) ikimashoo.

C Translate into English:
1 Senshuu eki de Nihonjin no gakusei ni aimashita. 2 Hikooki de Oosutoraria e ikimashita. 3 Anata wa Soren kara irasshaimashita ka. 4 Jimusho de shinbun o yomimasu. 5 Kanojo wa Furansujin ja arimasen. 6 O-tearai wa doko desu ka. 7 Honda san o go-shookai shimasu. 8 Okusan ni yoroshiku. 9 Anoko wa dare desu ka. 10 O-jama shimashita.

D Translate into Japanese:
1 Who is the Chinese student? 2 I bought a car yesterday. 3 Mr Brown came to Japan from Canada. 4 He [a child] goes to school by bus every day. 5 Did you make this out of paper? 6 Let's speak in English. 7 That is an aeroplane factory, isn't it? 8 I gave a magazine to the Japanese [language] teacher. 9 Let's meet at the university to-morrow. 10 Which one shall I give you?

DÁI YÓNKA

■ **BÉNRI NA HYOOGEN**

Itadakimásu̸   Gomen nasái.
Go-ch̸soosama désh̸ta   Yoroshíi desu̸ ka.
O-sómatsu̸sama desh̸ta.   Kékkoo desu̸.

BUNKEI

Koko ni hón to pén ga arimasu̸.   Teeburu no ue ni nánimo
                                    arimasén.

Jimúsho ni hísho ga imasu̸.   Shinbun wa kyuujuuen désu̸.
Hón wa hakó ni arimasu̸.   Dáre ga kimash̸ta ka.

■ **KAIWA**

1 A: Watashi no Nihongo no   B: Tsu̸kue no ué ni arimasén ka.
      jísho wa dóko ni
      arimasu̸ ka.
   A: Hái, arimasén.   B: Kinóo soko ni arimásh̸ta yo.

2 A: Ash̸ta no páatii ni   B: Ie, Tanaka san wa kimasén.
      Tanaka san ga kimásu̸
      ka.
   A: Sore déwa, dáre ga   B: Iida san to Yamanaka san ga
      kimásu̸ ka.   kimásu̸.

3 A: Suzuki san no o-uchi wa   B: Uenó-eki no ch̸káku ni
      dóko ni arimásu̸ ka.   arimasu̸.
   A: Ch̸katetsu de ikimashóo   B: Ie, básu de ikimashóo.
      ka.

4 A: Otootó wa máda Igirisu   B: Ítsu mukoo e ikimásh̸ta ka.
      ni imásu̸.
   A: Sannen máe ni   B: Ítsu Nihón e kaerimásu̸ ka.
      ikimásh̸ta.
   A: Rainen kaerimásu̸.

44

LESSON FOUR

USEFUL EXPRESSIONS

[Said at the beginning of a meal]	I'm sorry.
[Said by guest at end of meal]	Is it all right? Do you mind?
[Said by host in reply to above]	That's fine; It's quite all right.

SENTENCE PATTERNS

Here there are books and pens.   There is nothing on the table.

There is a secretary in the office.   The newspaper is ninety yen.
The book is in the box.   Who came?

CONVERSATIONS

1   A: Where is my Japanese   B: Isn't it on top of the desk?
       dictionary?
    A: No, it isn't.   B: It was there yesterday.

2   A: Is Mr Tanaka coming to   B: No, Mr Tanaka is not
       tomorrow's party?   coming.
    A: Then who is coming?   B: Mr Iida and Mr Yamanaka.

3   A: Where is Mr Suzuki's   B: It is near Ueno station.
       house?
    A: Shall we go on the   B: No, let's go by bus.
       underground?

4   A: My younger brother is   B: When did he go over there?
       still in England.
    A: He went three years ago.   B: When is he returning to
                                     Japan?

    A: Next year.

5 A: Sumimasén.

  A: Basɥtei wa dóko ni
     arimásɥ ka.

  B: Nán desɥ ka.

  B: Yuubínkyoku no yoko ni
     arimásɥ.

6 A: Kutsu-úriba wa dóko
     desɥ ka.

  A: Esɥkaréetaa wa gokai e
     ikimásɥ ka.

  B: Gokai ni arimásɥ.

  B: Iie, erebéetaa dake ikimásɥ.

7 A: Suzuki san wa nánnen ni
     umaremáshɹta ka.

  A: Sore wa seireki de
     nánnen desɥ ka.

  B: Shoowa nijúunen ni
     umaremáshɹta

  B: Sen kyúuhyaku yónjuugonen
     desɥ.

8 A: Tákɥshii de íkura desɥ
     ka.

  A: Jáa, tákɥshii de
     ikimashóo.

  B: Sen gohyakuen desɥ.

  B: Takɥshii-nóriba wa éki no
     máe ni arimasɥ.

5   A: Excuse me.   B: Yes, what is it?
    A: Where is the bus stop?   B: It is alongside the post office.

6   A: Where is the shoe   B: It is on the fifth floor.
            department?
    A: Does the escalator go to   B: No, only the lift does.
            the fifth floor?

7   A: What year were you   B: In the twentieth year of
            born, Mr Suzuki?   Shoowa.
    A: What year is that by the   B: It is 1945.
            Western calendar?

8   A: How much is it by taxi?   B: ¥1,500.
    A: Then let's go by taxi.   B: There is a rank in front of the
                                              station.

	'There is a B in A.'	'In A there is B.'

A ni	B ga	
Tookyoo	báa	
uchi	térebi	arimásu̸
hako no naka	enp̸ịtsu	
_____ ni	_____ ga	
daigaku	gak̸usei	
jimúsho	hísho	imásu̸
niwa	kodomo	

	'The A is in B.'	
		arimásu̸
A wa	B ni	
		imásu̸
Hón wa	hóndana ni	arimásu̸
Shachoo wa	jimúsho ni	imásu̸

Japanese makes a distinction between the verb 'to be' as a copula, i.e. when it means 'equals' or 'is equivalent to', as we saw in the last lesson, and when it means 'to be in a place', 'to exist'. In English the same verb is used for 'this is a book' and 'the book is in the drawer', but in Japanese we have

Kore wa hón dêsu̸ and *Hón wa h̸ịkidashi ni arimásu̸.*

A further distinction is made in Japanese according to whether the subject of the verb is animate or inanimate. *Imásu̸* is used for animate subjects (this includes not only persons and animals, but sometimes such things as cars, planes, etc., which are capable of movement under their own power) and *arimásu̸* for inanimate subjects.

As you can see from the above diagram the place in which the subject of the verb is situated is indicated by the particle *ni*, 'in' or 'at' (in addition to the meaning 'to' introduced in Lesson Two). This must not be confused with the place in which an *action* occurs, which is indicated by *de*:

Jimúsho de tegami o kakimáshɩta.	'He wrote the letter in the office.'
Jimúsho ni imasɩ.	'He is in the office.'

Irasshaimásɩ is used instead of *imásɩ* to show respect to the subject of the verb.

Ashɩta o-taku ni irasshaimásɩ ka.   'Will you be home tomorrow?'

The particle *ga* introduced in the first of the sentence patterns is the marker of the grammatical subject. The difference between the topic marker *wa* and the subject marker *ga* is perhaps the most difficult problem in Japanese grammar, and more will be said about it later. For the time being remember that if the place phrase comes before the subject use *ga*. This pattern is used when the subject is being introduced into the conversation for the first time. Once the subject has been mentioned it becomes a topic of the conversation and will therefore be followed by *wa*. The topic usually comes at the beginning of the sentence, but may sometimes be preceded by a time phrase. Often in this pattern the difference between *wa* and *ga* parallels the use of the definite article 'the' on the one hand and the indefinite article 'a' or 'an' plus 'there is' on the other. If you would use a 'there is' in English you must use *ga* after the subject in Japanese.

The locative construction with *désɩ* introduced in the last lesson can only be used with topics. [Noun] *wa* [place phrase] (without *ni*) '*désɩ*'.

Shachoo wa dóko desɩ ka.	'Where is the boss?'
Shachoo wa dóko ni imásɩ ka.	'Where is the boss?'

Notice that as question words specifically ask for new information they cannot be topics of sentences, so must be followed by *ga* if they occupy the subject position.

Dáre ga kimáshɩta ka?	'Who came?'
Dónata ga irasshaimáshɩta ka?	'Who came?' (respectful)

LOCATIONAL PHRASES

Japanese has only one particle, *ni*, to indicate the location of something. Sometimes the context will tell us whether it is 'in' as in *hɩkidashi ni arimásɩ* ('It's in the drawer'), 'on' as in *teeburu ni arimásɩ*

('It's on the table') or 'at' as in *kaisha ni imásų* ('He's at the office').
When there is a need to be more specific, i.e. to say 'near', 'under',
'behind', 'in front of', 'inside', 'on top of' and so on, Japanese uses a
noun followed by the particle *ni* and linked with the preceding noun
with the possessive particle *no*. In fact, this construction is very
similar to the use of phrases like 'on top of' in English.

chị́káku	(vicinity)	*no chị́káku ni*	'near'
shị́tá	(bottom)	*no shị́ta ni*	'under'
ushiro	(back)	*no ushiro ni*	'behind'
máe	(front)	*no máe ni*	'in front of'
náka	(inside)	*no náka ni*	'inside'
ué	(top)	*no ué ni*	'on top of'

Daigaku no chị́káku ni hón'ya ga   'There are many bookshops near
takụsán arimasụ.   the university.'

If the main verb is an action verb, of course, *ni* is replaced by *de*.

Daigaku no chikáku de   'I ate close to the university.'
tabemáshịta.

The use of *takụsán*, 'many', in the example above appears to be a
contradiction to the rule that descriptive words precede the words
they describe. Actually it is usual in Japanese for expressions of
quantity to occupy the adverb position. *Hón'ya ga takụsán arimasụ*
means literally 'there are bookshops to the extent of many'. *Takụsán*
modifies the verb whereas 'many' qualifies the noun. *Takụsán* can be
used in front of the noun, in which case it is often followed by *no*,
takụsan no hón'ya, 'many bookshops', but the adverbial usage is
more common.

NUMBERS

The Japanese numbers, used alone in counting and in combination
with suffixes such as *-en*, 'yen', *-nen*, 'years', *-ji*, 'o'clock', *-kai*,
'floors', and others introduced in Lesson Six, are as follows.

1 ichí	3 sán	5 gó
2 ní	4 shí/yon	6 rokú

7 shịchí/nána	17 juushịchí/juunána	60 rokujúu
8 hachí	18 juuhachí	70 nanájuu/
9 kú/kyúu	19 júuky/juukyúu	shichijúu
10 júu	20 níjuu	80 hachijúu
11 juuichí	21 níjuuichị	90 kyúujuu/
12 juuní	22 níjuuni	kujúu
13 júusan	30 sánjuu	100 hyakú*
14 juushí/juuyón	40 yónjuu/	1,000 sen†
15 júugo	shijúu	10,000 ichimán
16 juurokú	50 gojúu	100,000 juumán
		1,000,000 hyakumán
		100,000,000 ichíoku

*Sound changes occur in 300 *sanbyaku*; 600 *roppyaku*; 800 *happyaku*.
† Sound changes occur in 3,000 *sanzen* and 8,000 *hassen*.

Japanese dates

In addition to the Western system of counting years Japan still uses the traditional system of year periods. Since the Meiji Restoration of 1868 these periods correspond to the reign of the Emperor. The modern Japanese year periods are: *Méiji*, which began in 1868, *Taishoo* (1912), *Shóowa* (1926) and *Heisei* (1989). As 1868, 1912, 1926 and 1989 are the first years of their respective year periods, it is necessary to calculate from the year before each of these dates in converting to the Western calendar. For example, *Shóowa juukyúunen* is 1944 (1925 + 19) and 1979 is *Shóowa gojúuyonen* (1979–1925). Whether using the Western or traditional Japanese systems the suffix *-nen* is always used.

Here are some expressions of quantity. 'How much' (price) is *íkura*; for other question words *nan-* is combined with the suffix.

Are wa íkura desụ ka.	'How much is that?'
Gosénnanahyakuen désụ.	'It is ¥5,700.'
Késa rokúji ni okimáshịta.	'I got up at 6 o'clock this morning.'
Íma nánji desụ ka.	'What time is it now?'
Nánnen ni umaremáshịta ka.	'In what year were you born?'

Nánnen Róndon ni irasshaimáshḻta ka.	'How many years were you in London?'

Notice that *nánnen* can mean either 'what year?' or 'how many years', but in the former sense it is followed by *ni*. *Ni* is also used after *-ji*, 'o'clock'. In telling the time·the hours ('. . . o'clock') come first and the smaller divisions like *-hán*, 'half past' and the minutes (introduced in Lesson Six and Appendix 1) follow: *yóji hán*, 'half past four'.

INTERROGATIVE PRONOUNS FOLLOWED BY MO

The interrogative pronouns like *náni*, 'what', *dóko*, 'where', *dáre*, 'who', and *dónata*, 'who', when followed by the particle *mo* and combined with a negative verb at the end of the sentence, are like the English indefinite pronouns 'nothing', 'nowhere', 'nobody', etc. Sometimes *mo* occurs in these expressions after another particle, but it never occurs after *ga* and only very rarely after *o*.

Késa nánimo tabemasén deshḻta.	'I didn't eat anything this morning.'
Anóhḻto wa dáre nimo hanashimasén.	He doesn't speak to any one.'
Dónata mo irasshaimasén deshḻta.	'Nobody came.'
Dóko emo ikimasén deshḻta.	'I didn't go anywhere.'
Dóko kara mo kimasén deshḻta.	'They didn't come from anywhere.'

NOTES

Conversation 2   Notice that *wa* often replaces *ga* when the verb is negative, particularly if some kind of contrast is implied. This is explained in detail later.

Conversation 3   The honorific prefix *o-* attached to *uchi* is an indication of respect to the owner of the house. *O-uchi* (or *o-taku*, which is even more respectful), therefore, means 'your house' or 'his house', not 'my house'. *O-uchi* tends to be used by women, *o-taku* by both sexes. *Uchi* is also a general term for house.

VOCABULARY

heyá	room	*tomodachi*	friend
dóa	door	*páatii*	party
mádo	window	*seireki*	Western calendar
teeburu	table	*Méiji*	1868–1912
tsʉ́kue	desk	*Taishoo*	1912–26
isú	chair	*Shóowa*	1926–89
hóndana	bookshelf	*Heisei*	1989–
hakó	box	*ue*	top, above
hʉ́kidashi	drawer	*shʉ́ta*	bottom, below
jísho	dictionary	*náka*	middle, inside
shorui	papers, documents	*máe*	front
		ushiro	back, behind
nóoto	notebook, exercise book	*sóba*	next to, near
		tonari	next door to
mémo	memo, memo pad	*yoko*	side, beside
bóorupen	ball-point pen	*chʉ́káku*	vicinity, near
chʉ́katetsu	underground	*mukoo*	the other side, abroad
tákʉshii	taxi		
takʉshii-nóriba	taxi rank	*nánimo*	nothing
basʉ́tei (básu no teiryuujoo)	bus stop	*dáremo*	no one
		-en	yen
kʉ́tsú	shoes	*-nen*	year
uriba	department, counter	*-ji*	o'clock
		hán	half
kʉ́tsu-úriba	shoe department	*gokai*	fifth floor
esukaréetaa	escalator	*késa*	this morning
erebéetaa	lift	*ikura*	how much
o-taku	your house, your place	*takʉsán*	many, a lot
		daké	only
otokonohʉ́tó	man	*ga*	subject marker
onnanohʉ́tó	woman	*arimásʉ*	(there) is/are
kodomo	child	*imásʉ*	(there) is/are
otokónoko	boy	*umaremásʉ*	to be born
onnánoko	girl	*mimásʉ*	to see
hʉ́sho	secretary	*norimásʉ*	to ride, get onto (object takes *ni*)
otootó	younger brother		

EXERCISE 4

A Insert the word in brackets into the sentence and make any changes the sense demands:
1 Hikidashi ni boorupen ga arimasu. (naka) 2 Heya ni isu ga arimasu. (takusan) 3 Doko ni arimasu ka. (kutsu-uriba) 4 Shorui wa tsukue ni arimasu. (ue) 5 Gokai e ikimashoo. (esukareetaa) 6 Hisho wa imasu. (jimusho) 7 Yuubinkyoku no ushiro ni arimasu. (hon'ya) 8 Rokuji ni kaerimashita. (han) 9 Juukunen ni umaremashita. (Shoowa) 10 Mise wa eki ni arimasu. (chikaku)

B Supply the missing words:
1 Ima hisho wa jimusho ni ( ). 2 Eki ( ) mae ( ) takushiinoriba ( ) arimasu. 3 Enpitsu ( ) hako ( ) arimasu. 4 Doa ( ) soba ( ) isu ( ) arimasu. 5 Onnanokotachi ( ) gakkoo ( ) imasu. 6 Basu ( ) norimashita. 7 Yuubinkyoku ( ) ushiro ( ) hon'ya ( ) zasshi ( ) kaimashita. 8 Otooto ( ) kyonen mukoo ( ) imashita. 9 Boorupen ( ) nooto ( ) kakimashita. 10 Watanabe san ( ) Taishoo juunen ( ) umaremashita.

C Translate into English:
1 Memo wa itsumo teeburu no ue ni arimasu. 2 Erebeetaa de nanakai e ikimashoo. 3 Mainichi chikatetsu de kaisha e ikimasu. 4 Watashi no jisho o mimashita ka. 5 Go-chisoosama deshita. 6 Doa no ushiro ni nani ga arimasu ka. 7 Tanaka san wa Meiji sanjuunen ni umaremashita. 8 Otokonoko dake heya ni imashita. 9 Yoroshii desu ka. 10 Watashi no tomodachi wa mado no soba ni imasu.

D Translate into Japanese:
1 I'm sorry. 2 Where is the taxi rank? 3 My friend is going abroad next year. 4 I was born in 1943. 5 How much is the notebook? 6 The Japanese dictionary is ¥2,500. 7 The television set is ¥35,000. 8 I'll meet you at half-past nine in front of the post office. 9 I'm sorry it was such a simple meal. 10 My friend is a French teacher.

DÁI GÓKA

Chótto ukagaimásɥ ga . . .   . . . o meshiagarimásɥ ka.

. . . o kudasái.   . . . ikága desɥ ka.
O-negai shimásɥ.   Ikága deshɥta ka.

BUNKEI

Ano haná wa kírei desɥ.   Háyaku tsɥkimashɥta.
Shízuka na tokoro ni ikitai désɥ. Abe san wa Eigo ga
                                      wakarimasén.
Kono tokei wa tákaku nai desɥ.   Aói no wa anáta no desɥ.

■ KAIWA

1 A: Go-chɥsoosama déshɥta.   B: O-sómatsɥsama deshɥta.

   A: Ókɥsan wa ryóori ga   B: Iie, hetá desɥ.
      joozú desɥ né.

2 A: Kyóoto made nanjíkan   B: Sanjíkan desɥ.
      kakarimásɥ ka.
   A: Shinkánsen wa háyakɥ   B: Hontó ni sóo desɥ né.
      hashirimasɥ né.

3 A: Sɥshí o meshiagarimásɥ   B: Hái, itadakimásɥ.
      ka.
   A: Nihon-ryóori ga o-sɥki   B: Ée, dáisɥki desɥ.
      desɥ ka.

4 A: Chótto ukagaimásɥ ga.   B: Hái, nán desɥ ka.
   A: Kono hón o Oosɥtorária   B: Kookuubin desɥ ka, funábin
      ni okuritái desɥ. Íkura   desɥ ka.
      desɥ ka.
   A: Kookuubin de o-negai   B: Sén roppyakuen désɥ.
      shimásɥ.

56

LESSON FIVE

USEFUL EXPRESSIONS

I'd just like to ask . . ./Please tell me . . .

Please give me . . .

Please! I'd be grateful if you would . . .

Will you have some . . . ? [food]

How about . . .?

How was it?

SENTENCE PATTERNS

That flower is beautiful.

I want to go somewhere quiet.

This watch is not expensive.

I arrived early.

Mr Abe doesn't understand English.

The blue one is yours.

CONVERSATIONS

1 A: Thanks for the wonderful meal.

B: It was nothing.

A: You are very good at cooking!

B: No, I'm a poor cook.

2 A: How long does it take to Kyoto?

B: It's three hours.

A: The bullet train travels quickly, doesn't it?

B: Yes it really does.

3 A: Will you have some *sushi*?

B: Yes please!

A: Do you like Japanese food?

B: Yes, I love it!

4 A: Excuse me.

B: Yes, what is it?

A: I'd like to send this book to Australia. How much is it?

B: Airmail or sea mail?

A: Airmail please.

B: That's ¥1,600.

5 A: Suzuki san wa aói   B: Iie, watashi no wa minná
         wáishatsu ga arimásу   shirói desу.
         ka.

    A: Sore ja, kono aói no wa   B: Wakarimasén née.
         dáre no deshóo.

6 A: Ano jísho wa íkura desу   B: Sanzen sanbyakuen désу.
         ka.

    A: Takái desу née. Mótto   B: Kono usui no wa sén'en desу.
         yasúi no ga arimasén
         ka.

    A: Sore o kudasái.

7 A: Atamá ga itái desу.   B: Kaze o hуkimáshуta ka.

    A: Ie, yuube tomodachу to   B: Jáa, fуtsуkayoi désу née.
         takуsán nomimáshуta.

5   A: Do you have a blue shirt,   B: No, all mine are white.
         Mr Suzuki?

    A: Then whose is this blue   B: I don't know.
        one, I wonder?

6   A: How much is that   B: It is ¥3,300.
         dictionary?

    A: That's expensive! Don't   B: This thin one is ¥1,000.
        you have a cheaper
        one?

    A: Give me that one,
        please.

7   A: I have a headache.   B: Have you caught a cold?
    A: No, last night I drank a   B: Ah, it's a hangover then!
        lot with a friend.

ADJECTIVES AND DESCRIPTIVE NOUNS

We have seen how we can qualify a noun by placing in front of it another noun followed by *no*. This usually indicates a relationship in which the first noun owns the second – *tomodachi no kuruma*, 'my friend's car' – but often the first noun simply describes, or qualifies, the second: *natsu no hana*, 'summer flowers'.

The descriptive nouns function in the same way as this noun + *no* construction except that in meaning they correspond to what in English we would call adjectives and that instead of *no* they have the particle *na*.

Kírei na hana	'beautiful flowers'
Shízuka na tokoro	'a quiet place'
Hetá na Eigo	'poor English'

In the predicate, however, like all nouns they occur immediately before *desu* with no intervening particle:

Kono haná wa kírei desu.	'These flowers are beautiful.'
Suzuki san wa utá ga hetá desu.	'Mr Suzuki sings badly.'

And they undergo no changes in the negative form.

Anóhito ga amari sukí ja arimasén.	'I don't like him very much.'

In the vocabulary sections of this book the descriptive nouns are followed by the particle *na* to distinguish them from ordinary nouns. There are, however, some words which can be assigned to either category,

Shikakú na/no teeburu	'a square table'
Iroiro na/no hana	'various flowers'

When descriptive nouns occur before a verb other than *desu* they are followed by *ni*. This is the adverbial form.

Kírei ni kakimáshita.	'She wrote it beautifully.'

While the descriptive nouns share a number of characteristics with true nouns, the adjectives in many ways resemble verbs. They consist of a root and an ending. The present tense ending is *-i* and it is in this form that adjectives appear in dictionaries and the vocabularies of this book.

takái biru	'a high building'
Bíru wa takái desᵤ.	'The building is high.'

Adjectives come directly before the nouns they qualify and the same form occurs before *desᵤ*. It is in their negative and adverbial forms that adjectives reveal how different they are from the descriptive nouns.

Ano bíru wa tákaku arimasén.   'That building is not high.'
or
Ano bíru wa tákaku nai désᵤ.

Notice the alternative negative form and the fact that there is no *ja* (*dewa*) before *arimasén*. In the negative the *-i* ending is changed to *-ku*. This changes the adjective into an adverb, and it is this form which is used before all verbs, except the present affirmative, and probable forms of the copula, *desᵤ* and *deshóo*. *Deshóo* is explained in the notes below.

Bukka ga tákaku narimashᵢta.	'Prices have gone up/become higher.'
Heyá o óokiku shimashᵢta.	'We enlarged/made bigger the room.'
Késa háyaku okimashᵢta.	'I got up early this morning.'

Notice with the verbs *narimásᵤ*, 'to become', and *shimásᵤ*, 'to make', the English translation will often be an adjective in the comparative degree (. . . -er). With nouns (including the descriptive nouns) *ni* is used.

Kírei ni narimáshᵢta.	'It has become beautiful./It is cleaner.'
Senséi ni narimásᵤ.	'He will become a teacher.'
Kono heyá o jimúsho ni shimásᵤ.	'I'll make this room the office.'

Adjectives have a past tense. This is formed by adding the suffix *-katta* to the adjective root (what is left when you cut off the final *-i*). In the polite style of speech this is then followed by *desᵤ*.

Takái desᵤ.	'It is expensive.'
Tákakatta desᵤ.	'It was expensive.'

The negative past tense is either

Tákaku arimasen deshĮta   'It was not expensive.'
or
Tákaku nakatta desᵤ.

Descriptive nouns have no special past tense form.

Kírei deshĮta.   'It was beautiful.'

The adjectives *ookíi*, 'big', and *chiisái*, 'small', have alternate forms *óoki na* and *chíisa na*, but these differ from the descriptive nouns in that they do not occur before *désᵤ*. In predicates the true adjectives *ookíi* and *chíisai* or their adverbial forms *óokĮku* and *chíisakᵤ* must be used.

Kore wa chíisa na heyá desᵤ né.   'This is a little room isn't it?'
Kanojo wa mé ga ookíi desᵤ.   'She has big eyes.'

Before nouns the forms with *na* seem to carry connotations of softness and intimacy.

The adjective 'good' occurs in two forms, *íi* and *yói*, but the adverbial form is always *yóku*. In addition to the meaning 'well', *yóku* is frequently used in the sense of 'often'.

Yóku wakarimásᵤ.   'He understands well.'
Nihon ryóori o yóku tabemásᵤ.   'I often eat Japanese food.'

-tai, 'want to'

This is an adjective ending attached to the verb stem (what is left when you take off the *-masᵤ* ending). As the *-tai* form is an adjective its object should, strictly speaking, be marked by *ga*, but recently the use of the object marker *o* has become quite common before *-tai*, perhaps due to the influence of English grammar.

Hón ga/o kaitai desᵤ.   'I want to buy a book.'

As *-tai* implies a degree of subjective judgment it is not usually used to refer to third persons, and refers to the second person only in questions.

Ikitaku arimasén ka.   'Don't you want to go?'

GA AS AN OBJECT MARKER

A	WA	B		GA	Stative verb Descriptive noun + désʉ Adjective + désʉ	'A does B' 'A does B' 'A has . . . B'
		Nihongo			wakarimásʉ	'understands'
		o-kane	'money'		irimásʉ	'needs'
		kodomo	'child'		arimásʉ	'has'
		górufu	'golf'		dekimásʉ	'can do'
Suzuki	WA			GA		
san		bíiru	'beer'		sʉkí desʉ	'likes'
		shigoto	'work'		kirai désʉ	'dislikes'
		ryóori	'cooking'		joozú desʉ	'is good at'
		utá	'song'		hetá desʉ	'is bad at'
		mé	'eyes'		kírei desʉ	'has beautiful'
		se	'stature'		takái desʉ	'has high'

As you can see from the above diagram, apart from their use in front of nouns, many of these words function much like English verbs. Of the stative verbs, *wakarimásʉ* and *arimásʉ* have already been introduced. These and the other two listed above belong to a small group of verbs in Japanese which mark their objects with the particle *ga* and not *o*. All of them describe states rather than actions. Descriptive nouns and adjectives also take *ga* after the object. Note that when *arimásʉ* means 'to have' it may be used with either animate or inanimate objects.

Nihonjín no tomodachi ga arimásʉ.   'I have a Japanese friend.'

O-kane ga arimasén.   'I haven't any money.'

but

Shachoo wa jimúsho ni imásʉ.   'The director is in his office.'

Dekimásu̶, 'can do', as in *Nihongo ga dekimásu̶ ka*, 'Can you speak Japanese?', also occurs in a number of idiomatic expressions with the meaning of 'to be done', 'to be ready' or 'to be produced'.

Móo dekimáshḷta ka.	'Is it ready yet?'
Yasai ga takṵsán dekimáshḷta.	'We produced a lot of vegetables.'

'The . . . one'

Adjectives and nouns can be followed by *no* (not the particle but a noun meaning 'the one') to make expressions of the type 'the blue one', etc:

Yasúi no o kaimáshḷta.	'I bought the cheap one.'
Are wa watashi no désu̶.	'That is mine.'

With descriptive nouns *na* is used before *no*.

Kírei na no wa hḷkidashi ni arimásu̶.	'The clean ones are in the drawer.'

Demonstrative adjectives: 'this' and 'that'

In English we say 'this book' and 'this is a book', using the same demonstrative in each. In fact, the former is an adjective and the later a pronoun. We have already met the pronouns *kore*, *sore* and *are*. The demonstrative adjectives are *kono*, 'this . . .', *sono*, 'that . . .' and *ano*, 'that . . . over there'. These occur before a noun, or a noun with some descriptive word or phrase in front of it:

kono hón,	'this book';
kono atsui hón,	'this thick book';
ano Tookyoo dáigaku no shizuka na gakusei	'that quiet Tokyo university student'

The interrogative form of the demonstrative adjective is *dóno*, 'which'.

Dóno hon o agemashóo ka.	'Which book shall I give you?'

Onáji, 'same'

This is similar to the descriptive nouns, but appears before a noun without the particle *na*, *onáji hón* 'the same book'. It is also used with the particle *to* 'with' in the constructions, *A wa B to onáji desu* 'A is the same as B' and *A to B (to) wa onáji desu*.

MORE PARTICLES

To, 'with', 'and'

This particle is used in expressions such as

Watashi to (issho ni) tabemasén ka,	'Won't you eat with me?',
Tomodachi to (issho ni) ikimáshlta,	'I went with a friend' (the use with *issho ni* is very common),
Pén to enpltsu o kaimáshlta,	'I bought a pen and a pencil.'

It is important to remember that *to* in the sense of 'and' can be used only to join nouns. To join verbs *sore kara*, 'after that', or *soshlte*, 'and then', can sometimes be used:

Ginza e ikimáshlta.	'I went to Ginza and ate sushi.'
Soshlte sushí o tabemashlta.	

Made, 'as far as', 'until', 'to'

This particle is used with both expressions of space and time.

Kóobe made ikimáshlta.	'I went as far as Kobe.'
Rokúji made hatarakimásu.	'I work until six.'

It is often used with *kara* in expressions of the type, *A kara B made*, 'from A to B', 'from A till B'.

Juuníji kara ichíji made yasumimásu.	'I take a break from 12 to 1.'

With expressions of time *ni* is used after *máde* to indicate 'by [a certain time]',

Sánji made ni dekimásu.	'It will be ready by 3.'

Ka, 'or'

The particle *ka* coming between nouns is usually best translated by English 'or':

dóa ka mádo,	'a door or a window',
shachoo ka hĮsho,	'the director or the secretary', etc.
Pén ka enpĮtsu o kashimashóo ka.	'Shall I lend you a pen or pencil?'

This particle can also combine with *to* to form a compound particle, *tóka*, used to join nouns given as examples of a potentially longer list; e.g., *pén toka kamí toka*, 'pens and paper [and other things like that]'. It is usual to repeat *tóka* after each item in the list, but *nádo* is often used instead after the last noun listed.

Hón toka zasshi tóka shinbun nádo o kaimáshĮta.	'I bought books, magazines, newspapers and so on.'

Ya, 'and'

Another particle used to join nouns is *ya*. It is similar to *tóka* in that it joins nouns which are felt in some way to be connected, but does not make the same strong implication that more items have been left uncited.

Básu ya chĮkatetsu wa bénri desĮ.	'The bus and underground are convenient.'
Bíiru ya o-sake o kaimáshĮta ka.	'Did you buy the beer and sake?'

ALTERNATIVE QUESTIONS

Above we saw how *ka* is equivalent to 'or' when it occurs before nouns. In questions the use of 'or' in English can convey two different meanings. In speech the two are usually kept apart by intonation, but punctuation can also bring out the distinction in written English. For example, the sentence 'Shall I lend you a pen or a pencil?' can be shown to contrast with 'Shall I lend you a pen, or a pencil?'. The former simply means 'Shall I lend you something to write with?' while the latter means 'Shall I lend you a pen or shall I lend you a pencil?' In Japanese the use of *ka* between nouns can correspond only to the former. To convey the latter idea Japanese uses two separate questions: *Pén o kashimashóo ka. Enpḷtsu o kashimashóo ka.* Here are some more examples:

Kyoo irasshaimásṵ ka. Ashḷta irasshaimásṵ ka.	'Are you coming today, or tomorrow?'
Ríi san wa Kankokújin desṵ ka Chuugokújin desṵ ka.	'Is Mr Lee Korean, or Chinese?'
Ano jísho wa takái desṵ ka yasúi desṵ ka.	'Is that dictionary expensive or cheap?'

NOTES

Useful expressions Chótto ukagaimásṵ ga (literally, 'I am just asking, but . . .') employs the formal verb for 'to ask'. It is often used when requesting information. 'Excuse me, but I wonder if you could tell me . . .'

. . . o meshiagarimásṵ ka. The verb *meshiagarimásṵ* cannot be used with a first person subject as it shows special respect to the subject of the verb, which is usually 'you'.

O-negai shimásṵ, 'I request', is often used when asking a favour. It is usually used after the request has been made, something like, 'I'd be grateful if you would do that for me.'

Conversation 1 It is very common to reply to the compliment *joozú desṵ* with the modest *hetá desṵ*.

Conversation 3 When asking a respected person whether he likes something it is usual to supply the honorific prefix *o-* before *sṵki*. *Sṵkí* then loses its accent.

VOCABULARY

atamá	head	*shízuka (na)*	quiet
atamá ga ii	intelligent	*joozú (na)*	skilful, good at
mé	eye	*hetá (na)*	poor, bad at
sé	stature	*o-sṵki (na)*	(you) like
sé ga takai	tall (of people)	*sṵkí (na)*	to like
kaze	a cold; wind	*dáisṵki (na)*	to love;
futsṵkayoi	hangover		favourite
ryóori	cooking	*kirai (na)*	to dislike
Nihon-	Japanese	*shḭkaku*	square
ryóori	cooking	*(na)/(no)*	
sushí/	(raw fish etc. with	*iroiro (na)/(no)*	various
o-súshi	vinegared rice)	*onaji*	same
yasai	vegetables	*takái*	high,
haná	flower		expensive
natsú	summer	*yasúi*	cheap
fuyú	winter	*kurói*	black
áki	autumn	*shirói*	white
háru	spring	*akai*	red
tokoro	place	*aói*	blue, green
bíru	building	*kiiroi*	yellow
o-kane	money	*hayái*	fast; early
bukka	prices	*usui*	thin
wáishatsu	shirt	*atsui*	thick
tokei	watch, clock	*ookíi/óoki (na)*	big
jikan	time	*chiisái/chíisa*	small
-jíkan	hours	*(na)*	
utá	song, poem	*íi/yói*	good
shigoto	work	*yóku*	well, often
górufu	golf	*hontóo/honto*	true, real
densha	(electric) train	*chótto*	a bit, a little
shinkánsen	super express,	*miná/minna*	all
	'bullet' train	*sore déwa/sore*	then; in that
kookuubin	airmail	*já*	case
funabin	sea mail	*mótto*	more
kírei (na)	beautiful;	*yuube*	last night
	clean	*soshḭte*	and then

sore kara	and then	*kakarimásu*	to take; to cost
ka	or		
to	with, and	*hashirimśu*	to run
tóka	and	*kḷkimásu*	to hear, listen; ask
ya	and		
nádo	and so on, etc.	*ukagaimásu*	to ask, visit (formal)
máde	as far as, up to, until	*okurimásu*	to send
máde ni	by, before (time)	*kaze o hḷkimásu*	to catch a cold
kono	this	*narimásu*	to become
sono	that	*irimásu*	to need
ano	that over there	*hatarakimásu*	to work
		yasumimásu	to rest
dóno	which?	*okimásu*	to get up
amari	too . . . (not) very	*dekimásu*	to be able; to be done
tsḷkimásu	to arrive	*deshóo*	probably is

EXERCISE 5

A Change as indicated in brackets:
1 Kono tegami o kookuubin de okurimasu. (desiderative) 2 Koko wa shizuka desu. (negative) 3 Kyoo wa atsui desu. (negative) 4 Watashi no tokei wa takai desu. (past) 5 Kanojo wa Nihongo ga joozu desu. (negative) 6 Eiga wa yokatta desu. (negative) 7 Atama ga itai desu. (past) 8 Sukiyaki ga suki desu. (negative) 9 Abe san ni kikimashita. (negative desiderative) 10 Ano aoi waishatsu wa watashi no desu. (negative)

B Supply the missing particles:
1 Suzuki san ( ) okusan ( ) ryoori ( ) joozu desu. 2 Tookyoo ( ) Oosaka ( ) nankiro desu ka. 3 Kirei ( ) hana ( ) takusan kaimashita. 4 Watanabe san ( ) se ( ) takai desu. 5 Kyooto ( ) shinkansen ( ) kimashita. 6 Motto yasui ( ) o kaimashita. 7 Watashi ( ) uta ( ) amari joozu ( ) arimasen. 8 Buraun san ( ) Nihongo ( ) dekimasu ka. 9 Kaze ( ) hikimashita. 10 O-kane ( ) ikura irimasu ka.

C Translate into English:

1 Chuugoku-ryoori o meshiagarimasu ka. 2 Sumisu san to onaji fune de Nihon e kimashita. 3 Ano takai biru wa nan desu ka. 4 Sono yasai o sukoshi kudasai. 5 Kore wa natsu no waishatsu desu. 6 Rainen no fuyu Doitsu e ikimasu. 7 Kesa nanji ni okimashita ka. 8 Yuube atama ga itakatta desu. 9 Keiko san wa me ga kirei desu ne. 10 Ano onnanoko wa hontoo ni chiisai desu ne.

D Translate into Japanese:

1 Next autumn (autumn next year) I'd like to go somewhere quiet. 2 It takes one hour by train from Tokyo station. 3 Those boys work well. 4 Will my shirts be ready by five o'clock? 5 Do you like golf? 6 I always drink in the same bar. 7 What is that high building next to the post office? 8 I'm a poor singer. 9 Every day I work in a large factory from half past seven to half past three. 10 I need a better watch.

DÁI RÓKKA

BÉNRI NA HYOOGEN

Irasshaimáse.	Mata dóozo.
Irasshái.	O-ki o tsu̶kete.
Yóokoso irasshaimásh̶ta.	O-daiji ni.

BUNKEI

Buráun san wa ie ga níken to kuruma ga yóndai arimasu̶.
Máinichi sanjíkan benkyoo shimasu̶.
Suzuki san wa kodomo ga fu̶tari arimásu̶.
Ráigetsu (no) kokonoka ni Kánada ni ikimásu̶.
Tamágo o muttsu kaimash̶ta.
Ash̶ta éiga o mí ni ikimasu̶.

■ **KAIWA**

1 A: Ítsu Nihón e
      irasshaimásh̶ta ka.

   B: Séngetsu (no) yokka ni
      kimásh̶ta.

   A: Dono kúrai
      irasshaimasu̶ ka.

   B: Sankágetsu imasu̶.

2 A: Kyóoto-yuki no ki̶shá
      wa nánji ni demasu̶
      ka.

   B: Juurokúji sanpun ni demasu̶.

   A: Nánji ni Kyóoto ni
      tsu̶kimásu̶ ka.

   B: Juuhachíji sanjúppun ni
      tsu̶kimásu̶.

3 A: Kinoo Suzuki san to éiga
      o mí ni ikimash̶ta.

   B: Yókatta desu̶ ka.

   A: Máa máa desh̶ta.

4 A: Yúri chan wa o-iku̶tsu
      désu̶ ka.

   B: Kóngetsu no hatsu̶ka de
      fu̶tatsu ni narimásu̶.

   A: Ookíi desu̶ nee.

   B: Ée, yóku tabemasu̶ yo.

LESSON SIX

USEFUL EXPRESSIONS

Welcome! (shopkeeper to customer)

Please come again.

Welcome! Come in! (informal)

Take care; Have a good trip; Goodbye (etc.).

Welcome! Come in! (formal)

Look after yourself (to sick person).

SENTENCE PATTERNS

Mr Brown has two houses and four cars.
I study three hours every day.
Mr Suzuki has two children.
I'm going to Canada on the ninth of next month.
I bought six eggs.
I am going to see a film tomorrow.

CONVERSATIONS

1 A: When did you come to Japan?
   B: I came on the fourth of last month.
   A: How long will you be here?
   B: Three months.

2 A: What time does the train for Kyooto leave?
   B: It leaves at 16:03.
   A: What time does it arrive in Kyooto?
   B: It arrives at 18:30.

3 A: Yesterday I went to see a film with Miss Suzuki.
   B: Was it good?
   A: So so/Not bad (etc.)

4 A: How old is Yuri?
   B: She'll be two on the twentieth of this month.
   A: She is big, isn't she!
   B: Yes, she eats a lot, you know.

5 A: Kotoshi no natsu-yásumi   B: Yamá e ikimasʉ.
       ni dóko e ikimasʉ ka.

   A: Náze úmi e ikimasén ka.   B: Watashi wa hʲtogomi ga
                                          kirai désʉ.

6 A: Nichiyóobi ni   B: Nichiyóobi wa hito ga
       doobutsúen ni   -   oosugimásʉ.
       ikimashóo.

   A: Sore déwa doyóobi no   B: Jáa, món no máe de
       ása ni ikimashóo.   aimashóo.

7 A: Kayóobi no ban ni Abe   B: Áa, sóo desʉ ka. Asoko de
       san no tokoro e   náni o shimashʲta ka.
       ikimáshʲta.

   A: Osokú made máajan o   B: Abe san wa máajan ga sʉkí
       yarimashʲta.   desʉ née.

5 A: Where are you going for your summer holidays this year?

   B: I'm going to the mountains.

   A: Why don't you go to the sea?

   B: I hate crowds.

6 A: Let's go to the zoo on Sunday.

   B: On Sundays there are too many people.

   A: Then let's go on Saturday morning.

   B: Let's meet in front of the gate then.

7 A: I went to Mr Abe's place on Tuesday night.

   B: Did you? What did you do there?

   A: We played mahjong until late.

   B: Mr Abe likes his mahjong, doesn't he?

MORE NUMBERS AND NUMERAL CLASSIFIERS

In Lesson Four you learned the numbers and saw how they combined with the suffixes, *-en*, 'yen', *-nen*, 'years', and *-ji*, 'o'clock'. In Japanese, number words almost always combine with some suffix, the numeral classifier, which varies according to what is being counted, just as in English we say 'two head of cattle', 'six sheets of paper', 'three pairs of trousers' and so on. The quantative expression formed of the number and the appropriate numeral classifier usually occurs after the noun and particle; e.g., *jidóosha ga sándai arimasu̱*, 'I have three cars.' When the quantative expression comes before the noun it refers to, it is followed by *no*: *shichínin no samurai*, 'the seven samurai'.

Certain numbers undergo sound changes when followed by particular numeral classifiers. A list of the most important numeral classifiers and these sound changes is given in Appendix 1. Changes are most likely to occur after *ichi*, *san*, *roku*, *hachi* and *juu*, particularly before -h, -k, -t or -s.

-ka	'lesson'
dái íkka	'lesson one' (literally 'number one lesson')
dái rókka	'lesson six'
dái hákka	'lesson eight'
dái júkka/jíkka	'lesson ten'
-hyaku̱	100
sánbyaku̱	300
roppyaku̱	600
happyaku̱	800
-sén	1,000
sanzén	3,000
hassén	8,000

Although *ichí* and *hachí* often undergo sound changes *shi̱chí* never does. *Shi̱chí* is often replaced by *nána*.

Time and months

-gatsú is used for naming the months.

ichigatsú	January

nigatsú	February
sangatsú	March
shigatsú	April
gogatsú	May
rokugatsú	June
shichigatsú	July
hachigatsú	August
kugatsú	September
juugatsú	October
juuichigatsú	November
juunigatsú	December

-*kágetsu* is used for counting months.

ikkágetsu	'one month'
jukkágetsu	'ten months'
juuhakkágetsu	'eighteen months'

The form -*getsu* appears in the compounds, *séngetsu*, *kóngetsu* and *ráigetsu*, 'last month', 'this month', 'next month'.

The suffix -*jíkan*, 'hours', indicates duration of hours.

Sanjíkan yasumimáshιta.   'I rested three hours.'

-*fún*, 'minutes': the minutes from one to ten are *íppun*, *nífun*, *sánpun*, *yónpun*, *gófun*, *róppun*, *nanáfun*, *háppun*, *kyúufun*, *júppun/jíppun*. When telling the time the minutes are always given after the hour: *sánji háppun*, 'eight minutes past three'; *yóji gófun (sugi)*, 'five past four'. For minutes past the hour *súgi*, 'past', is optional, but *máe* is necessary to indicate minutes to the hour: *níji gofun mae*, 'five minutes to two'. This last might just as well be *ichíji gojuugofun*, 1:55, and in railway timetables and the like the twenty-four-hour clock is used, e.g. *nijúuji sánjuuroppun*, 20:36 or 8.36 p.m. *Gózen* is used for a.m. and p.m. is *gógo*. These come before the hours and minutes: *gózen rokuji*, '6.00 a.m.'

Some common numeral classifiers

A list of numeral classifiers combined with the numerals from one to ten is given in Appendix 1. Some of the common classifiers introduced in this lesson are as follows.

-nin	counter for people
-dai	counter for machines (cars, telephones, etc.)
-ken	counter for buildings (houses, shops, etc.)
-mai	'sheet', counter for thin flat objects (paper, plates, etc.)
-hon	counter for cylindrical objects (pens, bottles, etc.)
-satsu̧	counter for books
-tsuu	counter for letters
-hi̧ki	counter for animals (insects, fish, animals)
-too	'head', counter for large animals (horses, cattle, etc.)
-hai	'glassful', 'cupful'

Study Appendix 1 to see what sound changes occur when these are suffixed to the numerals. There is, in particular, great irregularity in the placing of the pitch accent. Here are some of the above in sentences.

Bíiru o íppon kudasai.	'One bottle of beer, please.'
Íi uma o sántoo kaimásḩta.	'He bought three good horses.'
Máinichi koohíi o goróppai nomimásu̧.	'Every day I drink five or six cups of coffee.'

Notice how to express the idea 'five' or 'six', etc. 'Two or three friends' is *tomodachi nisannin* even though 'two people' is *fu̧tarí*. 'One person' and 'two people', *hi̧tóri* and *fu̧tarí*, preserve the older Japanese numerals which were used before the present counting system was borrowed from China. The native Japanese numerals are now used only up to ten (except in a few compound words). They are used for counting boxes, pieces of furniture, round objects (eggs, fruit, etc.) and other miscellaneous objects without specific numeral classifiers. The native Japanese numerals are:

1 hi̧tótsu	2 fu̧tatsú	3 mittsú	4 yottsú	5 itsútsu̧
6 muttsú	7 nanátsu̧	8 yattsú	9 kokónotsu̧	10 tóo

The question word that goes with this series is *íku̧tsu*, 'how many?'. The native Japanese numerals are also used in counting years of age.

Anóko wa íku̧tsu desu̧ ka.	'How old is he?' (referring to a child)

Kokónotsu̥ desu̥.   'He is nine.'

After ten the usual Sino-Japanese numerals are used.

Suzuki san wa yónjuuni désu̥.   'Mr Suzuki is forty-two.'

There is, however, one exception. 'Twenty years old' is *hátachi*.

Counting days

Days are counted with a mixture of both systems of numerals. From the second to the tenth day the native Japanese numerals with some slight sound changes are used with the suffix -*ka*. The first day of the month is *tsuitachí*. To express the idea of one day's duration *ichinichi* is used, but for the other days the same word is used both for naming the day of the month and for expressing duration of days: *itsu̥ka*, 'the fifth [day of the month]' or 'five days'. With dates, *ni* is used where we would use 'on' in English.

Muika ni ̍kimáshi̥ta.   'I came on the sixth.'

The suffix -*kan* may be added where the meaning is days duration: *muika(-kan)* '[for] six days'.

Tsuitachí first day; *Ichinichí* one day	*Muika* sixth day; six days
Fu̥tsu̥ka second day; two days	*Nanoka* seventh day; seven days
Mikka third day; three days	*Yooka* eighth day; eight days
Yokka fourth day; four days	*Kokonoka* ninth day; nine days
Itsu̥ka fifth day; five days	*Tooka* tenth day; ten days

After ten the Sino-Japanese numerals are used followed by -*nichi* (*juuichinichí*, 'the eleventh', 'eleven days', etc.) but where the final unit is 'four' as in 'the fourteenth day', 'twenty-four days' etc. *júuyokka*, *níjuuyokka* and so on are used. 'Twenty days' or the 'twentieth of the month' is *hatsu̥ka*. 'How many days?' or 'What day of the month?' is *nánnichi*.

The days of the week

Nichiyóobi	Sunday
Getsuyóobi	Monday

Kayóobi	Tuesday
Suiyóobi	Wednesday
Mokuyóobi	Thursday
Kin' yóobi	Friday
Doyóobi	Saturday

NOUN + SHIMÁSU̧

Japanese has a class of verbs made up of a noun, usually originally borrowed from Chinese or English, and *shimásu̧*, 'to do': *benkyoo shimásu̧*, 'to study'; *ryóori shimasu̧*, 'to cook'; *ryokoo shimásu̧*, 'to travel, take a trip'; *kekkon shimásu̧*, 'to marry' (object followed by *to*); *unten shimásu̧*, 'to drive', etc. As the nouns also occur in other patterns without *shimásu̧*, as in *Benkyoo ga kirai désu̧*, 'I dislike study', the noun and verb are written separately, but the two usually function as a single unit and the noun is not followed by the object particle.

| *Máinichi Nihongo o sanjíkan benkyoo shimásu̧.* | 'I study Japanese for three hours every day.' |

VERB STEM + NI

The verb stem is formed by cutting off the *-másu̧* ending. This results in a verbal noun which can be followed by the particle *ni* and used in conjunction with a verb of motion (usually *ikimásu̧* or *kimásu̧*) to express the idea of going or coming in order to do something.

| *Tenránkai o mí ni ikimashḭta.* | 'I went to see the exhibition.' |
| *Su̧shí o tábe ni ikimashóo.* | 'Let's go and eat *sushi*.' |

With some verbs the stem can function like an independent noun.

| *Anóhḭto wa hanáshi ga joozú desu̧ né.* | 'He is good at speaking, isn't he?' |

But as this is by no means true of all verbs, such words are marked separately in the vocabularies. As the stem is in fact a noun, it follows that with verbs of the type, noun plus *shimásu̧*, *ni* is placed straight after the noun and *shimásu̧* is dropped altogether.

| *Nihón e benkyoo ni kimáshḭta.* | 'I came to Japan to study.' |

Notice that where a place phrase is present it is followed by *e*.

Depáato de kaimáshĮta.   'I bought it at the department
                                   store.'

But

Depáato e kai ni ikimáshĮta.   'I went to buy it at the depart-
                                   ment store.'/'I went to the
                                   department store to buy it.'

NOTES

Conversation 4 'In' or 'on' with time expressions is usually *de* when the main verb is *désĮ* or *narimásĮ*. This is because we are dealing with the idea of time accumulated 'by' a certain date and not with an action taking place at a single specific point of time.

   Conversation 5 Expressions like 'this summer holiday', 'next Tuesday' are usually expanded into two nouns linked with *no*, e.g. *Kotoshi no natsu-yasumi, raishuu no Kayóobi.*

VOCABULARY

tamágo	egg	*hĮtogomi*	crowd
ringo	apple	*kamí*	paper
míkan	mandarin orange	*món*	gate
orénji	orange	*samurai*	samurai, warrior
depáato	department store	*natsu-yásumi*	summer holiday
tenránkai	exhibition	*ása*	morning
doobutsúen	zoo	*hirú*	noon
doobutsu	animal	*ban*	night
sáru	monkey	*yuugata*	evening
umá	horse	*hirumá*	daytime
kĮshá	(steam) train, long-distance train	*yóru*	night time
		o-híru	lunch; noon
yamá	mountain	*góhan*	meal, cooked rice
úmi	sea	*asa-góhan*	breakfast
hanashí	story, talk	*hiru-góhan*	lunch

ban-góhan/ *yuugóhan*	dinner	*-dai*	(numeral classifier for machines)
máajan	mahjong		
unten suru	to drive	*-ken*	(numeral classifier for buildings)
kekkon suru (*to* after object)	to marry		
		-mai	(numeral classifier for thin flat objects)
ryokoo suru	to travel		
benkyoo suru	to study		
óoi	numerous		
sʉkunái	few, not many	*-hon*	(numeral classifier for cylindrical objects)
yarimásʉ	to do, to play (games)		
demásʉ	to go out (to leave)	*-satsʉ*	(numeral classifier for books)
dóozo	please		
náze	why	*-tsuu*	(numeral classifier for letters)
dóoshʉte	why		
gózen	before noon, a.m.		
gógo	afternoon, p.m.	*-hʉki*	(numeral classifier for small animals)
osoku	late		
hʉtóri	one (person)		
hʉtóri de	alone, by oneself	*-too*	(numeral classifier for large animals)
oosugimásʉ	to be too many	*-hai*	glassful, cupful
		-nichi/-ka	days
fʉtarí	two people	*-fun*	minutes
-nin	(numerical classifier for people)	*-kan*	(duration suffix)
		-ka	lesson
		-yuki	bound for –, to –
-gatsú	months (of the year)	*dái-*	number – (ordinal prefix)
-kágetsʉ	months (duration)		
		sugi	past
-getsʉ	month (compounds)	*áa*	Ah!
		máa máa	so so; not bad

kúrai/gúrai	about	*hatsɨka*	twentieth day
dono kurai	How long? How		of the month
	far? How much?	*hátachi*	twenty years
tsuitachí	first day of the		old
	month		

EXERCISE 6

A Supply the number and appropriate numeral classifier:
1 Jidoosha o (3) kaimashita. 2 Tomodachi (2) to issho ni eiga o mi ni ikimashita. 3 Ringo o (8) to tamago o (10) kudasai. 4 Konoaida ii hon o (3) yomimashita. 5 Sono chiisai sakana o (6) kudasai. 6 Hikidashi ni boorupen ga (6) to kami ga (4) arimashita. 7 Kono chikaku ni hon'ya ga (3) arimasu. 8 Kesa tegami o (3) dashimashita. 9 Kono daigaku ni gakusei ga (how many) imasu ka. 10 Suzuki san no kodomo wa (how old) desu ka.

B Substitution, expansion and transformation practice. Substitute the words in brackets for the words in italics, or expand the sentence by incorporating the word in brackets or transform as indicated in brackets. In all cases make any other changes the sense demands.
1 *Doyoobi* ni *eiga* o *mi* ni ikimasu. (senshuu; tomodachi; aimasu) 2 *Hakone* e *gorufu* o *yari* ni ikimashita. (Hokkaidoo; uma; kaimasu) 3 Kesa *tegami* o santsuu *dashimashita*. (koohii; nomimasu) 4 Ookina *kuruma* ga nandai irimasu ka. (kami) 5 Yuube osoku made tomodachi to *hanashimashita*. (maajan) 6 Kanojo wa dare ni *aimashita* ka. (kekkon) 7 Nihon de benkyoo shimasu. (kimashita) 8 Depaato de mikan o kaimasu. (ikimasu) 9 Chuugoku-ryoori o tabe ni ikimasu. (hortative) 10 Tenrankai o mi ni ikitai desu. (negative past)

C Translate into English:
1 Tookyoo kara Oosaka made hitori de unten shimashita. 2 Mikka mae ni tenrankai de Sumimoto san ni aimashita. 3 Doobutsuen de Nihon no saru o goroppiki mimashita. 4 Yoru itsumo nijikan gurai

benkyoo shimasu. 5 Dooshite maajan o yarimasen ka. 6 Nihongo no jisho ga sansatsu arimasu. 7 O-ki o tsukete. 8 Mokuyoobi no ban ni tomodachi to issho ni yuugohan o tabe ni ikimashita. 9 Kyoo wa shigatsu tsuitachi desu. 10 Karuizawa made jidoosha de nanjikan gurai kakarimasu ka.

D Translate into Japanese:
1 Welcome. How about a cup of coffee? 2 Where shall we go to eat German food/cooking? 3 Let's meet at the gate of the zoo at a quarter to eleven on Wednesday morning. 4 Did you see Mr Tanaka's three white horses? 5 The sea is beautiful in the evening, isn't it? 6 Shall we have lunch together in that big department store near the station? 7 How many books did you read last month? 8 Where would you like to travel? 9 I have breakfast at ten past seven every morning. 10 I am going to play golf in Karuizawa on the twentieth of next month.

DÁI NÁNAKA

■ **BÉNRI NA HYOOGEN**

O-dekake désu̶ ka.   Itte irasshái.

Ée, chótto.   Tadáima.
Itte mairimásu̶.   O-kaeri nasái.

BUNKEI

Abe san wa hataraite imásu̶ ga Míki san wa yasúnde imasu̶.
Kodomo ga benkyoo shi̶te imásu̶ kara shízuka ni shi̶te kudasai.
Ginza e itte yoofu̶ku o kaimáshi̶ta.
Kono misé wa yásu̶ku̶te oishii désu̶.
Hi̶kidashi ni háitte imasu̶.
Hako ni irete arimásu̶.

■ **KAIWA**

1 A: Íma náni o shi̶te imasu̶   B: Chi̶chi ni tegami o káite
      ka.   imasu̶.
   A: Otóosan wa dóko ni   B: Íma Róndon ni súnde imasu̶.
      irasshaimasu̶ ka.

2 A: Nódo ga kawakimáshi̶ta.   B: Ano ki̶ssáten de júusu o
                                        nomimashóo.
   A: Sandoitchi mo tabetái   B: Watashi wa onaka ga suite
      desu̶.   imasén kara nanimo
                                        tabemasén.

3 A: Óngaku ga su̶kí desu̶ ka.   B. Ée, koten-óngaku ga dáisu̶ki
                                        desu̶.
   A: Íma íi no o yatte imasu̶   B: Zéhi ki̶ki ni iki̶tái desu̶.
      yo.

4 A: Oishii tenpura o tabetái   B: Íi mise o shi̶tte imásu̶ kara,
      desu̶.   oshiete agemásu̶ yo.
   A: O-negai shimásu̶.

86

LESSON SEVEN

USEFUL EXPRESSIONS

Going somewhere?

Yes, just [down the road].
Goodbye (by person leaving the house)

Goodbye (by person staying in the house)
I'm back!
Welcome home.

SENTENCE PATTERNS

Mr Abe is working, but Mr Miki is resting.
The children are studying so please be quiet.
I went to the Ginza and bought some clothes.
This shop is cheap and the food tastes good too.
It is in the drawer.
It has been put into the box.

CONVERSATIONS

1 A: What are you doing now?

   B: I'm writing a letter to my father.

   A: Where is your father?

   B: He is living in London at present.

2 A: I'm thirsty.

   B: Let's have a soft-drink in that coffee shop.

   A: I want to have a sandwich too.

   B: I'm not hungry, so I shan't have anything to eat.

3 A: Do you like music?

   B: Yes, I love classical music.

   A: There is something good on now.

   B: I want to be sure to hear that.

4 A: I'd like to eat some good *tempura*.

   B: I know a good place. I'll take you there.

   A: Please do.

5 A: Ano nékᴜtai o mísete
kudasai.

   B: Dóre desᴜ ka.

  A: Ano hósokᴜte aói no
desᴜ.

   B: Kore wa Furansᴜsei désᴜ
kara kánari takái desᴜ.

  A: Okurimono désᴜ kara
kamaimasén.

6 A: Nihongo o oshiete
kudasái.

   B: Íi desᴜ yo. Oshiete agemásᴜ.
Ítsu hajimetái desᴜ ka.

  A: Suiyóobi no ban wa
íkaga desᴜ ka.

   B: Suiyóobi wa osokú made
hatarakimásᴜ kara
mokuyóobi ni shimashóo.

  A: Kékkoo desᴜ. Hachíji
ni o-taku ni
ikimásᴜ.

7 A: Dóko de Nihongo o
benkyoo shᴉte imásᴜ
ka.

   B: Jibun de benkyoo shᴉte
imásᴜ.

  A: Taihen muzukashii
deshóo.

   B: Ie, máda amari muzukashᴉku
nái desᴜ.

  A: Kore kara muzukashᴉku
narimásᴜ yo.

5 A: Show me that tie.

     B: Which one?

     A: The narrow, blue one.

     B: This is pretty expensive. It's made in France.

     A: It doesn't matter. It's a present.

6 A: Teach me Japanese, please.

     B: All right, I'll teach you. When do you want to start?

     A: What about Wednesday night?

     B: I work late on Wednesdays. Let's make it Thursday.

     A: That's fine. I'll come to your place at eight.

7 A: Where are you studying Japanese?

     B: I'm studying it by myself.

     A: It must be very difficult.

     B: No, it isn't very difficult yet.

     A: It will get a lot more difficult later.

THE FORMATION OF THE '-TE FORM'

	Stem*			Ending	'-te form'
	'eat'	tabe	mású		tábete
	'see'	mi	mású		míte
Group I	'get up'	oki	mású	-te	ókíte
	'to come'	ki	mású		kíte
	'to do'	shi	mású		shíte
	'lend'	kashi	mású		kashíte
	'write'	†kaki	mású	-ite	káite
	'hurry'	isogi	mású	-ide	isóide
	'wait'	machi	mású		mátte
Group II	'cut'	kiri	mású	-tte	kítte
	'meet'	ai	mású		átte
	'read'	yomi	mású		yónde
	'die'	shini	mású	-nde	shinde
	'fly'	tobi	mású		tonde

*Italics indicate assimilation of the syllable into the ending.
†*Ikimású* has an irregular *-te* form, *itte*.

The chart shows the formation of the '-*te* form', sometimes called the gerund, which occurs in a number of very common constructions, some of which are given below. The ending varies according to which of the two groups (conjugations) a verb belongs and, in the case of the Group II verbs, on the final consonant of the stem. For example, the '-*te* form' of the Group I verb *okimású*, 'to get up', is *ókíte*, but the '-*te* form' of the Group II verb *okimású*, 'to put', is *oite*. More will be said about the verb conjugations in the next lesson and you will be able to tell at a glance to which group most verbs belong. In the meantime, the list below of all Group I verbs with stems ending in -*i* (all verbs with stems ending in -*e* belong to Group I) which have been introduced so far should enable you to make the '*te* forms' of all the verbs you know.

Group I (and irregular)

Verbs with stems ending in -i

kimás̸ (irreg.)	'to come'
shimás̸ (irreg.)	'to do'
imás̸	'to be'
mimás̸	'to see'
karimás̸	'to borrow'
okimás̸	'to get up'

For Group I verbs *-te* is added directly to the stem: *mimás̸*, 'to see'; *míte*, 'seeing' (this is only a tag translation; the '*-te* form' seldom corresponds to the English gerund); *kimás̸*, 'to come'; *kĭte*, 'coming'; *shimás̸*, 'to do'; *shĭte*, 'doing'.

In the case of Group II verbs sound changes occur resulting from the assimilation of the last syllable of the stem into the '*-te*' of the ending. The only Group II verbs which preserve the final syllable of the base intact are those ending in *-shi*: *kashimás̸*, 'to lend'; *kashĭte*, 'lending'. Verbs with base-final *-ki* lose the *-k-* when *-te* is added: *kakimás̸*, 'to write'; *káite*, 'writing'. Verbs with *-gi* drop the *-g-* and the *-te* becomes *-de*: *isogimás̸*, 'to hurry'; *isóide*, 'hurrying'. Verbs with the stem-endings *-chi*, *-ri* or a vowel followed by *-i* have their '*-te* forms' ending in *-tte*: *karimás̸*, 'to mow, to cut', and *kaimás̸*, 'to buy', have identical '*-te* forms'; *katte* and *kachimás̸*, 'to win', is only distinguished from the other two by a difference in the pitch accent, *kátte*. Notice some verbs have accented *-te* forms while others do not. The verb given in the chart above, *kirimás̸*, is the normal verb 'to cut'.

Verbs with base-final *-bi*, *-mi* and *-ni* have '*-te* forms' in *-nde*: *tobimás̸*, 'to fly', becomes *tonde*, 'flying'; *yomimás̸*, 'to read', becomes *yonde*, 'reading'; and *shinimás̸*, 'to die', the only verb with a base ending in *-ni*, becomes *shinde*, 'dying'.

Note that the '*-te* form' of *ikimás̸*, 'to go', is irregular. It is *itte*, 'going', and not *iite* as expected.

The '-te form' of adjectives

The '*-te* form' of adjectives is made by adding *-te* to the adverbial *-ku* ending. If the dictionary form of the adjective (the plain present tense) is accented, the accent shifts one syllable to the left when *-ku*, or *-kṵte*, is added. If the dictionary form is unaccented the vowel before the *-kṵte* ending gains an accent.

| takái | tákaku | tákakṵte |
| akai | akaku | akákṵte |

The '-te form' of désṵ

The '-*te* form' of *désṵ* is *de*. This form is also used in making the '-*te* form' of the descriptive nouns, *kírei de*, 'quiet and . . .'

THE FUNCTIONS OF THE '-*TE* FORM'

-te imásṵ: the present continuous tense

You will remember that with most verbs the *-másṵ* ending conveys habitual action, a general truth or future action. With a very small number of verbs known as the stative verbs (those which mark their objects with *ga*), like *wakarimásṵ*, the *-másṵ* ending does describe the actual present situation. With all other verbs, in order to describe a present state, such as an action in progress, the *-te* form followed by *imásṵ* is used.

Háha wa zasshi o yónde imasṵ.　　'My mother is reading a magazine.'

Just as the present continuous tense in English can be used to cover an activity which continues over a long period, even though it might not actually be taking place at the time of speaking (as in 'I am studying Japanese now, you know'), the *-te imásṵ* form is used in Japanese: *Íma Nihongo o benkyoo shṵte imásu yo*. Some verbs which in English are stative and hence do not occur in the 'is . . . ing' construction behave as active verbs in Japanese and therefore need the *-te imasṵ* construction in order to describe present states,

Abe san wa okṵsan o ái shṵte　　'Mr Abe loves his wife.'
imásṵ.

This is true of most Japanese verbs. Compare the active and stative forms of the following:

tsɰkaremásɰ	'to get tired'	*tsɰkárete imasɰ*	'to be tired'
yasemásɰ	'to get thin'	*yasete imásɰ*	'to be thin'
fɰtorimásɰ	'to get fat'	*fɰtótte imasɰ*	'to be fat'
yoimásɰ	'to get drunk'	*yótte imasɰ*	'to be drunk'
haremásɰ	'to fine up'	*hárete imasɰ*	'to be fine'
oboemásɰ	'to memorize, learn'	*obóete imasɰ*	'to remember'
shirimásɰ	'to get to know'	*shɰtte imásɰ*	'to know'

Shɰtte imásɰ does not occur in the negative, but this does not apply to *obóete imasɰ* or, it seems, to any other verb which can appear in the *-te imásɰ* form.

Shízuko san o shɰtte imásɰ ka.	'Do you know Shizuko?'
Iie, shirimasén.	'No, I don't.'
Watashi o obóete imasɰ ka.	'Do you remember me?'
Iie, obóete imasen.	'No, I don't.'

As a general rule the *-te imásɰ* form with transitive verbs (those which can have objects followed by *o*) indicates an activity in progress and with intransitive verbs describes a present state. So the *-te imásɰ* form of the intransitive verb *ikimásɰ*, 'to go', does not describe an action in progress but a present state: *Amerika ni itte imasɰ*, 'He is in America'; 'He has gone to America', etc. The intransitive verb *hairimásɰ*, 'to enter', has a *-te imasɰ* form meaning 'to be in . . .',

Pén ga hako ni háitte imásɰ.   'The pen is in the box.'

Similarly, in *Mádo ga aite imásɰ*, 'The window is open', we see the stative form of *akimásɰ* 'to become open, to open'.

te arimasɰ, completed state

This construction is used only with transitive verbs and it describes a state arising from a completed action: *Kanji ga kokuban ni káite arimasɰ*, 'Characters are written on the blackboard' or 'Characters have been written on the blackboard.' In some cases a transitive verb in the *-te arimásɰ* form has a close counterpart in an intransitive verb in the *-te imásɰ* form. For example, from *iremásɰ*, 'to put in', we get *Pén ga hako ni irete arimásɰ*. The difference between this sentence and the one with *háitte imasụ* given above is that the *-te arimásụ* construction strongly suggests an agent. It means, 'The pen has been put into the box by someone' or 'Someone has put the pen in the box'.

Of course the *-te* form can be followed by the past tense of the auxiliary to indicate continuous action or completed state in the past.

Kinoo Tanaka senséi wa Doitsugo no hón o yónde imashịta.	'Yesterday Dr Tanaka was reading a German book.'
Kanji ga móo kokuban ni káite arimashịta.	'The characters were already written on the blackboard.'

-te kudasái, **please**

Kudasái after the *-te* form makes a polite request, 'please . . . for me'.

Moo sụkóshi yukkuri hanáshịte kudasai.	'Please speak a little more slowly.'

(Note the use of *moo* in front of an adverb of quantity in the sense of 'more' (see Lesson Eight).)

Mata ashịta irasshátte kudasai.	'Please come again tomorrow.'

Remember, too, that *kudasái* can take a direct object, in which case it means 'please give me':

Ano ringo o kudasái.	'Please give me that apple.'

-te agemásụ, **'I shall . . . for you'**

Agemásụ, 'to give' (to a respected person), used after the *-te* form, is often used for 'I shall . . . for you'.

Misete agemásụ	'I shall show it to you.'

-te **linking clauses, 'and'**

We have seen how 'and' joining nouns is *to*, *inú to néko* (a dog and a cat). To join clauses the verb at the end of the first clause is put into the *-te* form.

Résutoran ni itte sutéeki o   'We went to the restaurant and
  tabemáshita.   ate steak.'

The *-te* form has no tense. This is supplied by the main verb at the
end of the sentence.
  Sumimasén after the *-te* form means 'I'm sorry I . . .'

O-kane o takusán tsukatte   'I'm sorry I spent [so] much
  dóomo sumimasén.   money!'

'Thank you for . . . ing' is usually expressed by *-te kudasátte arígatoo gozaimasu/gozaimashita.*

Irasshátte kudasatte arígatoo   'Thank you for coming.'
  gozaimashita.

It is in this function of linking clauses that we find the '-*te* form' of
the adjectives and *désu*. Two or more adjectives coming before a
noun are usually joined with the '-*te* form', but one also hears
sequences of adjectives in the plain present-tense form, with a slight
pause after each: *Takákute shirói bíru,* or *Takái, shirói bíru,* 'a high,
white building'. Where there is no noun present the '-*te* form' must
be used.

Kore wa shírokute are wa akai   'This is white and that is red.'
  désu.

De, the '-*te* form of *désu*, is used in sentences of the type

Anáta wa senséi de watashi wa   'You are a teacher and I am a
  gakusei désu.   student.'

Often the '-*te* form' suggests a mild causal relationship.

Takákute kaimasén deshita.   'It was expensive so I did not
                                      buy it.'

An adjective in the '-*te* form' followed by *íi desu* is used much as
we use 'nice and . . .' in English.

Yásukute ii desu.   'It is nice and cheap.'
                                    [Literally, 'Being cheap it is
                                      good.']
Koko wa shízuka de íi desu.   'This place is nice and quiet.'

-TO SHITE, 'AS'

The '-*te* form' of *shimásu* is used after a noun followed by the particle *to* in the sense of 'as . . .', 'in the capacity of'.

Eigo no senséi to shite Nihon ni kimashita.	'He came to Japan as an English teacher.'
Hako o teeburu to shite tsukaimáshita.	'We used the box as a table.'

GA, KEREDOMO, 'BUT'

Ga and *Keredomo* are used to link contrasting clauses like English 'but' or 'however'. They belong to the preceding clause and are pronounced as if they were attached to the verb they follow. You can pause after *ga* or *keredomo* but not before them. Clause final particles like *ga* and *keredomo* coordinate and subordinate clauses to the main verb at the end of the sentence.

Kore wa yasúi desu ga sore wa takái desu.	'This is cheap but that is expensive.'
Tanaka san o shitte imásu keredomo Abe san wa shirimasén.	'I know Mr Tanaka, but I don't know Mr Abe.'

KARA, 'BECAUSE'

This clause-final particle indicates that the clause preceding it gives a reason for the action or state described in the main verb. It is like the English 'because', or 'as', but remember that you must reverse the order of the Japanese clauses when translating into English. If you stick to the Japanese clause order 'and so' is a more appropriate translation.

Íma jikan ga arimasén kara ashitá ni shite kudasái.	'Please come tomorrow because I haven't any time now.'
	'I haven't any time now so make it tomorrow please.'

VOCABULARY

résutoran	restaurant	*sumimásu*	to live
kissáten	tea shop, café	*hairimasu*	to enter
júusu	(orange) juice	*iremásu*	to put in
sandoítchi	sandwich	*akimásu*	to come open,
sutéeki	steak		open
tenpura	(fish and	*akemásu*	to open
	vegetables	*shimemásu*	to close, to shut
	deep-fried	*shimarimásu*	to close
	in batter)		(intransitive),
nódo ga	(I'm) thirsty		become
kawakimashita			closed
o-naka ga	(I'm) hungry	*oshiemásu*	to teach, inform
sukimáshita		*misemásu*	to show
yoofuku	(Western)	*shirimásu*	to get to know
	clothes	*shitte imásu*	to know
nékutai	tie	*shirimasén*	to not know
okurimono	present	*oboemásu*	to remember
inú	dog	*hajimemásu*	to begin (transit)
néko	cat	*kashimásu*	to lend
kanji	Chinese	*karimásu*	to borrow
	character		(Group I)
kokuban	blackboard	*isogimásu*	to hurry
óngaku	music	*arukimásu*	to walk
koten-óngaku	classical music	*aruíte*	on foot,
mádo	window		walking
chichí	(my) father	*oyogimásu*	to swim
háha	(my) mother	*tobimásu*	to fly
otóosan	(your/his)	*tsukaimásu*	to use
	father	*machimásu*	to wait for
okáasan	(your/his)	*shinimásu*	to die
	mother	*okimásu*	to get up
ai shimásu	to love		(Group I)
oishii	delicious,	*okimásu*	to put
	tasty	*kirimásu*	to cut
muzukashii	difficult	*karimásu*	to mow, to cut
hosói	narrow, thin,	*haremásu*	to fine up
	slim	*tsukaremásu*	to get tired

yasemásu	to get thin	*moo*	more
futorimásu	to get fat	*kánari*	fairly, rather
yoimásu	to get drunk	*taihen*	very
kamaimasén	it doesn't matter	*kore kara*	(from) now (on)
		-sei	made in –
-te agemásu	I do . . . for you/him	*zéhi*	certainly, definitely
-te kudasái	please, (you) do for me	*jibun de*	(by) oneself
		ga	but
to shite	as, in the capacity of	*keredomo*	but
		kara	because

EXERCISE 7

A Change the following to continuous or stative verb forms:
1 Kissaten de juusu o nomimasu. 2 Koten-ongaku o kikimashita. 3 Kanojo wa yasemasu. 4 Moo okimasu ka. 5 Oishii sandoitchi o tabemasu. 6 Ano mado ga akimasu. 7 Chichi wa ongaku o oshiemasu. 8 Hikooki ga tobimasu. 9 Nani o tsukaimasu ka. 10 Doko de machimashita ka.

B Supply what is missing inside the brackets and give the correct forms of the verbs italicized:
1 Kokuban ni kanji ga *kakimasu* ( ). 2 Anokata o *oboemasu* ( ). 3 Abe san wa kanari *tsukaremasu* ( ) ne. 4 Ginza ( ) *ikimasu* yoofuku ( ) kaimashita. 5 Shachoo wa ima Amerika ( ) *ikimasu* imasu. 6 Akai nekutai wa ano ooki ( ) hako ( ) *irete* ( ). 7 Sono jisho ( ) *kashimasu* kudasai. 8 Kono mise no tenpura wa *oishii* yasui ( ). 9 Shizuko san ( ) *futorimasu* imasu ( ) Haruko san ( ) *yasemasu* imasu. 10 Itsumo doko ( ) *oyogimasu* ni irasshaimasu ( ).

C Translate into English:
1 O-kaeri nasai. 2 Daigaku de nani o oshiete imasu ka. 3 Michiko san no okaasan o shitte imasu ka. 4 Watashi wa nodo ga kawakimashita kara ano kissaten e koohii o nomi ni ikimashoo. 5 Kono

nekutai o chichi e no okurimono to shite kaimashita. 6 Ano ooki-kute kuroi inu wa dare no desu ka. 7 O-dekake desu ka. 8 Kodomo no neko ga shinimashita kara moo ippiki kai ni kimashita. 9 Mainichi o-taku kara kaisha e aruite irasshaimasu ka. 10 Ima wa jikan ga arimasu keredomo niji kara kaisha e dekakemasu kara isoide kudasai.

D Translate into Japanese:
1 Please teach me some Japanese. 2 Where are you living now? 3 We went to the sea for a swim. 4 This restaurant is cheap and [the food is] tasty. 5 The dictionaries have been put on that bookshelf. 6 He was a little bit drunk last night. 7 The door is closed, but the window is open. 8 Please lend me ¥2,000 because I want to buy that tie. 9 It's fine today so let's go to the zoo. 10 Please use my pen. I'm not using it now.

DÁI HÁKKA

■ **BÉNRI NA HYOOGEN**

Dóo shimashịta ka.
Daijóobu desụ.
Damé desụ.

Tanoshími desụ.
Go-shinpai náku.
Taihen désụ.

BUNKEI

Háyaku okíru koto ga
dekimasén.
Nihón e itta kotó ga arimasen.
Unten shịte iru hịto wa dáre
desụ ka.

Ashịta ikụ kotó ni shimashịta.

Asátte kúru deshoo.
Yuube míta éiga wa
omoshírokatta desụ.

■ **KAIWA**

1 A: Konogoro kaigai-ryókoo
o suru hịto ga
fuemáshịta né.

B: Ée, o-kane to hima no áru
hịto ga óoi desụ yo.

A: Jitsú wa watashi mo
ráigetsu Yooroppa e
ikimásụ.

B: Urayamashíi desụ né.

2 A: O-káasan ni tegami o
kakimashịta ka.

B: Iie, konogoro wa benkyoo
de isogáshịkụte káku
hima ga arimasén.

A: O-káasan wa shinpai
shịte iru deshóo.

B: Iie, nárete imasụ kara
daijóobu desụ.

3 A: Sore wa Suzuki san ga
tótta shashin désụ ka.

B: Ée, kyónen no haru-yásumi
ni Itaria de torimáshịta.

A: Taihen késhịki no kírei
na tokoro desụ né.

B: Ée kono shashin déwa
wakarimasén ga subarashíi
machí desụ.

100

LESSON EIGHT

USEFUL EXPRESSIONS

What's the matter?
It's all right.
It's no good.

[I'm] looking forward to it.
Please don't worry.
It's terrible!

SENTENCE PATTERNS

I can't get up early.

I've never been to Japan.
Who is the person driving?

I've decided to go tomorrow.

He'll probably come the day
  after tomorrow.
The film I saw last night was
  interesting.

CONVERSATIONS

1 A: There are a lot more
        people going abroad
        these days, aren't
        there?

   A: Actually I am going to
        Europe next month
        too.

   B: Yes, there are a lot of
        people with money and
        spare time.

   B: Half your luck!/I envy you!

2 A: Did you write to your
        mother?

   A: Your mother must be
        worried.

   B: No, lately I've been busy
        with study and haven't
        had time to write.

   B: No it's all right. She's used
        to it.

3 A: Did you take that
        photograph, Mr
        Suzuki?

   A: It's a place with
        beautiful scenery,
        isn't it?

   B: Yes, I took it when I was on
        holiday in Italy last
        spring.

   B: Yes, you can't tell from this
        photograph, but it is a
        glorious town.

4 A: Shachoo wa
    irasshaimásɥ ka.

   A: Iie, kyuu ni Tookyoo e
    kimásh̬ta kara.

B: Hái imásɥ ga, kyóo wa
   taihen isogashíi desɥ.
   Yakɥsoku ga arimásɥ ka.

B: Sumimasén ga kyóo wa áu
   jikan ga arimasén kara
   mata ash̬ta irasshátte
   kudasai.

5 A: Raishuu kúru h̬to wa
    dáre desɥ ka.

   A: Kyónen átta h̬to desɥ
    ka.

B: Kámera o yushɥtsu sh̬te iru
   kaisha no hanbai-búchoo
   desɥ.

B: Iie, chigau h̬to deshóo.

6 A: Ash̬ta inaka e doráibu
    ni iku deshóo?

B: Ie, raishuu ikɥ kotó ni
   shimash̬ta.

   A: Náze desɥ ka.

B: Kónban kara tomodachi ga
   uchi e tomari ni kimásɥ.

4 A: Is the director in?

B: Yes, but he's very busy today. Do you have an appointment?

A: No. I suddenly found myself in Tokyo.

B: I am sorry, but he hasn't time to see you today. Please come back tomorrow.

5 A: Who is the man coming next week?

B: He is the sales manager of a company which exports cameras.

A: Is he the man we met last year?

B: No, probably somebody else.

6 A: You're going for a drive in the country tomorrow, aren't you?

B: No, I've decided to go next week.

A: Why?

B: We've got a friend coming to stay from tonight.

PLAIN PRESENT TENSE: 'DICTIONARY FORM'

In this lesson we meet the plain present and past forms of the verb. These occur in the polite style of speech as non-final verbs. A final verb in one of the -*másu* or *désu* forms·is sufficient to make most Japanese sentences polite, but as we have seen it is usual for the verb at the end of a clause ending in *ga*, 'but', and *kara*, 'because', to be in the same style as the final verb. Before discussing the uses of the plain-style verbs let us see how these verbs are formed.

The plain present tense is formed by attaching the suffix -*(r)u* to the verb root.

In Japanese verbal suffixes can be divided into those which are attached to the stem and those which are attached to the root, so it is important to grasp this distinction. The verb root of Group I verbs is the same as the stem (simply take off the -*másu*) and ends in either one of the vowels *i* or *e*. Group I verbs, then, are known as the vowel-root verbs. Verbs of Group II have roots ending in consonants and for that reason they are called the consonant-root verbs. To find the root of most verbs of Group II cut off the final -*imásu*; e.g., *kakimasu* has the root *kak*-. Verbs which after the -*imásu* has been removed end in -*ch* or -*sh* change these to -*t* and -*s* respectively; e.g., *machimasu* has the root *mat*- and *hanashimásu* becomes *hanas*-. Verbs of Group II which have -*a* or -*o* before the -*imásu* ending are actually consonant-root verbs ending in -*w*, but this appears in the pronunciation and hence in the romanization only before *a*. The root of *aimásu* is *aw*-, and *omoimásu*, 'to think', has the root *omow*-. When the present tense -*ru* ending is attached to a consonant-root verb the -*r* of the suffix drops. The only other point to note is that *u* does not occur after *t* – so verbs with roots ending in *t*- have their present tense forms ending in *tsu*-. *Kimásu*, 'to come', and *shimásu*, 'to do', have present forms *kúru* and *suru*. *Irasshaimásu* is also formed irregularly from the plain present form *irassháru*. The plain form of *désu* is *dá*.

The formation of the plain present tense is summarized in the chart. As this plain present-tense form is the form in which words are listed in dictionaries it is also called the 'dictionary form'. From now on this is how verbs will appear in the vocabularies of this book. You will notice that some verbs have an accent in their dictionary forms while others do not. As even accented verbs lose their accent when the -*másu* endings are attached it is not possible to tell the accent of a verb from the -*másu* form. You should, therefore, learn verbs in their dictionary forms. Accented verbs have the accent mark on the penultimate (last but one) syllable.

-*másu* form	Root	Present tense suffix	Plain present tense of verb (dictionary form)
Vowel-root			
tabemásu	tábe-		tabéru
mimásu	mí-		míru
imásu	i-		iru
Irregular			
shimásu	su-	-(r)u	suru
kimásu	kú- (kó-)		kúru
Consonant-root			
ka*k*imásu	kák-		káku
ka*sh*imásu	kas-		kasu
*machi*másu	mát-		mátsu
aimásu	aw-		á*u*
irasshaimásu	irasshár		irassháru

Note Take special note of the italicized sound changes.

It is usually possible to tell from the dictionary form of a verb whether it belongs to Group I (the vowel-root verbs) or Group II (the consonant-root verbs). Most verbs ending in -*eru* or -*iru* belong to Group I. Those which do not are listed in the vocabularies of this book with a hyphen after the stem. Here are some common consonant-root verbs ending in -*eru* and -*iru*.

káer-u	'to return [home]'	kaerimásu
her-u	'to decrease'	herimásu
ir-u	'to need'	irimásu
kír-u	'to cut'	kirimásu
háir-u	'to enter'	hairimásu
hashír-u	'to run'	hashirimásu
shir-u	'to get to know'	shirimásu

The English infinitive is used as a convention in referring to verbs, but it must be remembered that the dictionary form in Japanese is the plain-style, present-tense form. The *-(r)u* ending which indicates the present tense also occurs after the polite-style suffix *-más-* in the *-másʮ* ending.

THE PLAIN PAST TENSE

The plain past-tense suffix is *-ta*. We have already met it in *-máshʮta*, *déshʮta* and *-katta* (past tense of adjectives). It is subject to the same sound changes as the '*-te* form', so simply change the *-e* of the '*-te* form' to *-a*: *itte*, 'going'; *itta*, 'went'.

Verbs which are unaccented in the dictionary form are unaccented in the '*-te* form' and in the past tense: *ireru*, 'to insert'; *ireta*, 'inserted'; *tobu*, 'to fly'; *tonda*, 'flew'. With accented vowel roots (i.e. accented in the dictionary form) the addition of the *-te* or *-ta* ending pushes the accent mark one syllable to the left: *tabéru*, 'to eat'; *tábeta*, 'ate'; *kazoéru*, 'to count'; *kazóeta*, 'counted'.

The dictionary form and the plain-style past-tense form are used in the polite style of speech for non-final verbs only. The use of the plain style in final verbs will be dealt with in a later chapter.

KOTÓ GA DEKIMÁSʮ, 'CAN'

One way of indicating the potential is to use *kotó ga dekimásʮ* after the dictionary form of the verb. In this construction *kotó* is a noun meaning 'thing' or 'fact', which has the function of nominalizing the verb so it can be followed by the particle *ga* and the whole phrase can become the object of the stative verb *dekimásʮ*, 'to be able', 'to be produced', etc.

Nihongo o hanásʮ kotó ga   'Can you speak Japanese?'
   dekimásʮ ka.

With noun-plus-*shimásʮ* (noun + *suru*) verbs *dekimásʮ* is used without *suru kotó*.

Kuruma no unten ga dekimásʮ   'Can you drive a car?'
   ka.

In this case the noun (*unten*, etc.) is linked to the preceding noun by *no*. Literally it means, 'Can you do the driving of a car?'

Koko wa shízuka de benkyoo ga   'I can study here because it's
   dekimás.   quiet.'

Dekimás is also used directly after nouns denoting languages, when it means 'to be able' to speak.

Nihongo ga dekimás ka.   'Can you speak Japanese?'

KOTÓ NI SHIMÁS, 'TO DECIDE TO'

This is another construction with *kotó* used after the dictionary form.

Rainen Nihón ni ik kotó ni   'I have decided to go to Japan
   shimáshta.   next year.'

ADJECTIVAL CLAUSES

One of the most common uses of the plain forms of the verb is in adjectival clauses. An adjectival clause is like the relative clause in English (starting with 'who', 'whose', 'whom', 'which' or 'that') in that it qualifies a noun phrase, but it differs from the English and follows a general rule of Japanese structure, in that it precedes the noun it qualifies. Actually we have already met the adjectival clause in dealing with the adjective. *Takái bíru* means 'a building which is high'. Here the adjective is in the present tense, but it may be in the past tense: *muzukáshkatta shkén*, 'the examination which was difficult' (but is not any more), etc. In the same way a verb in the plain present or past-tense form may be used to describe a following noun.

Míru tokoro ga óoi des.   'There are lots of places to see.'

The verb may come at the end of a long clause.

Ototói no ban Suzuki san no   'I telephoned the woman I met
   páatii de átta onnanohtó ni   the night before last at Mr
   denwa shimáshta.   Suzuki's party.'

    Japanese adjectival clauses do not specify the relationship to the

noun they qualify as precisely as the relative clause does in English.
Taken out of context, *míta hĳto* could mean 'the man whom I saw' or
'the man who saw me'. This ambiguity can be removed by including
the subject or object of the verb: *Watashi ga míta hĳto*, 'the man I
saw', and *Watashi o míta hĳto*, 'the man who saw me'. Ambiguity
often occurs when an indirect object is involved – *Tegami o okĳtta
hĳto*, 'the man who sent the letter' or 'the man to whom I sent the
letter'. Usually the context will make it clear which meaning is
intended. If there is likely to be any misunderstanding include the
subject of the adjectival clause. The subject of an adjectival clause
can be followed by either *ga* or *no*.

watashi ga/no shĳtte iru hĳto	'someone I know'
benkyoo ga/no kirai na gakĳsei	'a student who dislikes study'
ḿe ga/no kírei na onnanohĳto	'a woman with beautiful eyes'
sé ga/no takái otokonoko	'a tall boy'

Sé ga takái is one of a number of adjectival phrases in Japanese
which function like a single adjective. Others are: *haba ga hirói*, 'to
be wide'; *haba ga semái*, 'to be narrow' (*haba* is a noun meaning
width); and *sé ga hĳkúi*, 'to be short'. The expressions with *sé*,
'stature', are used only when talking about people.

NOMINALIZATION

Just as an adjectival clause ending in a plain form verb can be used
to describe a noun, a clause can be nominalized, so that it can
become the subject or object of another verb, by the addition of the
particle *no*. This is the same *no* we met in Lesson Five meaning 'the
one' in expressions like *akai no*, 'the red one', etc. So, *míta no*
means 'the one I saw'; *ashĳta kau no*, 'the one I'm going to buy
tomorrow'; and *ototói tomodachi ni okĳtta no*, 'the one I sent to my
friend the day before yesterday'. Often when the nominalized clause
is the subject or object of another verb, the English gerund gives a
more appropriate translation.

Sensei ga tegami o káite iru no o mimáshĳta.	'I saw the teacher writing a letter.'
Nihongo o hanásu no wa muzukashii désĳ ka.	'Is speaking Japanese difficult?'
	'Is it difficult to speak Japanese?'

You have now learned five ways to qualify a noun in Japanese. They are summarized in the chart. The use of negative verbs in adjectival clauses is treated in Lesson Eleven.

EXPANSION OF THE NOUN

1	Demonstrative adjective			*kono*	'this'	
				sono	'that'	
				ano	'that over there'	
2	Noun	+ no		*gakųsei no*	'the student's'	
3	Descriptive noun	+ na	noun	*rippa na*	'splendid'	*hon*
						'book'
4	Adjective root	+ tense		*taká-i*	'expensive'	
				taka-katta	'was expensive'	
5	Verb root	+ tense		*yóm-u*	'reads'	
				yón-de irų	'is reading'	
				yón-da	'read'	

Adjectival clauses can be used before the noun *no*, 'the one', just as adjectives can: *akai no*, 'the red one'; *kinóo míta no*, 'the one I saw yesterday.'

KOTÓ GA ARIMÁSŲ, 'TO HAVE EXPERIENCED'

Kotó ga arimásų after the plain, past tense of a verb means, 'to have experienced', 'to have done', etc. In interrogative and negative sentences this construction corresponds to English expressions with 'ever' or 'never'.

Inaka ni súnda koto ga arimasų.	'I have lived in the country.'
Sashimí o tábeta koto ga arimásų ka.	'Have you ever eaten *sashimi?*'
Kono óngaku o kiita kotó ga arimasen.	'I've never heard this music.'

Kotó ga dekimasų, kotó ni shimasų and *kotó ga arimasų* can, of course, occur in adjectival clauses, in which case they appear in the plain style.

Nihongo o hanásɥ kotó ga dekiru gaikokújin ga kánari óoi desɥ.

'There are quite a lot of foreigners who can speak Japanese.'

Kinóo Nihón ni súnda koto no aru gakɥsei ni aimáshɥta.

'Yesterday I met a student who has lived in Japan.'

Dá, the dictionary form of *desɥ*, is not used in adjectival clauses. It is replaced by *no*, as in *Shachoo no Suzuki san*, 'Mr Suzuki the Director' (the *no* indicating apposition, introduced in Lesson Three) or in more formal speech by the full form *de aru*:

Watashi no hɪsho de aru Ueda san.

'Miss Ueda who is my secretary.'

The plain past-tense form, however, is used:

Watashi no untenshu dátta hɪto.

'The person who used to be my driver.'

DESHÓO

This is the polite probable form of *désu*, introduced in Lesson Five. It can occur as the main verb of a sentence in the sense of 'probably is', 'I suppose . . . is', etc.

Anóhito wa Nihonjín deshoo.

'He is probably Japanese.'

It can also be used after a verb in the plain style to mean 'probably does', 'probably did', etc.

Kinóo kɪta deshoo.

'I suppose he came yesterday.'

If said with a rising intonation, *deshóo* is something like the sentence-final particle *né*, and means 'don't you think?', 'isn't it so that?' It is rather less positive than *né*, as when 'aren't you?', 'isn't he?' etc. are pronounced with a rising intonation in English.

Ashɪta ikú deshóo?

'You are going tomorrow, aren't you?'

Where there is a question word in the sentence and no *ka* at the end, *deshóo* means 'I wonder'.

Ashɪta nánji ni kúru deshoo [falling intonation].

'I wonder what time he'll be coming tomorrow.'

Anóhito wa dáre deshoo.   'I wonder who he is.'

Where *ka* is used after *deshóo*, the sentence becomes an indirect (and therefore polite) request for information: 'I wonder if you could tell me . . .', etc.

AshĮta irassháru deshóo ka.   'I wonder if you would mind telling me if you are coming tomorrow?'

AnóhĮto wa dáre deshóo ka.   'Would you mind telling me who he is?'

MÓO AND MÁDA

We have met *móo* in the sense of 'already': *Móo dekimashĮta*, 'It is ready.'/'It is already done.' With a negative verb it means 'no longer', 'any more', 'not now'.

Móo yasúi no o kau kotó ga dekimasén.   'You can't buy cheap ones any more.'

In questions it is often equivalent to English 'yet'.

Móo kimáshĮta ka   'Has he come yet?'

Moo (this time without the accent) coming before an adverb of quantity (including the numerals and numeral classifiers) means 'more'.

Moo hĮtótsĮ kudasái.   'Give me one more, please.'

Moo sĮkóshi itadakimásĮ.   'I'd like a little more [food], please.'

Moo does not usually occur before *takĮsán*, 'a lot', but *móo* does. So *Móo takĮsán desĮ* is a common way of saying 'I've had sufficient' (literally, 'already a lot'), though the expression *Móo kékkoo desĮ* which means the same thing is preferable as it is more polite. Notice the difference in meaning between *móo* and *moo* in the following:

Móo sannen imásĮ.   'I've been here three years already.'

Moo sannen imásĮ.   'I'll be here for another three years.'

Máda with a negative verb means 'not yet': *Máda kimasen*, 'He has not come yet' (or, with future reference, 'He won't be coming for a while yet'). There is also a strong tendency to use *-te imasén* after *máda* in the senses of 'have not yet': *Máda yónde imasén*, 'I have not read it yet'. In this case, even with transitive verbs the *-te iru* ending indicates a present state rather than an activity in progress. With an affirmative verb it usually means 'still': *Máda kimasu*, 'There are still more coming'. But *máda desu* means 'not yet'.

Móo shigoto ga owarimáshlta ka.	'Have you finished work yet?'
Máda desu.	'Not yet.'

NOTES

Useful expressions   *Tanoshimi désu* is shortened from the full form *tanoshimi ni shlte imasu* which is also very commonly heard.

VOCABULARY

kàmera	camera	*rippa na*	splendid, fine
shashin	photograph	*damé na*	no good
késhlki	scenery	*sé ga hlkúi*	short (of people)
inaka	countryside		
haru-yásumi	spring holiday	*haba ga hirói*	wide
doráibu	drive	*haba ga semái*	narrow
untenshu	driver	*hijoo ni*	very, extremely
kaigai-ryókoo	overseas trip	*omoshirói*	interesting, amusing
gaikokujin/ gaijin	foreigner	*isogashíi*	busy
yunyuu	import	*subarashíi*	wonderful
yushltsu	export	*urayamashíi*	enviable, be envious
hanbai	sales		
hanbai-búchoo	sales manager	*yunyuu suru*	to import
denwa	telephone	*yushltsu suru*	to export
hima	free time	*denwa suru*	to telephone
yaklsoku	appointment, promise	*yaklsoku suru*	to promise
		fuéru	to increase
sashimí	raw fish	*heru*	to decrease

naréru	to get used to	*dátta*	was
kazoéru	to count	*jitsú wa*	in fact
tóru	to take	*kyuu ni*	suddenly
tomaru	to stay, to stop	*kotó ga áru*	to have done
chigau	to be different (from)	*kotó ga dekíru*	to be able
omóu	to think	*kotó ni suru*	to decide to
dá/de áru	to be		

EXERCISE 8

A Combine the following into a single sentence using an adjectival clause:

1 Kinoo kissaten de tomodachi ni aimashita. Kare mo Nihongo o benkyoo shite imasu. 2 Shachoo no heya de hito ga matte imasu. Untenshu desu. 3 Anohito wa Suzuki san desu. Itsumo omoshiroi hanashi o shimasu. 4 Tegami o kakimasen. Hima ga arimasen. 5 Kamera o yushutsu shite imasu. Sono kamera wa taihen ii desu. 6 Nihonjin ga kaigairyokoo o shimasu. Sono hitotachi ga fuemashita. 7 Yuube paatii de onnanohito ni aimashita. Kanojo wa daigaku de Eigo o oshiete imasu. 8 Kore wa shashin desu. Yushutsu-buchoo ga torimashita. 9 Kinoo sashimi o tabemashita. Sore wa ikaga deshita ka. 10 Nihon ni gaijin ga kimasu. Karetachi wa sugu Nihon-ryoori ni naremasu.

B Expand the following sentences by incorporating the words in brackets. Make any other changes the sense demands:

1 Nihon de Nihongo o benkyoo shimasu. (koto ni suru) 2 Jidoosha o unten shimasen. (dekiru) 3 Yooroppa no inaka ni sumimashita ka. (koto ga aru) 4 Sono hako o akemasen ka (dekiru) 5 Moo machimasen. (dekiru) 6 Hanbai-buchoo wa rippa na uchi ni sunde imasu. (deshoo) 7 Yama no keshiki ga kirei desu. (deshoo) 8 Otoosan wa oyogimasu ka. (dekiru) 9 Kono subarashii jidoosha o mite urayamashii desu. (-katta deshoo) 10 Konban wa koten-ongaku o kiki ni ikimasu. (koto ni suru)

C Translate into English:

1 Ashita no kaigi ni dare ga deru deshoo. 2 Tanaka sensei ga unten shite iru jidoosha wa subarashii desu ne. 3 Igirisu ni irasshatta koto ga arimasu ka. 4 Kono kamera de wa amari ii shashin o toru koto ga dekimasen. 5 Ashita inaka e doraibu ni iku koto ni shimashita. 6 Nihongo o benkyoo suru jikan ga herimashita. 7 Mainichi ga isogashikute taihen deshoo. 8 Nihon kara no jidoosha no yunyuu wa hijoo ni fuemashita. 9 Kyonen no haru-yasumi ni itta tokoro e moo ichido ikimashoo. 10 Doo shimashita ka.

D Translate into Japanese:

1 Give me another [= one more] glass of whisky, please. 2 Who is the short man over there? 3 She could not marry the man she loves. 4 How many cameras do you export a year? 5 I've decided to stay two more days. 6 Can you eat *sashimi*? 7 This room is narrow. 8 Do you really think so? 9 Please open that box and count the pens inside it. 10 What time are you free on Friday?

DÁI KYÚUKA

■ **BÉNRI NA HYOOGEN**

. . . go-zónji desu̥ ka.　　　　Shibáraku desu̥ né.
Móshimoshi.　　　　　　　　O-hisashiburi désu̥ né.
O-matase shimáshi̥ta.　　　　Go-búsata shi̥te imásu̥.

BUNKEI

Shashin o tótte mo íi desu̥ ka.　　Sore o tábete wa ikemasén.
Súgu itta hóo ga íi desu̥.　　　　Dónna hi̥to desu̥ ka.
Náze sonna ni isóide imasu̥ ka.　Ashi̥ta áme ga fúru kamo
　　　　　　　　　　　　　　　shiremasen.

■ **KAIWA**

1　A: Kyóo wa taihen samúi　　B: Ée, sóra ga kumótte ite iyá
　　　　desu̥ né　　　　　　　　　na ténki desu̥ né.
　　A: Ashi̥ta yuki̥ ga fúru　　　B: Iie, sonna ni sámuku nai
　　　　kamo shiremasen.　　　　　desu̥.

2　A: Moo hi̥tótsu itadaite mo　B: Ée, mochíron. Dóozo.
　　　　íi deshoo ka.

　　A: Konna ni oishii o-káshi o　B: Hontoo ni sonna ni oishii
　　　　tábeta koto ga　　　　　　désu̥ ka.
　　　　arimasén.

3　A: Dónna hi̥to to kekkon　　B: Hánsamu de, shínsetsu de,
　　　　shi̥tai désu̥ ka.　　　　　o-kane ga áru hi̥to ga íi
　　　　　　　　　　　　　　　　desu̥.
　　A: Sonna hi̥to wa imasén　　B: Éiga dewa sonna hi̥to o yóku
　　　　yo.　　　　　　　　　　　mimasu̥ yo.

4　A: Koko wa hakubútsu̥kan　B: Hái sóo desu̥.
　　　　desu̥ ka.
　　A: Kono dóa kara háitte　　B: Iie, damé desu̥. Omote no
　　　　mo íi desu̥ ka.　　　　　iriguchi o tsu̥katte
　　　　　　　　　　　　　　　　kudasái.

LESSON NINE

USEFUL EXPRESSIONS

Do you know. . . ?
Hello (on telephone)
[Sorry] I've kept you waiting.

It's been quite a while, hasn't it?
It's a long time, isn't it?
Sorry I've been out of touch.

SENTENCE PATTERNS

May I take a photograph?
You had better go immediately.
Why are you in such a hurry?

You mustn't eat that!
What kind of person is he?
Perhaps it will rain tomorrow.

CONVERSATIONS

1   A: It is very cold today, isn't it?

    B: Yes, it is horrible cloudy weather, isn't it?

    A: It might even snow tomorrow.

    B: No, it is not that cold.

2   A: I wonder if you would mind if I had one more.

    B: Of course you may. Please help yourself.

    A: These are the most delicious cakes I've ever eaten.

    B: Are they really as good as all that?

3   A: What sort of person do you want to marry?

    B: I'd like someone who is handsome, kind and rich.

    A: There aren't any people like that!

    B: You often see people like that in films!

4   A: Is this the museum?

    B: Yes, it is.

    A: Can we go in this door?

    B: No, use the front entrance, please.

5 A: Taihen o-matase shimásh̥ta.

   A: Dónna res̥toran ni ikimashóo ka.

   B: Dóo itashimash̥te. Watashi mo s̥kóshi okuremásh̥ta.

   B: Kónban wa Supein-ryóori o tabetái des̥.

6 A: Móshimoshi. Hanbai-búchoo irasshaimás̥ ka.

   A: Sore déwa kotozuké o-negai shimás̥.

   B: Tadáima kaigichuu dés̥.

   B: Hái, dóozo.

7 A: Koko de tabako o s̥tte mo kamaimasén ka.

   B: Iie, s̥tté wa ikemasén. Koko wa kin'en dés̥.

5 A: Sorry I've kept you waiting.

B: It doesn't matter. I was a bit late myself.

A: What sort of restaurant will we go to?

B: Tonight I'd like to have Spanish food.

6 A: Hello. Is the sales manager there?

B: He's in conference at the moment.

A: Then I'd like to leave a message.

B: Yes. Go ahead!

7 A: May I smoke here?

B: No you mustn't. This is a non-smoking area.

-té mo	íi desɯ	'may'
-té wa	ikemasén damé desɯ	'must not'
-ta hóo ga	íi desɯ	'had better'

Here are some more common uses of the '-te form' and the plain past tense.

PERMISSION

The '-te form' followed by the particle *mo* means 'even if'.

Íma déte mo ma ni aimasén.   'Even if we leave now we will
                                                      not be in time.'

This is often used with *íi desɯ* (or *kamaimasén*, 'it does not matter') to express permission: *Itté mo íi desɯ ka*, 'May I go?', 'Do you mind if I go?' (literally, 'Is it all right even if I go?').

Kyóo wa háyaku káette mo   'You may go home early today.'
  kamaimasén.

PROHIBITION

The idea 'must not' is conveyed by *-té wa ikemasén* or *-té wa damé desɯ*.

Koko de tabako o sɯtté wa damé   'You must not smoke here.'
  desɯ.
Hanáshɪte wa ikemasén   'You must not speak.'

ADVICE

The noun *hóo*, 'side' or 'direction', is used after the plain past tense of the verb in the expression *-ta hoo ga ii désɯ*, 'it would be better to', 'had better', etc. As we shall see in Lesson Eleven, *hóo* is often used in comparisons, where it suggests a choice between two 'sides' or 'directions'. In this construction the choice is between doing something or not doing something.

Ash̩ta háyaku ók̩ta hoo ga íi   'You had better get up early
   desu yo.   tomorrow.'

Notice the past tense is used even if the action is in the future.

MORE DEMONSTRATIVES

Japanese has another set of demonstrative adjectives meaning 'this kind of', 'that kind of', etc. They parallel *kono, sono* and *ano*.

Konna	'this kind of'
Sonna	'that kind of'
Anna	'that kind of' (over there, by a third person)
Dónna	'what kind of'

Konna monó wa yakú ni   'This kind of thing is useless'
   tachimasén.

Dónna óngaku ga s̩kí des̩ ka.   'What kind of music do you
                                like?'

Dóno, the question word which goes with *kono, sono* and *ano*, is more specific.

Dóno rekóodo ga s̩kí des̩ ka.   'Which [of these] record[s] do
                                you like?'

   'What colour' is usually *dónna iro*.

Míchiko san no kimono wa   'What colour is Míchiko's
   dónna iro des̩ ka.   kimono?'

These demonstrative adjectives are converted into adverbs by adding *ni: konna ni*, 'this much'; *sonna ni*, 'that much' (referring to a second person or something mentioned earlier in the conversation); *anna ni*, 'that much' (third person); *dónna ni*, 'how much'.

Konna ni oishii nikú o tábeta   'I've never eaten such delicious
   kotó ga arimasen.   meat.'

Sometimes these are used as exclamations, just as we use 'that much!' in English.

ShĮkén wa sonna ni   'Was the examination [really]
  muzukashĮkatta desĮ ka.   so/that difficult?'

Alternative forms of these demonstrative adjectives often used in conversation are *koo yuu*, 'this kind of'; *soo yuu*, 'that kind of'; *aa yuu*, 'that kind of'; *dóo yuu*, 'what kind of'.

Soo yuu hĮto to kekkon shĮtaku   'She doesn't want to marry a
  nái desĮ.   person like that.'

Sometimes the even longer forms *koo yuu fúu na; soo yuu fúu na*, etc. are used.

THE DEMONSTRATIVE ADVERBS

We have met *soo*, 'like that, so', in expressions like *Sóo desĮ ka*, 'Is that so', and *Soo shimashóo*, 'Let's do that'. In the same series of demonstrative adverbs are *koo*, 'like this', *aa*, 'like that', and *dóo*, 'how, like what'.

Kono oishii shokuji o dóo   'How did you make this
  tsĮkurimáshĮta ka.   delicious food?'
Koo kaíte mo íi desĮ ka.   'Can I write it like this?'

The longer forms, *koo yuu fúu ni*, *soo yuu fúu ni* and *dóo yuu fúu ni*, are also very common, but do not occur before *désĮ*.

Soo yuu fúu ni hanáshĮte wa   'You mustn't talk like that.'
  ikemasén.

A full list of demonstratives is given in Appendix 4.

THE INDEFINITE PRONOUNS

The interrogative pronouns followed by *-ka* form a series of indefinite pronouns.

náni	'what'	*nánika*	'something'
dáre	'who'	*dáreka*	'someone'
dóko	'where'	*dókoka*	'somewhere'
dóre	'which one'	*dóreka*	'one of'
íkĮtsu	'how many'	*íkĮtsuka*	'a few' (number)
íkura	'how much'	*íkuraka*	'a bit, a little' (quantity)

We have met the interrogative pronouns followed by *-mo* to form the negative pronouns, *nanimo*, 'nothing', *daremo*, 'nobody', etc. Paralleling these is a set of emphatic pronouns ending in *demo* used in conjunction with a final affirmative verb meaning 'any . . . [at all]': *nándemo*, 'anything'; *dáredemo*, 'anybody'; *dókodemo*, 'anywhere', etc.

After a noun *démo* means 'even' or 'or something'.

Watashi démo dekimásu yo.	'Even I can do it.'
Sandoítchi démo tabemashóo.	'Let's have a sandwich or something.'

This *démo* should not be confused with the two particles *de mo*, each of which retains its original meaning as in *Nihongo dé mo káku kotó ga dekímasu*, 'I can write it in Japanese, too', or *Ano mise dé mo utte imásu*, 'They sell it at that shop, too'.

-KÁMO SHIREMASEN, 'PERHAPS'

This sentence ending follows the plain present or past forms of the verb.

Eigo ga wakáru kamo shiremasen.	'Perhaps he understands English.'
Móo tábeta kamo shiremasen.	'Perhaps he has already eaten.'

It is also used after a noun or a descriptive noun (without the *na*) in the sense, 'perhaps it is', etc.

Doroboo kámo shiremasen.	'Perhaps it's a burglar.'
Utá ga joozú kamo shiremasen.	'Perhaps he sings well.'

NOTES

Conversation 3   The compound particle *dewa* is simply *de* 'in' and *wa* indicating contrast: 'as far as films are concerned'.

Conversation 6   *Kaigichuu*, 'in conference', has the suffix *-chuu*, 'in the middle of', 'throughout', which appears in a number of words such as *denwachuu*, 'on the telephone'; *hanashichuu*, 'engaged' (telephone); *shigotochuu*, 'at work'; *gozenchuu*, 'in/all/throughout the morning'. In some words it appears as *-juu*: *ichinichijuu*, 'all day

[long]'; *kyoojuu*, 'during/throughout today'; *ichinenjuu*, 'all year', etc. Words with the *-chuu/-juu* suffix are unaccented.

VOCABULARY

ténki	weather	*kumóru*	to become cloudy
áme	rain	*okureru*	to be late
yukí	snow	*suu*	to inhale, smoke, suck
sóra	sky		
o-káshi	cakes	*kiru*	to wear
hakubutsúkan	museum	*tátsu̥*	to stand
omoté	the outside	*yakú ni tátsu̥*	to be useful
iriguchi	entrance	*ma ni áu*	to be in time (for =*ni*)
déguchi	exit		
káigi	conference	*mochíron*	of course
kaigichuu	in conference	*súgu*	immediately
kotozuké	message	*tadáima*	just now, at present
tabako	cigarette		
kin'en	no smoking	*konna/koo yuu*	this kind of
nikú	meat	*sonna/soo yuu*	that kind of
sh̥kén	examination	*anna/aa yuu*	that kind of
doroboo	robber, thief	*dónna/dóo yuu*	what kind of
Itaria/Itarii	Italy	*koo/koo yuu fúu ni*	like this
S̥péin	Spain		
kimono	kimono	*soo/soo yuu fúu ni*	like that
rekóodo	record		
iró	colour	*dóo/dóo yuu fúu ni*	how
monó	thing		
iyá na	nasty, unpleasant	*-té mo íi des̥*	may
hánsamu na	handsome	*-té wa ikemasén*	must not
shínsetsu na	kind		
atsúi	hot	*-ta hóo ga íi des̥*	had better
samúi	cold (of weather)		
shokuji suru	to have a meal	*kámo shiremasen*	perhaps
fúru	to fall (of rain and snow)		

EXERCISE 9

A Expand the following sentences using the words in brackets and making any other changes the sense demands:
1 Asa hayaku okimasu. (hoo ga ii) 2 Kore wa yaku ni tachimasu. (ka mo shiremasen) 3 Sore o tabemasu. (ikemasen) 4 O-kane o sonna ni tsukaimasu. (ikemasen) 5 Ima hanashimasu ka. (kamaimasen) 6 Oishii o-kashi o tabemasu ka. (-tai) 7 Kyoo no gogo ame ga furimasu. (deshoo) 8 Moo hitotsu itadakimasu. (ii desu ka) 9 Ano resutoran de shokuji shimasu. (hoo ga ii) 10 Kyoo wa atsuku narimasu. (kamo shiremasen)

B Fill in the blanks:
1 Koko ( ) tabako ( ) sutte ( ) ii desu ka. 2 Rainen no natsu-yasumi ni Itaria ( ) iku ka ( ) ( ). 3 Iriguchi no soba ni tatte ( ) hito ( ) dare ( ) ka. 4 Ashita mo atsu( ) ( ) deshoo. 5 Inagaki sensei ( ) doo ( ) kotozuke ( ) arimashita ka. 6 Motto akarui iro ( ) kimono ( ) kita ( ) ga ii desu. 7 Sonna uta no rekoodo ( ) kiite ( ) ikemasen. 8 Ano hashitte ( ) otokonohito wa doroboo ( ) shiremasen. 9 Tadaima kaigi( ) de au ( ) ( ) dekimasen. 10 Hayaku shokuji ( ) ( ) ga ii desu yo.

C Translate into English:
1 Suzuki sensei o gozonji desu ka. 2 Taihen o-matase shimashita. 3 Ashita wa donna tenki ni naru deshoo. 4 Sukoshi okurete mo ii desu ka. 5 Chikatetsu no naka de tabako o sutte wa ikemasen. 6 Ima hakubutsukan de omoshiroi tenrankai o yatte iru kamo shiremasen. 7 Sora ga kumotte imasu ne. 8 Sumisu san wa moo Rondon ni kaetta kamo shiremasen. 9 Koo yuu tenki wa iya desu ne. 10 Hayaku kaetta hoo ga ii desu.

D Translate into Japanese:
1 This little camera is extremely useful. 2 What kind of a person is Mr Miki? 3 Of course you may smoke. 4 There is a message written on the memo by the telephone. 5 It has been a long time, hasn't it? 6 He is kind and handsome. 7 Perhaps he likes Spanish cooking. 8 What kind of meat would you like to eat? 9 You had better make it of wood. 10 It might snow tomorrow.

DÁIJÚKKA

■ BÉNRI NA HYOOGEN

Senjitsu wa dóomo.

Chótto shị́ta o-miyage désị.
Tsumaránai monó desu ga,
dóozo.

Taihen kékkoo na mono o
itadaite.
O-medetoo gozaimásị.
Dóomo go-shínsetsu ni.

BUNKEI

Tábete kara dekakemásị.

Káre ga kúru to tanoshíi desị.
Háyaku neru tsumori désị.

Irassháru máe ni denwa shị́te
kudasái.
Sánji ni tátsu yotei désị.
Ashị́ta kúru soo desị.

■ KAIWA

1 A: Ashị́ta náni o suru
      tsumori désị ka.
   A: Watashi wa kokuritsu-
      gékijoo ni ikị́ tsumori
      désị.

   B: Betsu ni yotei ga arimasén
      ga.
   B: Íma íi shibai o yatte iru soo
      désị yo.

2 A: Shokuji shị́te kara súgu
      dekakeru tsumori
      désị.
   A: Kamaimasén ga taikị́tsị
      suru deshóo.

   B: Watashi mo issho ni itte mo
      íi desị ka.
   B: Iie, watashi wa kabuki ga
      dáisị́ki desị.

3 A: Sumimasén ga,
      kokuritsu-gékijoo wa
      dóchira deshóo ka.

   B: Kono michi o massúgu ikị́ to
      koosáten ga arimásị.
      Soko o migi e magatte
      hyaku méetoru gúrai ikị́
      to hidarigawa ni arimásị.

   A: Dóomo go-shínsetsu ni.

   B: Dóo itashimashị́te.

LESSON TEN

USEFUL EXPRESSIONS

Thanks for the other day.

[Thank you] for the lovely gift.

It's just a little souvenir.
It's nothing much, but please . . .

Congratulations.
That was very kind of you.
   Thanks.

SENTENCE PATTERNS

I'll leave after I've eaten.

Please ring before you come.

It's fun when he comes.
I intend to go to bed early.

I plan to leave at 3 o'clock.
I hear he is coming tomorrow.

CONVERSATIONS

1 A: What do you intend to do tomorrow?

     A: I intend to go to the National Theatre.

B: I haven't planned anything in particular.

B: Apparently there is a good play on at the moment.

2 A: I intend to set out straight after dinner.

     A: No, but you'll probably be bored.

B: Do you mind if I come with you?

B: No, I love *kabuki*.

3 A: Excuse me. I wonder if you could tell me where the National Theatre is?

     A: Thank you. You're very kind.

B: If you go straight along this road you'll come to an intersection. Turn right there and it is about 100 metres down, on the left-hand side.

B: Not at all.

4 A: Konna tokoro e kúru to
   tanoshíi desu né.

A: Shibai ga hajimaru máe
   ni júusu demo
   nomimashóo ka.

B: Ée, hontoo ni kimochi ga íi
   desu né.

B: Ée, atsúi desu kara nánika
   tsumetai monó o nomitái
   desu.

5 A: Kyóo wa yuumei na
   yakusha ga déru soo
   desu yo.

A: Onna no yakú ga totemo
   joozú da soo desu.

B: Áa sóo desu ka. Sore wa
   tanoshími desu née.

B: Áa onnagata désu ka.

6 A: Kono heya wa kurákute
   hón o yómu koto ga
   dekimasén.

A: Móo tsukete arimasu yo.

B: Dénki o tsukéru to akarui
   désu.

B: Mádo no sóba no sutándo
   mo tsuketa hoo ga íi desu.

4 A: It's fun to come to a place like this.

B: Yes it really is a nice feeling.

A: Shall we have a soft drink or something before the play starts?

B: Yes, it's hot! I'd like something cool to drink.

5 A: They say there is a famous actor appearing today.

B: Is there? That will be worth seeing, won't it!

A: Apparently he is very good at female roles.

B: Oh, he's a female impersonator, is he?

6 A: This room is dark. I can't read my book.

B: It's bright if you put the light on.

A: The light is on already.

B: You'd better put on the standard lamp by the window too.

V-te	kara	'after . . . ing'
V-(r)u	máe ni	'before . . . ing'
	to	'whenever', 'if', 'when'
	yotei désy̌	'plan to . . .'
	tsumori désy̌	'intend to . . .'
V-(r)u/-ta Adj-i/-katta N da/datta DN da/datta	soo desy̌	'I hear that . . .', 'they say that . . .', etc.

This chart summarizes the uses of the *-te* form, the dictionary form and the plain past-tense form, introduced in this lesson. 'V' indicates a verb stem, 'Adj' an adjective root, 'N' a noun and 'DN' a descriptive noun.

-te kara, 'after . . . ing

This is a clause-final construction indicating that the action of the next clause follows directly the action of the verb before *kara*. There is always a feeling of prearrangement or planning between the actions linked by the *-te kara* construction.

Shokuji shỵte kara térebi o mimashỵta.	'I watched television after having my meal.' 'I had dinner and then watched television.'
Suzuki san ga kỵte kara soodan shimashóo.	'Let's discuss it after Mr Suzuki comes.'
Nihón ni tsúite kara súgu Nihongo no benkyoo o hajimeru tsumori désỵ.	'I intend to start studying Japanese immediately after I arrive in Japan.'

A sentence such as *Senséi ga káette kara Fújiko san ga kimáshỵta*, 'Fujiko came after the teacher had gone home', would indicate that Fujiko had timed her arrival to occur after the teacher's departure. Other ways of expressing the English 'after' will be introduced in a later lesson.

-(r)u máe ni, 'before . . . ing'

Máe ni after the dictionary form of the verb indicates that the action of that verb takes place before that of the main verb at the end of the sentence.

Sore o chuumon suru máe ni denwa de nedan o shirábeta hoo ga íi desu̹.	'Before you order that you had better ring up and find out the price.'
Sonna kotó o yuu máe ni yóku kangáete kudasai.	'Think carefully before you say things like that.'
Sotsugyoo suru máe ni kekkon shimáshl̹ta.	'I got married before I graduated.'

-(r)u to, 'whenever', 'if', 'when'

To is another clause-final particle which follows the dictionary form of the verb. When the verb of the main clause (the final verb) is in the present tense, *to* indicates that the verb in the following clause occurs as a natural or habitual consequence of the verb preceding *to*.

Hi ga déru to akaruku narimásu̹.	'When the sun comes up it gets light.'
Ása okíru to mázu koohíi o nomimasu̹.	'When I get up in the morning the first thing I do is have some coffee.'
Massúgu iku̹ to shingoo ga arimásu̹.	'If you go straight ahead you'll come to some traffic lights.'

The *to* construction is not used where the main verb expresses the speaker's determination, a request or a command.

When the final verb is in the past tense, there is not necessarily an antecedent and consequent relationship between the clauses connected with *to*, but there is a feeling of surprise that the action of the second clause should have happened. Often a phrase like 'I saw that' or 'I realized that' seems to be implied.

Mádo kara sóto o miru to áme ga fu̹tte imashl̹ta.	'When I looked outside through the window it was raining.'
Uchi ni káeru to kodomo ga byooki de nete imáshl̹ta.	'When I got home my child was sick in bed.'

Note that the past tense does not occur before this use of *to*. The noun *toki*, 'time', does not indicate surprise. It can also be used when there is no antecedent-consequent relationship or when the main verb is a request or command.

Ryokoo ni iku tokí imootó o tsurete ikimásu.	'When I go for trips I take my sister with me.'
Káeru toki ni wa dóa ni kagí o kákete kudasai.	'When you leave please lock the door.'

Although all the examples given above show *to* after the dictionary form of a verb, it should be noted that it can also occur after adjectives.

Takái to kaimasén.	'When things are expensive I don't buy them.'
Osoi to komarimásu.	'We'll be in trouble if it is late.'

-(r)u yotei désu, -(r)u tsumori désu, 'plan to', 'intend to'

Adjectival clauses qualifying the nouns *yotei*, 'plan', and *tsumori*, 'intention', often occur with a final copula (*désu*, etc.) to express the idea 'plan to' or 'intend to'.

Isshookénmei hataraku tsumori désu.	'I intend to work flat out.'
Hikóoki wa sanji han ni tsuku yotei desu.	'The plane is scheduled to arrive at 3.30.'
Denpoo o útsu tsumori désu.	'I intend to send a telegram.'

Of course, these nouns also occur independently.

Yotei o tsukurimáshita.	'I made a plan', 'I drew up a schedule.'
Sono tsumori ja arimasén deshita.	'That was not my intention.'

Soo désu, indicating hearsay

Soo désu is often used as a final predicate to indicate hearsay. It can usually be translated by a phrase such as 'they say that,' 'I hear that', etc. It follows the plain, present or past forms of the verb adjective or copula.

Atarashíi seihin ga déru soo desu̥.	'They say there is a new product coming out.'
Jíko ga atta soo desu̥.	'Apparently there was an accident.'
Fujisan wa taihen kírei da soo désu̥ né.	'I believe Mt Fuji is very beautiful.'
Karada ga nakanaka yowái soo desu̥.	'Apparently he is very frail.' 'I hear his health is very poor.'
Anóhi̥to wa Chuugokújin da soo desu̥.	'I understand he is Chinese.'

NOTES

Conversation 3 Michi o iku. 'Along', 'through', 'by', 'over', etc., with verbs of linear motion, that is, verbs like 'walk', 'run', 'swim', 'fly', 'go', 'pass', etc., which describe continuous movement over a certain distance, are expressed in Japanese with the object particle *o*.

Michi o arukimásu̥.	'I walk along the road.'
Hikóoki ga uchi no ue o tobimásh̥ta.	'A plane flew over our house.'
Táku̥shii wa daigaku no món no máe o tóotta.	'The taxi went past the gate of the university.'
Sanji ni heyá o demásh̥ta.	'I went out of the room at 3 o'clock.' 'I left the room at 3 o'clock.'

VOCABULARY

kokuritsu (no)	national	*yaku̥sha*	actor
gekijoo	theatre	*onnagata*	actor of female roles in *kabuki*
kokuritsu-gékijoo	National Theatre		
shibai	play	*imootó*	younger sister
kabuki	kabuki	*kimochi*	feeling
yakú	role, part	*kimochi ga íi*	to feel good
		karada	body, health

byooki	illness, disease	*kesu*	to switch off; extinguish
chįkará	strength		
jíko	accident	*tátsu*	to leave
nedan	price	*útsu*	to hit; send (telegram)
seihin	product		
kagí	key	*yuu* (ste, *ii-*, root *w-*)	to say
sįtándo	standard lamp		
dénki	electricity; light (traffic) signal	*kangáeru*	to think, to consider
shingoo			
denpoo	telegram	*shirabéru*	to investigate, to find out
gásu	gas, cooker		
sóto	outside	*hajimaru*	to begin (intransitive)
monó	thing		
nánika	something	*dekakeru*	to go out
dáreka	some one	*tóoru*	to pass, go past
nándemo	anything	*neru*	to go to bed; to lie down
dáredemo	anybody		
o-miyage	gift, souvenir	*uru*	to sell
tsumori	intention	*komáru*	to be in a fix
yotei	plan	*taikįtsų suru*	to get bored
tokí	time; when	*soodan suru*	to discuss
yuumei na	famous	*chuumon suru*	to order
taikįtsu na	boring	*sotsugyoo suru*	to graduate
akarui	bright, light	*kagí o kakeru*	to lock
kurai	dark	*tsurete iku*	to take (a person)
yowái	weak	*migi*	right
tsuyoi	strong, tough	*hidari*	left
chįkará ga tsuyói	strong (of people)	*migigawa*	right-hand side
		hidarigawa	left-hand side
tsumetai	cold (of objects)	*mázu*	first
tanoshíi	enjoyable, pleasant	*betsu ni*	(not) in particular
		nakanaka	(not) very
osoi	late; slow	*totemo/tottemo*	very
tsumaránai	uninteresting, trifling	*isshookénmei*	with all one's might
tsųkéru	to switch on; attach	*massúgu*	straight (ahead)

-(r)u tsumori *désu̸*	to intend to	-(r)u to -te kara	when, whenever after
-(r)u soo *desu̸*	they say, I hear	toki	time, when

EXERCISE 10

A Make into a single sentence incorporating the words in brackets:
1 Ashita kokuritsu-gekijoo ni ikimasu. (yotei desu) 2 Byooki desu.
Soto e deru koto ga dekimasen. (kara) 3 Denki o tsukemasu.
Akaruku narimasu. (to) 4 Chuumon shimasu. Yoku kangaeta hoo
ga ii desu. (mae ni) 5 Daredemo dekimasu. (soo desu) 6 Doa ni kagi
o kakemashita. Mon o demashita. (kara) 7 Ikimasu. Denpoo o
uchimasu. (mae ni) 8 Fuyu ga kimasu. Samuku narimasu. (to) 9
Eiga ga hajimarimasu. Koohii o ippai nomimashoo. (mae ni) 10
Rainen sotsugyoo shimasu. Furansu e iku tsumori desu. (kara)

B Fill in the blanks:
1 Massugu iku ( ) shingoo ( ) arimasu. 2 Shibai ( ) mi ( )
ikimashoo. 3 Anohito ( ) yuumei ( ) yakusha ( ) soo desu. 4
Betsu ( ) yotei ( ) arimasen. 5 Denki-sutando ( ) tsukeru
( ) akaruku narimasu. 6 Ano mise ( ) nedan ( ) takai desu ( )
asoko de kaimasen. 7 Suzuki san ( ) kodomo ( ) karada
( ) yowai soo desu. 8 Sonna takai mono ( ) kau ( ) ni moo
sukoshi shirabeta ( ) ga ii desu yo. 9 Nodo ( ) kawaite imashita
( ) kissaten ( ) tsumetai juusu o nomimashita. 10 Hidarigawa ( )
aru biru ( ) yuubinkyoku ( ) soo desu.

C Translate into English:
1 Senjitsu wa doomo. 2 Tsukue no soba no denki o tsuketa hoo ga ii
desu. 3 Ano chiisa na baa de tsumetai biiru demo ippai nomimashoo. 4 Sotsugyoo shite kara nani o suru tsumori desu ka. 5 Amari
nagaku benkyoo suru to me ga itaku narimasu. 6 Tsumaranai mono
desu ga, doozo. 7 Neru mae ni doa ni kagi o kakete gasu o keshite
kudasai. 8 O-medetoo gozaimasu. 9 Konoaida no kaigairyokoo wa
tanoshikatta desu ka. 10 Kabuki o mita koto ga arimasu ka.

D Translate into Japanese:

1 Let's order quickly. I'm hungry. 2 I haven't anything in particular planned for tomorrow so let's go and see a play. 3 They say he is very strong, but not very intelligent. 4 Please send me a telegram before you leave London. 5 I was up till late working last night so tonight I intend to go to bed early. 6 First let us investigate the prices. 7 I don't want to read such a boring book. 8 Before you sell the products perhaps you had better discuss it with the director. 9 Tomorrow I'm intending to take the children to the zoo. 10 They probably sell souvenirs at that little shop on the right.

DÁI JUUÍKKA

■ BÉNRI NA HYOOGEN

O-machidoosama déshįta.
O-tsįkaresama déshįta.
Go-kúroosama deshįta.

O-sewasamá deshįta.
Zannén deshįta.
Ganbátte kudasai.

BUNKEI

Ikanai kotó ni shimáshįta.
Shinpai shináide kudasai.

Máda ìkanákįte mo íi desį.
O-kane ga nái to komarimásį.

Pán wa báta yori yasúi desį.

Pán no hóo ga yasúi desį.

■ KAIWA

1 A: Korewa muzukashíkįte
    dekimasén.
  A: Mótto benkyoo shinai to
    damé desį né.

  B: Sonna kotó o iwanaide
    kudasái.
  B: Ganbátte kudasai.

2 A: Íma harawánai to damé
    desį ka.
  A: Ítsu haraimashóo ka.

  B: Iie, máda harawánakįte mo
    íi desį.
  B: Káeru máe ni harátte
    kudasai.

3 A: Kono tori wa amari
    oishíku nái desį.
  A: Démo tabénai to onaka
    ga sįkimásį.

  B: Tabénakįte mo íi desu yo.
  B: Jáa, hoka no monó o
    chuumon shįte kudasái.

4 A: Nihongo wa fįkuzatsu
    de oboéru kotó ga
    dékimasén.
  A: Sóo shįtai desu ga
    Nihonjín o hįtóri mo
    shirimasén.

  B: Dekiru daké Nihonjín to
    shaberánai to damé desį
    yo.
  B: Uchi no kaisha ni tsįtómete
    iru hįto o shookai
    shimashóo.

138

LESSON ELEVEN

USEFUL EXPRESSIONS

Sorry to have kept you waiting.   Thank you for your help.
You must be tired.   What a pity!
Thanks for your efforts.   Stick to it! Work hard!

SENTENCE PATTERNS

I've decided not to go.   You needn't go yet.
Please don't worry.   You're in a mess without
                                           money.

Bread is cheaper than butter.   Bread is the cheaper.

CONVERSATIONS

1 A: I can't do this. It's   B: Don't say things like that.
      difficult!
   A: I'll have to study harder,   B: Keep at it (and you'll be all
      won't I?   right).

2 A: Do we have to pay now?   B: No, you needn't pay yet.

   A: When shall I pay you?   B: Pay before you leave,
                                            please.

3 A: This chicken isn't very   B: You needn't eat it, you
      good.   know.
   A: But if I don't I'll get   B: Then order something else.
      hungry.

4 A: I can't memorize any   B: You have to talk to Japanese
      Japanese. It's   people as much as you
      complicated!   can.
   A: I'd like to do that, but I   B: Then let me introduce you to
      don't know a single   one working in our
      Japanese.   company.

5 A: Taiséiyoo wa taihéiyoo
yori hirói deshoo.

B: Iie, taihéiyoo no hóo ga
hirói desɥ.

A: Chízu de míru to
ryoohootómo sugóku
hirǫi desu né.

B: Sóo desu. Táiriku yori úmi
no hóo ga zutto hirói desɥ.

6 A: Mótto kuwashíi shíryoo
ga nái to komarimásɥ
né.

B: Ée, kore daké ja tarimasén
né.

A: Kore yori íi no ga
arimasén ka.

B: Ée, tsɥkuránai to arimasén.

7 A: O-cha o motte-
kimashóo ka.

B: Wázawaza irenákɥte mo íi
desɥ.

A: Kyóo wa irimasén ka.

B: Íya, shokudoo de
nomimásɥ.

5 A: The Atlantic is bigger than the Pacific, isn't it?

B: No, the Pacific is the larger.

A: When you see them on the map they are both very big.

B: Yes, they are. The [area of] sea is much greater than that of the continents.

6 A: We'll be in a mess if we don't have more detailed data.

B: Yes. This isn't enough, is it?

A: Haven't we got anything better than this?

B: No, not unless we make some.

7 A: Shall I bring some tea?

B: You needn't make any especially.

A: Don't you want any today?

B: Yes, but I'll have it in the canteen.

THE PLAIN NEGATIVE FORM

The plain present-tense negative of a verb is formed by adding the ending -(a)nai to the verb root. The initial vowel of the suffix is dropped when the verb root ends in a vowel. Consonant roots ending in -w (i.e. those which have a vowel before -imásu̧) retain the -w before the negative suffix.

Plain present affirmative		Plain present negative	
káku	'writes'	kakánai	'does not write'
iku	'goes'	ikanai	'does not go'
tabéru	'eats'	tabénai	'does not eat'
akeru	'opens'	akenai	'does not open'
kau (root kaw-)	'buys'	kawanai	'does not buy'
mátsu (root mát-)	'waits'	matánai	'does not wait'

Notice that accented verbs have accented negative forms and unaccented verbs have unaccented negative forms. The irregular verbs kúru and suru have the negative forms kónai, 'does not come', and shinai, 'does not do'.

The -(a)nai suffix is, in form, an adjective and takes the usual adjectival inflections. The plain negative past tense is formed with -(a)nákatta: kawanai, 'does not buy'; kawanákatta, 'did not buy'.

Shinbun o yománakatta   'Explain it to those who did not
  hı̧totachi ni setsumei shı̧te   read the newspaper.'
  kudasái.

Nái occurs as a predicate in its own right as the negative form of *áru*, 'to have', 'to be', which does not take a negative form.

O-kane ga áru hı̧to   A man who has money
O-kane ga nái hı̧to   A man who does not have
                money
O-kane ga nákatta hı̧to   A man who did not have money

Nái is also used after *ja, dewa* (or simply *de*) to form the negative of the copula and the descriptive nouns.

  Sensei ja nái hı̧to   A man who isn't a teacher
  Shoojiki ja nái hı̧to   A dishonest man

or

> *Shoojíki de(wa) nái hļto*   A dishonest man

We have already met its use after the *-ku* form of adjectives: *Ano tatemono wa tákaku nai desψ.* Notice that *nái* loses its accent if the adjective or descriptive noun preceding it is accented: *akaruku nái heya*, 'a room which is not light', but *tákaku nai hón*, 'an inexpensive book.'

The suffix *-(a)nai* differs from other adjectives in having two *-te* forms, *-(a)nákψte* and *-(a)náide*. The full predicate *nái* (the negative of *áru*), however, has only *-nákψte*.

O-kane ga nákψte komátte imasψ.	'I'm in a fix as I don't have any money.'

This, too, is the only form used with adjectives and descriptive nouns.

Oishļku nákψte zannén deshļta.	'It is a pity the food wasn't good.'

The suffix *-(a)nákψte* is used for joining clauses, particularly if the subjects are different, or if there is an implied cause and effect relationship between the clauses.

Nihongo ga yóku wakaránakψte komátte imasψ.	'I'm having difficulty because I don't understand Japanese very well.'

It is this form that is used in the expression . . . *-(a)nákψte mo íi desψ*, 'need not' (literally, 'even if not . . . it is all right.')

Móo kψsuri o nománakψte mo íi desψ.	'You need not take the medicine any longer.'
Máda kaeránakψte mo íi desψ ka.	'Don't you have to go [back home] yet?'

-(a)náide

The most important use of *-(a)náide* is in the polite, negative request form *-(a)náide kudasai*, 'Please don't . . .'

Sonna ni isogánaide kudasai.	'Please don't be in such a hurry.'

It is also used for joining clauses, in which case it can usually be paraphrased as 'without _____ -ing'. In this construction the subject is the same for both clauses.

Gakkoo ni ikanáide éiga o mí ni ikimáshḷta.	'He went to see a film instead of going to school.'

Compare this with

Musḷko ga gakkoo ni ikanákḷte komátte imasḷ.	'My son doesn't go to school and it is causing me trouble.'

-(a)nai to komarimásḷ, -(a)nai to damé desḷ, (a)nai to ikemasén, 'must'

Negative *to* clauses can combine with a final verb like *komarimásḷ*, 'to be in trouble', 'to be at a loss', etc.; *damé desḷ*, 'it's no good', or *ikemasén*, 'it will not do', to indicate obligation, 'must': *Háyaku ikanai to damé desḷ*, 'I must go quickly.' (literally, 'If I do not go quickly it will be no good.').

COMPARISON OF ADJECTIVES

There is no change in the form of adjectives to indicate the comparative or superlative degree. Instead, the comparison is suggested by the use of particles, the noun *hóo*, 'side', 'direction', and a set of demonstrative pronouns.

Yori, 'than'

Tookyoo wa Róndon yori ookíi desḷ.	'Tokyo is bigger than London.'

A comparison of the type 'A is . . . er than B' becomes *A wa B yori . . .* in Japanese.

Dótchi, 'which [one of two]?'

Tookyoo to Róndon to dótchi ga ookíi desḷ ka.	'Which is the bigger, Tokyo or London?'

A question of the type 'Which is . . . er, A or B?' is expressed as *A to B to dótchi ga . . . desu̜ ka*. Corresponding to the question word *dótchi* and its more formal equivalent *dóchira* are the demonstrative pronouns *kotchí/kochira*, 'this [one of two]; *sotchí/sochira*, 'that [one of two]'; *atchí/achira*, 'that [one of two over there]'. These words, particularly those ending in *-ra*, which are more polite, are also often used to indicate direction or location.

Kochira e dóozo.	'This way please.'
Dóchira ni súnde imasu̜ ka.	'Where do you live?'

No hóo ga

Tookyoo no hóo ga ookíi desu̜.   'Tokyo is bigger.'

To emphasize one of two things compared the noun *hóo*, 'side', 'direction' can be used. *A no hóo ga . . . desu̜*, 'A is [the] . . . er', literally means 'The A side is . . .' and is often used, as in the example above, to answer a question when only one of the two items compared is mentioned in the reply. When special emphasis is needed this construction may be used even though both items in the comparison are mentioned, as in Conversation 5. Where neither of the items compared is specifically mentioned, the adverb *mótto*, 'more', can be used before the adjective.

Mótto yasúi no o kudasái.   'Please give me a cheaper one.'

Ichiban, 'the most'

Ichiban, literally 'number one', is used to make superlatives: *ichiban takái tokei*, 'the most expensive watch'; *ichiban abunai su̜póotsu̜*, 'the most dangerous sport'.

A to B to C no naka de dóre ga   'Which is . . . est, A, B or C?'
  ichiban . . . desu̜ ka.

As you see from this example, when more than two things are compared, *no naka de*, 'among', is used after the last item in the list and the question word used is *dóre*, 'which [of many]?' In statements the ordinary demonstrative pronouns *kore*, *sore* and *are* are used.

Dóre ga ichiban ookíi desu̜ ka.	'Which is the biggest?'
Kore ga ichiban ookíi desu̜.	'This is the biggest.'

Notice that in the comparative and superlative constructions, where a question word like *dótchi* or *dóre* is used, the topic marker *wa* is used in neither the question nor the reply. Nor is *wa* used after . . . *no hóo*.

Gúrai, 'as', 'as . . . as'

In expressions of the type 'A is as . . . as B', Japanese uses a construction with *gúrai*, *A wa B gúrai . . . désu*.

Kore we Párii de tábeta ryoori gúrai oishii désu.	'This cooking is as good as that I ate in Paris.'
Áni wa chįchi gúrai sé ga takái desu.	'My elder brother is as tall as my father.'

After an expression of quantity, *gúrai* means 'about': *sankiro gúrai*, 'about three kilometres/kilograms'; *sanjikan gúrai*, 'about three hours'. *Gúrai*, however, is not used when referring to a point of time; 'at about' is *góro(ni)*; e.g., *sanji góro*, 'about 3 o'clock'. Both *gúrai* and *góro* always retain their accent, and any accent on the word preceding them is lost: *sanjíkan*, but *sanjikan gúrai*.

Hodo, '[not] as . . . as'

In negative sentences of the type 'A is not as . . . as B' *hodo* replaces *gúrai*: *A wa B hodo . . . ku nái desu*.

Otootó wa watashi hodo omoku nái desu.	'My younger brother is not as heavy as I am.'

NOTES

Conversation 7 O-cha o ireru is used for 'to make tea'.

VOCABULARY

pán	bread	*setsumei suru*	to explain
báta/bátaa	butter	*shokuji suru*	to have a meal
gyuunyuu	milk	*zutto*	far, all the time/ way
chíizu	cheese		
satóo	sugar	*sugóku*	terribly, very
tori	chicken; bird	*wázawaza*	expressly, specially
kusuri	medicine		
supóotsu	sport	*íya*	no
karate	sport	*démo*	even, or something
ténisu	tennis		
chízu	map	*hitóri mo*	no one, (not) even one person
táiriku	continent		
Taihéiyoo	Pacific Ocean	*góro*	(at) about
Taiséiyoo	Atlantic Ocean	*ryoohoo (tomo)*	both
kíro	kilometre/ -gram	*dótchi/ dóchira*	which (of two), which way
tatemono	building	*kotchí/ kochira*	this (of two), this way
shokudoo	dining-room, cafeteria	*sotchí/ sochira*	that (of two), that way
shíryoo	materials, data	*atchí/ achira*	that (of two), that way
bunpoo	grammar	*yori*	than
fukuzatsu na	complicated	*hóo*	direction, side
shoojíki na	honest	*gúrai*	extent, as . . . as
hoka (no)	other	*hodo*	extent, not as . . . as
uchi no	our(s), my/mine		
kuwashíi	detailed, know in detail	*ichiban*	most, 'number one'
abunai	dangerous		
anzen na	safe	*kotó ni suru*	to decide to
haráu	to pay	*-(a)náide kudasai*	please don't . . .
shabéru	to speak, talk		
tariru	to be enough	*dekiru daké*	as much as possible
motte kúru	to bring		
ganbáru	to persist, stick to a task		
tsutoméru	to work (in, for = ni)		

EXERCISE 11

A Change the following sentences into the negative:
1 Ashita kite kudasai. 2 Kono shiryoo wa kuwashii desu. 3 Oosaka-yuki no kisha ni ma ni atta soo desu. 4 Chizu o motte itta soo desu. 5 Haratte kudasai. 6 Otooto wa watashi gurai se ga takai desu. 7 Kono kusuri o nonde mo ii desu ka. 8 Matsu tsumori desu. 9 Kore de tariru soo desu. 10 Kono supootsu wa abunai desu.

B Fill in the blanks and give the correct forms of the words in italics:
1 Tookyoo ( ) Oosaka ( ) hiroi desu. 2 Moo o-sake ( ) nomanai ( ) ni shimashita. 3 Kono tori ( ) amari *oishii* nai desu. 4 Motto *kuwashii* setsumei ( ) kudasai. 5 Shokudoo ( ) *tabemasen* hoo ( ) ii desu. 6 Moo *haraimasen* ( ) dame desu. 7 Gorufu ( ) tenisu ( ) dotchi ( ) suki desu ka. 8 Bata ( ) chiizu ( ) takaku arimasen. 9 Dekiru ( ) hayaku *tsukurimasu* kudasai. 10 Jikan ( ) *arimasen* komatte imasu.

C Translate into English:
1 Supeingo to Furansugo to dotchi ga muzukashii desu ka. 2 Soo yuu fukuzatsu na koto wa kuwashiku setsumei shinai to dame desu. 3 O-kane ga tarinakute komatte iru soo desu. 4 Shoojiki na hito ga sukunai desu. 5 Kono kusuri yori yasui no ga arimasen ka. 6 O-tsukaresama deshita. 7 Hoka no hito ni shaberanaide kudasai. 8 Hitori mo konakatta soo desu. 9 O-machidoosama deshita. 10 Donna kaisha ni tsutomete imasu ka.

D Translate into Japanese.
1 Thank you for your help. 2 The train is much cheaper than the plane. 3 Which do you prefer [=like better], fish or chicken? 4 That building is as large as the post office. 5 Please don't show this material to anyone else. 6 It was a pity I couldn't meet you yesterday. 7 Which is the most detailed map? 8 Karate is not a dangerous sport. 9 My house is about two kilometres from the station. 10 At the cafeteria you have to pay before you have your meal.

DÁI JUUNÍKA

■ **BÉNRI NA HYOOGEN**

O-saki ni dóozo.   Dóozo o-hairi kudasái/nasái.
O-saki ni dóomo.   Dóozo o-agari kudasái/nasái.
Gomen kudasái.   O-jáma shimasu.

BUNKEI

Íma jimúsho ni iru hazu desu.   Móo Amerika ni itta hazu désu.

Dóoshite kuruma o urú n' désu   Chichí wa bengóshi na n' desu.
ka.
Watashi ga shimásu.   Nihonjín wa yóku
                                    hatarakimásu.

■ **KAIWA**

1 A: Nímotsu no haitatsu ga   B: Ée. Choodo rásshu de michi
      osoi désu né.   ga kónde iru n' desu yo.

   A: Misé e denwa shita hóo   B: Iie, móo misé o déta hazu
      ga íi desu ka.   desu.

2 A: Kono hako ni tabako ga   B: Okashíi desu né. Nijúppon
      juukyúuhon shika   háitte iru hazu désu.
      arimasén.
   A: Futsuu yori sukóshi   B: Dákara sóo ná n' deshoo.
      yásukatta n' desu
      ga . . .

3 A: Kono koojóo dewa   B: Jimúin o irenáide yónhyaku
      nannin gúrai yatótte   gojúunin desu.
      imasu ka.
   A: Jimu-kánkei wa nánnin   B: Tatta júunin shika inái n'
      imasu ka.   désu.

150

LESSON TWELVE

USEFUL EXPRESSIONS

After you.	Please come in.
Excuse my going first.	Please come in.
Hello!; Anyone home!	Thank you. (in reply to above)

SENTENCE PATTERNS

He should be in the office now.

I expect he's already gone to America.

Why are you selling the car?

My father is a lawyer, you see.

I shall do it.

The Japanese work hard.

CONVERSATIONS

1 A: The delivery of the goods is late, isn't it?

B: Yes. We're right in the rush-hour and the traffic is congested.

A: Would it be better if I rang the shop?

B: No, they must already have left the shop.

2 A: There are only nineteen cigarettes in this box.

B: That's funny! There should be twenty.

A: Actually, they were a little cheaper than usual.

B: That must be the reason, then!

3 A: How many people do you employ in this factory?

B: Not counting the office staff, we have 450.

A: How many on the clerical side?

B: There are only ten people.

151

4 A: Ameriká jin wa
      tabesugíru n' desu né.

   B: Ée. Shikáshi konogoro wa
      kenkoo ni ki o tsukete iru
      hito ga óoi soo desu.

   A: Áa sóo desu ka. Sore wa
      íi keikoo désu né.

   B: Sóo desu. Tóku ni, chuunen
      no hito ni futorisugi wa
      ikenái n' desu.

5 A: Kono kaban wa igai to
      karui désu né.

   B: Sóo na n' desu. Nanimo
      háitte inái n' desu.

   A: Dóoshite kara no kaban
      o motte ikú n' desu
      ka.

   B: Mukoo de kaimono o
      takusán suru tsumori
      désu.

6 A: Shúuri ni dáshita
      puréeyaa o tóri ni
      kimáshita.

   B: Ítsu motte kitá n' desu ka.

   A: Mikka máe desu kara
      móo dékite iru hazu
      désu.

   B: Íma shirabemásu kara chótto
      mátte kudasai.

4 A: The Americans eat too much, don't they?

B: Yes. But I hear these days there are a lot of people who are careful about their health.

A: Really? That is a good trend, isn't it?

B: Yes. In particular, being too fat is bad for the middle-aged.

5 A: This bag is surprisingly light, isn't it?

B: That's just it. There is nothing in it, you see.

A: Why are you taking an empty bag?

B: I intend to do a lot of shopping over there.

6 A: I've come to pick up the record-player I put in for repair.

B: When did you bring it?

A: Three days ago, so it should be ready by now.

B: I'll check now. One moment, please.

N' DESѱ, 'THE THING IS'

N' desѱ, a contraction of the more formal, written form *no desѱ*, is used after the plain present or past tense of the verb or adjective to add a connotation of explanation or elaboration. The meaning of the expression is close to 'the thing is . . .', but often the idea is conveyed in English by 'you know', 'you see', 'let me explain that' or the like. It fixes a sentence within the wider conversational or situational context.

Compare the sentences *Ashí ga itái desѱ* and *Ashi ga itái n'desѱ*. Although both have the basic meaning 'my foot hurts', the former is a simple statement of fact, probably a piece of information with no particular connection with the present conversational situation. The latter, however, is an explanation, perhaps in reply to the question 'Why are you walking so slowly?'

Here are some more examples.

Ashѱta shѱppatsѱ surú n'desѱ.	'I'm leaving tomorrow, you see [and that's why I'm busy packing].'
Kaze o hiitá n' desѱ.	'I've got a cold, you see [and that's why my voice is husky].'
Kѱsuriya de kattá n' desѱ.	'I bought it at the chemists [that's why I called in there on the way home].'

The use of *n' desѱ* is particularly common in questions beginning with *dóoshѱte* or *náze* (both meaning 'why) and in reply to such questions. It is often used as a stylistic device to add life and continuity to a conversation, relieving the monotony of a *-másѱ* form at the end of every sentence. *Dá*, the simple present tense (dictionary form) of *désѱ*, is replaced by *ná* before *n' desѱ*.

Ashѱtá wa watashi no tanjóobi ná n' desѱ.	'Tomorrow is my birthday, you see.'

This also applies to the descriptive nouns.

Kánojo ga sѱki ná n' desѱ.	'The thing is, I'm fond of her.'

But the past tense form *dátta* does occur before *n' desѱ*.

Ano byooin wa mukashi keimusho dátta n' desụ̈.	'You see, that hospital used to be a prison.'

HAZU DESỤ̈, 'IT IS EXPECTED THAT', 'SHOULD BE', 'OUGHT TO'

This form is used after the plain present or past tense of the verb or adjective to indicate expectation, supposition or assertion. It often corresponds to an English expression with 'should', 'ought' or 'must', but is not to be confused with the 'should', etc., which conveys obligation or moral judgment, as in 'You should study harder.'

Hyakkáten de katta hóo ga yasúi hazu desụ̈.	'It should be cheaper to buy it at a department store.'
Kinoo no ban made ni káetaa nazu desụ̈.	'I expect he came back last night.'
	'He should have come back last night [and probably did].'
Sonna kotó wa nái hazu desụ̈.	'That sort of thing shouldn't happen.'
	'Surely that can't be right!'
Kyuukyúusha wa sanjuppun máe ni demáshịta kara móo jikogénba ni tsúite iru hazu desụ̈.	'The ambulance left thirty minutes ago so it should be at the scene of the accident by now.'
Shorui o íma súgu okurimásụ̈ kara asátte todóku hazu desụ̈.	'I'll send the papers right now, so they should reach you the day after tomorrow.'

MORE ABOUT WA AND GA

It might be useful at this stage to summarize the uses of *wa* and *ga*, two particles which are often confused by non-native speakers of Japanese.

Wa has two functions when it occurs after a noun. The one we have met already, and by far the most common, is its use to indicate the topic of discourse. In addition *wa* is used to indicate contrast.

Wa the topic marker

A topic is something the speaker assumes the hearer is acquainted with, either because it has been introduced earlier in the conversation, or because it is part of their shared knowledge and experience. For this reason it is used after unique natural phenomena like 'sun', 'moon', 'autumn' and for generalizations likely to be known by both speaker and hearer, like 'Englishmen', 'roses', 'mankind', etc., even though they have not been introduced earlier in the conversation. Often, because topics tend to be definite, their English equivalents are nouns preceded by the definite article 'the', but, particularly in the case of generalizations, English often employs the indefinite article, or no article at all.

Hi wa higashi kara déte nishi ni hairimásu̦.	'The sun rises in the east and sets in the west.'
Igirisújin wa inú ga su̦ki desu̦.	'The English like dogs.'
Ningen wa kangáeru doobutsu désu̦.	'Man is a thinking animal.'

Wa indicating contrast

Another use of the particle *wa* is to show that the noun occurring before it is being contrasted with something else which may or may not be mentioned in the same sentence.

Inú wa súkí desu̦.	'Dogs I do like.'
	'I like *dogs* [but not cats].'
Sakana wa tabemásu̦.	'I eat *fish* [but not meat].'
Yuki wa fu̦tte imasen.	'It's not *snowing* [but it is raining].'

Notice that in this usage *wa* replaces *o* or *ga*.

THE USES OF GA

The particle *ga* has three uses: (1) to mark the object of adjectives, descriptive nouns and stative verbs; (2) to mark the subject in neutral descriptions; and (3) to emphasize that the subject alone is involved in the action of the verb. Let us now look at these three in more detail.

Ga as an object marker

This use of *ga* was introduced in Lesson Five. The main stative verbs, i.e. those which mark their objects with *ga*, are *wakáru*, 'to understand', *áru*, 'to have', *iru*, 'to need', *dekíru*, 'to be done', 'be able to do'.

Nihongo ga dekimásᵤ ka.	'Can you speak Japanese?'
O-tétsudaisan ga irimásᵤ.	'We need a maid.'
Mátchi ga arimásᵤ ka.	'Have you got a match?'

Those adjectives and descriptive nouns which can take an object mark their objects with *ga*. Of the adjectives in this category common examples are *hoshíi*, 'to want', *umái*, to be good at', *kowai*, 'to be frightened of', *urayamashíi*, 'to be envious of'. The adjectival suffix *-tai*, 'to want to', may take either *ga* or *o* after its object, but the recent trend is towards the use of *o* and it seems that with some verbs, like those formed of a noun plus *suru*, *ga* is unacceptable. The negative suffix *-(a)nai* (also an adjective in form) does not influence the choice of the object marker. In this case, whether the object is marked with *o* or *ga* depends on the verb or adjective to which *-(a)nai* is attached. However, the independent verb *nái* (the plain negative form of *áru*) marks its object with *ga*. Here are some examples of the above.

Mótto jikan ga hoshíi desᵤ.	'I want more time.'
Suiei ga umái desᵤ.	'He is good at swimming.'
Kúmo ya hébi ga kowái desᵤ.	'I'm frightened of spiders and snakes.'
Káre no seikoo ga urayamashíi desᵤ.	'I envy his success.'
Nihongo ga/o naraitái desᵤ.	'I want to learn Japanese.'
Nihongo o benkyoo shitái desᵤ.	'I want to study Japanese.'
Gyuuniku o tabénai n' desᵤ.	'The thing is they don't eat beef.'
Roshiago ga wakaránai n' desᵤ.	'I don't understand Russian, you see.'
Hima ga nái n' desᵤ.	'You see, I don't have the spare time.'

You are well acquainted with the use of *ga* to mark the object of descriptive nouns like *sᵤkí*, 'to like', *kirai*, 'to dislike', *joozú*, 'to be

good at', *hetá*, 'to be bad at', and more examples are given in the
exercises. It should be remembered that *wa* can replace *ga* (or *o*) in
the above examples if some kind of contrast is implied; e.g. *Hima
wa nái n' desu̜* would mean 'The thing is I don't have the *time* [but I
do have the money].'

Ga in neutral descriptions

For objective descriptions of observable actions or states the subject
is marked with *ga*. This is how new information is introduced into
the conversation. 'It is raining', 'the telephone is broken', 'John is
washing the car', 'an old man is reading the paper', 'the sky is
cloudy', etc. are neutral descriptions which would have Japanese
equivalents with subjects marked with *ga*: *áme ga fu̜tte imasu̜*; *denwa
ga kowárete imasu̜*; *Jón ga kuruma o aratte imásu̜*; *o-jíisan ga
shinbun o yónde imasu̜*; *sóra ga kumótte imasu̜*; etc. *Ga* is usually
used after the subject of a subordinate clause.

Mású̜ko san ga ki̜te kara dekakemashóo.	'Let's go out [set out] after Masuko comes.'
Are wa áni ga káita e desu̜.	'That is the picture my elder brother painted.'

Ga emphasizing the subject

When special emphasis is to be placed on the subject it is followed
by *ga*. This is what the linguist Kuno calls the 'exhaustive listing
function' of *ga*. It indicates that the subject and the subject alone is
involved in the action of the verb. As interrogative words always
receive strong emphasis they are followed by *ga* when they occur in
the subject position: *Dóko ga suzushíi desu̜ ka*, 'Where is it cool?';
Dáre ga soo iimáshi̜ta ka, 'Who said so?' *Watashi ga shimásu̜* means
'I am the one who will do it', 'I and I alone shall do it'. *Ríi san ga
Chuugokújin desu̜* means 'It is Mr Lee [and he alone] who is the
Chinese.' This use of *ga* singles out the subject. It should not be
confused with the contrastive use of *wa*, which always implies a
contrast with something else. If we compare two sentences like *kore
wa denwachoo désu̜* and *kore ga denwachoo désu̜*, both meaning
'this is a telephone directory' we find that the former is a straight-

forward statement, perhaps in answer to the question 'What is that?', while the latter places strong emphasis on 'this' and might well be the reply to the question 'Which of these is a telephone directory?' The former example, in the correct context, might be interpreted as an instance of the contrastive use of *wa*. In this case it would form the reply to a question such as 'I know what this is, but what is that?' or it might be a partial answer to 'What is this and what is that?' Often where there is likely to be confusion between the *wa* marking the topic and the *wa* indicating contrast, the noun preceding the contrastive *wa* is pronounced with strong stress.

Sometimes there is ambiguity between the *ga* of natural description and the *ga* of 'exhaustive listing'. *Jón ga kuruma o aratte imásu* might be a simple objective description – 'John is washing the car' – or an assertion singling out John – 'It is John who is washing the car.' Context usually makes it clear which meaning is intended.

TERMS INDICATING FAMILY RELATIONSHIPS

You will no doubt have noticed that there are often two words to express a single family relationship. We have already met *otóosan* and *chíchi*, both meaning 'father', and *oníisan* and *áni*, both meaning 'elder brother'. Japanese distinguishes a neutral term used when referring to one's own father, elder brother, etc., when speaking to people outside one's own family circle, or when referring to fathers, elder brothers, etc., in general; and an honorific term which is used when referring to other people's relations or when addressing one's own. The following is a list of the more common kinship words.

Plain form	Honorific form	Address form	
chíchi	otóosan	otóosan	'father'
háha	okáasan	okáasan	'mother'
ryóoshin	goryóoshin		'parent'
áni	oníisan	oníisan	'elder brother'
ane	onéesan	onéesan	'elder sister'
otootó	otootosan	(name used)	'younger brother'
imootó	imootosan	(name used)	'younger sister'
kyóodai	gokyóodai		'brothers and sisters'
sófu	ojíisan	ojíisan	'grandfather'

sóbo	obáasan	obáasan	'grandmother'
oji	ojisan	ojisan	'uncle'
oba	obasan	obasan	'aunt'
kodomo	okosan	(name used)	'child'
musʉko	musʉkosan	(name used)	'son'
musumé	musumesan/	(name used)	'daughter'
	ojóosan		
shújin/otto	goshújin	(name) or	'husband'
		anáta	
kánai/nyóobo	ókʉsan	(name used)	'wife'
itóko	oitokosan	(name used)	'cousin'

NOTES

Useful expressions O-saki ni dóomo is short for *o-saki ni dóomo sumimasén*, 'very sorry [I went/I'm going] first.' Although it is less common than the first expression given here it is used when one discovers, for example, that one has gone through a door before a superior. This phrase or the simple *o-saki ni* is used in the sense of 'good-bye' when leaving one's place of work etc. *O-saki ni shʉtsúrei shimasʉ*, the full form, is also often used.

Dóozo o-agari kudasái is literally 'please come up' and would be said to a guest stepping up from the entrance hall into a Japanese house. *O-hairi kudasái* is used when asking someone to come into a room.

VOCABULARY

hi/táiyoo	sun	o-jiisan	old man
hi	day	ningen	man, human being
tsʉkí	moon, month		
higashi	east	ashí	leg, foot
nishi	west	kenkoo (na)	health(y)
minami	south	suiei	swimming
kʉta	north	chuunen	middle age
mushi	insect	fʉtorisugi	too fat
kúmo	spider	o-tétsudai	maid, household help
hébi	snake	(san)	

byooin	hospital	umái	to be good at
keimusho	prison	okashíi	funny
bengóshi	lawyer	karui	light
kaban	bag, case	urayamashíi	enviable, to envy
nímotsu	luggage	kowái	to be frightened
kyuukyúusha	ambulance	hĮku	to catch (a cold)
jiko-génba	scene of an accident	arau	to wash
		motte iku	to take
shorui	papers, documents	kowaréru	to get broken
		kowásu	to break
gyuuniku	beef	kómu	to get crowded
butaniku	pork	narau	to learn
booeki	trade	uru	to sell
booeki-gáisha	trading company	muku	to face
denwachoo	telephone directory	noru	to appear (in paper)
denwa-bángoo	telephone number	sugíru	to go past, go over
bangoo	number	-sugíru	to be too . . .
kootsuu	traffic	mukashi	in the old days, long ago, formerly
rásshu	rush-hour		
mátchi	matches		
é	picture	shĮkáshi	but
puréeyaa	record-player	choodo	exactly, just
purézento	present	fĮtsuu (ni)	usually
tanjóobi	birthday	fĮtsuu no	usual
kaimono (suru)	(to do) shopping	sórosoro	soon, shortly
haitatsĮ suru	to deliver	táda/tatta	only
seikoo (suru)	(to succeed), success	igai to/ni	unexpectedly
		toku ni	specially, in particular
shúuri suru	to repair	saki ni	first, in front, before
jama suru	to be a nuisance		
shĮppatsĮ suru	to leave, set off	dákara	that's why; and so
		désĮ kara	(polite form of above)
todóku	to reach, be delivered		
kara (no)	empty	sore démo	even so
ironna	various	shĮka (negative)	only
hoshíi na	to want		

EXERCISE 12

A Expand the following sentences using the forms in brackets.
Make any other changes necessary:
1 Asatte wa otooto no tanjoobi desu. (n' desu) 2 Kono heya wa nishi
ni muite imasu kara natsu wa atsusugimasu. (hazu desu) 3 Sono kara
no kaban o motte kimasu. (kudasai) 4 Dooshite ma ni aimasen
deshita ka. (n' desu) 5 Kaimono ga kirai desu. (n' desu) 6 Ano
tatemono wa keimusho desu. (soo desu) 7 Oji wa ashita kimasen.
(hazu desu) 8 Byooin no denwa-bangoo wa ano denwachoo ni notte
imasu. (hazu desu). 9 Futorisugi wa karada ni yoku arimasen. (n'
desu). 10 Kyonen katta pureeyaa wa moo kowarete imasu kara
tsukau koto ga dekimasen. (n' desu).

B Fill in the blanks:
1 Taiyoo (   ) higashi (   ) dete nishi (   ) hairimasu. 2 Abe san (   )
o-neesan (   ) suiei (   ) umai desu. 3 Dare (   ) anata no nimotsu
(   ) motte kita n' desu ka. 4 Matchi (   ) arimasu ga tabako
(   ) arimasen. 5 Konban no shokuji (   ) futsuu (   ) takakatta desu
ne. 6 Mukashi Igirisu (   ) kita no hoo no kaisha (   ) tsutome-
mashita. 7 Sobo (   ) minami (   ) koko e kimashita. 8 Konogoro
Nihongo (   ) naratte iru hito (   ) fuemashita. 9 Ani (   ) e
(   ) joozu desu. 10 Sono kowareta pureeyaa (   ) shuuri (   ) dashita
(   ) ga ii desu.

C Translate into English:
1 Kumo wa kirai desu ga hebi wa kirai ja arimasen. 2 Ato sanpun de
shuppatsu suru hazu desu. 3 Ano hyakkaten wa takakute ookii
mono shika haitatsu shimasen. 4 O-jama shimasu. 5 Ano mise de
oishii gyuuniku o utte imasu. 6 Ningen wa hoka no doobutsu yori
iroiro na mono o taberu koto ga dekiru n' desu. 7 Anohito wa
mukashi bengoshi deshita ga ima wa keimusho ni haitte imasu. 8
O-saki ni doozo. 9 Chiisa na booeki-gaisha de jimu no shigoto o
shite imasu. 10 Gomen kudasai.

D Translate into Japanese:

1 It is very chilly here in winter so we often catch colds. 2 I [am the one who] took your luggage to the hospital. 3 I envy your being able to go abroad every year. 4 Does your sister like beef? 5 Can you deliver it by 3 o'clock the day after tomorrow? 6 He is overweight so he should take care of his health. 7 My father is over sixty, but he still goes for a swim every morning. 8 How many children are there in your family? 9 You see, I've walked eight kilometres and my feet are sore. 10 The traffic is congested, but even so we should get there by 6 o'clock.

DÁI JUUSÁNKA

■ **BÉNRI NA HYOOGEN**

Osóre irimasu ga . . .   Dóozo o-kake kudasái.
Go-méiwaku desu ga . . .   Dóozo go-yukkúri.

O-tesúu desu ga . . .   Okáwari wa ikága desu̶ ka.

BUNKEI

Íma detara ki̶shá ni ma ni áu to iimásh̶ta.
Áme ga furánakattara umibé e ikimashóo.
Soku̶tatsu de okuréba yókatta no ni.
Nihongo de hanasánakereba narimasen.
O-sake o nómeba nómu hodo su̶kí ni narimasu̶.
Sore nára yamemásu̶.

■ **KAIWA**

1 A: Ejinbara-yuki no ki̶shá   B: Áto gófun de demásu̶.
        wa n̶ánji ni demásu̶ ka.   Hash̶tte ittára ma ni
                                                              aimásu̶ yo.

   A: Dóno hóomu kara   B: Sanbánsen kara desu̶.
        demásu̶ ka.

2 A: Kinoo katta omócha wa   B: Sonna yasumono o
        móo kowaremásh̶ta.   kawanákereba yókatta no
                                                              ni.

   A: Kodomo ga doosh̶témo   B: Ítsumo kodomo no yuu tóori
        hoshíi to yuu kara   ni shináku̶te mo íi deshoo.
        kawanákereba
        naránakatta n' desu̶.

3 A: Ash̶ta dókoka e   B: Ée, kodomo o doobutsúen e
        irasshaimásu̶ ka.   tsurete iku̶ tsumori désu̶.
   A: Ténki ga yókereba íi   B: Tenki-yóhoo ni yoru to
        .desu̶ né.   átsu̶ku náru soo desu̶.

164

LESSON THIRTEEN

USEFUL EXPRESSIONS

I am very grateful, sorry, etc.

I'm sorry to bother you,
   but . . .

I'm sorry to trouble you,
   but . . .

Please sit down.

Please make yourself at home.

Would you like another
   helping?

SENTENCE PATTERNS

He said if we leave now we'll be in time for the train.
If it doesn't rain, let's go to the seaside.
You should have sent it express delivery.
You must speak Japanese.
The more you drink *saké* the more you like it.
In that case I'll leave it.

CONVERSATIONS

1 A: What time does the Edinburgh train leave?

    B: It leaves in five minutes. If you run you'll make it.

    A: What platform does it leave from?

    B: Track three.

2 A: The toy I bought yesterday is broken already.

    B: You shouldn't have bought such cheap rubbish.

    A: The children insisted, so I had to buy it.

    B: You don't always have to do as the children say, you know.

3 A: Are you going anywhere tomorrow?

    B: Yes, I intend to take my boy to the zoo.

    A: It'll be nice if the weather is fine.

    B: According to the forecast it is going to be hot.

4 A: O-tesúu desu ga, kono
      pánfuretto o kachoo
      ni watashịte kudasái.

   B: Sumimasén ga, watashi wa
      yosó e ikanákereba
      narimasén.

   A: Sore nára watashi ga áto
      de watashimásụ.

   B: Dóomo osóre irimasụ.

5 A: Kono senpúuki wa
      kịkimasén yo.

   B: Átsụkereba watashi no heyá
      ni irasshátte kudasai.

   A: Yahári koko wa suzushíi
      desụ ne.

   B: Ée, atarashíi kúuraa o ireta
      bákari desụ.

6 A: Ópera no kén ga nímai
      té ni hairimáshịta.

   B: Watashi ga kai ni itta tokí wa
      móo urikire déshịta.

   A: Yókattara issho ni
      irasshaimasén ka.

   B: Go-méiwaku de nákattara
      zéhi ikịtai désụ né.

4 A: Sorry to trouble you, but
would you mind
giving this pamphlet
to the head of section?

B: Sorry, but I have to go
somewhere else.

A: In that case I'll give it to
him later.

B: I'm terribly sorry.

5 A: This fan doesn't work.

B: If you're hot come to my
room.

A: You're right. It's cool
here.

B: Yes. I've just put in a new
room cooler.

6 A: I managed to get two
tickets for the opera.

B: When I went to buy some
they were already sold
out.

A: If you like, please come
with me.

B: If it is no trouble, I'd really
love to go.

-TÁRA, 'IF'

Japanese has a number of ways of expressing temporal and conditional clauses. We have already met *to*, 'whenever', 'when', 'if'. Perhaps the most commonly used conditional is the suffix *-tára*, which attaches itself to the stem of verbs and adjectives and undergoes the same sound changes as the *-te* and *-ta* endings. In other words, simply add *ra* to the past tense forms: *hanáshḷtara*, 'if speak'; *máttara*, 'if wait'; *tábetara*, 'if eat'; *isóidara*, 'if hurry'; *aketára*, 'if open'; *akákattara*, 'if red'; *tákakattara*, 'if expensive'; *déshḷtara*, 'if be' (formal); *dáttara*, 'if be'. Accented verb and adjective roots have the accent mark on the same syllable as in the plain past form and this overrides the accent on *-tára*. Unaccented adjectives have an accent before the stem suffix – *kat* as in the past tense. The basic meaning of the *-tára* conditional is 'if or when the action of the subordinate verb is completed the action of the main verb follows.'

O-kyaksḷsan ga kḷtara watashi ni oshiete kudasái.	'Please let me know when the guests have arrived.'

The main verb may refer to either future or past time.

Sono sakana o tábetara onaka ga ḷtaku narimasu yo.	'If you eat that fish you'll get a stomach ache.'
Uchi ni káettara tomodachi ga kḷte imáshḷta.	'When I returned home my friend was there.'

Where the main verb is in the past tense, the *-tára* construction usually suggests surprise that the action of the main verb should have taken place. It is as if '[I] noticed that' or '[I] was surprised to see that' had been left out of the sentence. Usually the subjects of the two clauses are different. In this respect it resembles the use of *to* in past-tense sentences. *-tára*, however, refers to a single specific action or event. It is not used in the sense of 'whenever' and differs from *to* in that it can be used in sentences in which the main verb is a request or a command.

Fuyú ni náru to sḷkíi ni ikimasḷ.	'I go skiing when winter comes [i.e. every winter].'
Fuyú ni náttara sḷkíi ni ikimasḷ.	'When winter comes [has come], I'm going skiing.'
Sámukattara kono móofu o kákete kudasai.	'If you are cold, put this blanket over you.'

Colloquial Japanese is also available in the form of a course pack (ISBN 0-415-04741-2), containing this book and an accompanying audio cassette. The pronunciation guide, readings, conversations and idiomatic phrases contained in the book have been recorded by native speakers of Japanese, making the cassette an invaluable aid to speaking and comprehension.

If you have been unable to obtain the course pack the cassette can be ordered separately through your bookseller or, in case of difficulty, cash with order from Routledge Limited, ITPS, North Way, Andover, Hants SP10 5BE, price £7.95 including V.A.T., or from Routledge, Chapman and Hall Inc. 29 West 35th Street, New York, N.Y. 10001, U.S.A.

For your convenience an order form is attached.

CASSETTE ORDER

Please supply one/two/ . . . . . cassette(s) of

Clarke and Hamamura, *Colloquial Japanese*

ISBN 0-415-04740-4

Price £7.95 inc V.A.T.

☐ I enclose payment with order.

☐ Please debit my Access/Mastercharge/Visa/American Express account number

Name . . . .

Address . . . .

. . . .

Order to your bookseller or to . . .

ROUTLEDGE
ITPS
North Way
Andover, Hants.
SP10 5BE
ENGLAND

ROUTLEDGE INC.
29 West 35th Street
New York
NY 10001
USA

Of the conditional expressions *-tára* has the widest application. In a number of constructions, however, the suffix *-(r)éba* (*-kereba* with adjectives) is attached to the root to make another conditional form. The *-r* of *-(r)eba* is dropped when it follows a verb root ending in a consonant: *kákeba*, 'if write'; *ikéba*, 'if go'; *tabéreba*, 'if eat'; *nákereba*, 'if not'. *Désµ*, *dá* and the polite *-másµ* ending do not take the *-(r)éba* suffix, though the non-contracted copula *de áru* has the conditional *de áreba*.

-(A)NÁKEREBA NARIMASEN, -NÁKEREBA IKEMASEN, 'MUST', 'HAVE TO'

A common use of the *-(r)éba* suffix is in this double negative construction, 'if one does not . . . it will not do' which results in a strong connotation of obligation as in English 'must', 'have to', etc.

Kyóo wa shinseki ga kimásµ   'Today I have a relation coming
kara háyaku kaeránakereba   so I'll have to leave early.'
narimasen.

The use of *ikemasén* is rather stronger, suggesting moral judgment.

Ashµta wa shµkén desµ kara   'Tomorrow's the exam, so I'll
isshookénmei benkyoo   have to study for all I'm
shinákereba ikemasen.   worth.'

This word is often used alone as an exclamation: *Ikemasén*. 'Stop it!' 'Don't do that!'

(R)ÉBA (ÍI) NO NI, 'SHOULD', 'OUGHT TO'

In conversational Japanese *-(r)éba* often combines with *no ni* at the end of the sentence, conveying the idea 'should' or 'should have', lamenting a lost opportunity or unachieved action.

Háyaku irassháreba ma ni.   'If you had come earlier you
aimáshµta no ni   would have been in time.'
                       'You should have come earlier.'

It is more often used in familiar speech with a plain form of the verb or adjective, preceding *no ni.*

Ganbáreba seikoo shĮta no ni.   'If you had really worked at it
                                    you would have succeeded.'

Háyaku ieba yókatta no ni.   'I should have said so earlier.'

The use of the plain style is covered in Lesson Twenty.

-(R)ÉBA . . . HODO . . ., 'THE MORE . . . THE MORE'

The *-(r)éba* conditional is used in combination with *hodo*, 'extent', in sentences of the kind: *Róndon ni súmeba súmu hodo sĮki ni narimásĮ,* 'The more you live in London, the more you like it' (literally, 'If you live in London you come to like it to the extent that you live there').

The *-(r)éba* conditional is also used with the emphatic particle *sáe*, 'only', in expressions of the type *o-kane sáe areba*, 'if only I had the money'; *jikan sáe áreba*, 'if only there were time.' Notice, *sáe* replaces other particles.

Sáe sureba can be used after the stem of a verb to convey 'if only [just] something happens', 'if only [just] something is done'.

Koko ni namae to júusho o káki   'If you just write your name and
sae sureba áto de haitatsĮ   address here, we'll deliver it
shimásĮ.   later.'

Máinichi nijikan zútsu benkyoo   'You'll be all right if you just
shĮ sáe sureba daijóobu desu   study two hours every day.'
yo.

Zútsu in the example above means 'each'. It is often used in conjunction with a numeral or quantity word.

Ringo to orénji o niko zútsu   'I bought two each of the apples
kaimáshĮta.   and oranges.'

SĮkoshi zútsu tábete kudasai.   'Eat it a little at a time.'

Kodomotachi ni ame o hĮtotsu   'I gave the children one sweet
zútsu agemashĮta.   each.'

The accent of *zútsu* dominates the accent phrase, removing any accent from the word it follows.

NÁRA, 'IF', 'PROVIDED THAT', 'SUPPOSING THAT'

Nára, a conditional form of the plain-present copula *dá*, is often used after nouns and descriptive nouns. Sometimes it is used to develop a topic and is like an emphatic *wa*.

Sore nára íi desu.	'*That* one will be fine.'
	'In that case it will be all right.'
Watashi nára sonna kotó o shimasén.	[If I were you] *I* would not do such a thing.'
Ashlta áme nara ikimasén.	'If it rains tomorrow I shan't go.'
Sore ga hontoo nára íi desu ga.	'I hope that is true.'(literally, 'If that is true it will be good, but . . .').

When *nára* comes at the end of a clause after the plain form of a verb or adjective it means 'if it is true that', 'if it is a fact that' and like the *n' desu* form (sometimes *no* or *n'* is inserted before *nára* also) it links the sentence with something said before. In this construction the verb of the main clause represents the speaker's intention, assertion, command or question.

Anóhito ni dekíru nara watashi ni mo dekimásu.	'If he can do it so can I.'
Dóose iku nára háyaku itte kudasái.	'If you are going anyway, go early [or quickly].'
Honda san ga kúru nara watashi wa kaerimásu.	'If Mr Honda is coming I'm going home.'
Kore ga damé nara dóo sureba íi desu ka.	'If this is no good, what should we do?'

MÓSHI, 'IF'

Sometimes to add emphasis to a conditional, *móshi*, 'if', is used at the beginning of the *-tára*, *-(r)éba* or *nára* clause.

Móshi ashlta áme nara píkunikku o raishuu ni shimashóo.	'If it rains tomorrow let's make the picnic next week.'
Móshi jikan ga áttara uchi ni yotte kudasái.	'If you have time please drop in to my place.'

TO, 'THAT'; THE QUOTATIVE PARTICLE

The particle *to*, 'that', 'thus', is used before verbs of saying, thinking, knowing, etc., to indicate that the preceding words are reported speech or thought.

Ashḷta kúru to iimáshḷta.	'He said he is coming tomorrow.'
Nihongo ga muzukashii to omoimásḷ ka.	'Do you think Japanese is difficult?'
'Dustbin' o Nihongo de nán to iimásḷ ka? 'Gomibáko' to iimásḷ.	'How do you say "dustbin" in Japanese?' 'We say "gomibako".'

To express an indirect or reported command *-te kudasái to* or the plain present tense of the verb followed by *yóo ni* (without *to*) may be used.

Kabin ni sawaranáide kudasai to iimáshḷta	'He said not to touch the vase.'

or

Kabin ni sawaranai yóo ni iimáshḷita.

(Note the verb *sawaru*, 'to touch', takes an indirect object.)

Indirect questions usually drop *to* altogether.

Ítsḷ ikḷ ka [to] kḷkimáshḷta.	'I asked him when he is going.'
Dóo sureba íi ka wakarimasén.	'I don't know what I should do.'

Questions of the type 'whether or not . . .' use *ka dóo ka* usually without *to*.

Doyóobi no ban ni éiga o mí ni ikḷ ka dóo ka kḷkimáshḷta.	'I asked him whether he was going to see the film on Saturday night or not.'

NOTES

Conversation 1 Áto gófun de is an expression indicating time duration rather than a specific point of time, so *de* is used.

Conversation 2 To yuu kara. The present tense is used here instead of the expected *to itta kara*. Often the present tense is used in Japanese to dramatize a past event. Here it might be used to indicate that the saying was not a single event in the past, but an habitual action. As the final verb is in the past tense and there is no particular emphasis of completion in the subordinate clause there seems to be no need for the past tense in this sentence. Of course, *itta kara* is equally possible.

Conversation 5 Yahári and the more colloquial form *yappári*, very common in Tokyo, are frequently used in conversation. They express the idea, 'as expected', 'sure enough', 'you're right', 'I might have guessed', 'just as I thought', etc.

VOCABULARY

senpúuki	(electric) fan	*renshuu suru*	to practise
kúuraa	cooler	*kantan na*	simple, easy
móofu	blanket	*yosó*	somewhere else
tenki-yóhoo	weather report	*tóori*	way, as; road
sɪkíi	skiing	*asú*	tomorrow
píkunikku	picnic	*attakái/*	warm
kása	umbrella	*atatakái*	
umibé	seaside	*suzushíi*	cool
ópera	opera	*atarashíi*	new
kén	ticket	*furúi*	old
urikire	sold out	*tsurete iku*	to take (a person)
hóomu	platform	*yaméru*	to cease, give up,
-bánsen	track number . . .		abandon
sokɪtatsu	express	*watasɪ*	to hand over, pass
	delivery	*kɪku*	to work, be
omócha	toy		effective
ame	sweet, candy	*sawaru*	to touch
yasumono	cheap article	(takes *ni*)	
júusho	address	*kakéru*	to put over, hang
pánfuretto	pamphlet	*denwa o*	to ring up
kachoo	section head	*kakéru*	
gomibáko	dustbin	*denwa ga*	to be rung up
kabin	vase	*kakáru*	
shinseki	relation	*naku*	to cry

omóu	to think	*nára*	if
wasureru	to forget	*dooshḷtémo*	no matter what
yoru (ni)	to drop in, call in (at)	*yahári*	as expected, sure enough
hashḷtte	running	*dóosei*	anyway, in any case
-ta bákari desu̦	to have just	*sáe*	(if) only
-tára	if, when, provided that	*móshi*	if
-(r)éba	if, when	*to*	that, quotative particle
-kereba	if, when		

EXERCISE 13

A Join the following sentences using the forms in brackets and making any other changes the sense demands:

1 Terebi ga kowarete imasu. Shuuri ni dashita hoo ga ii desu. (nara)
2 Jon ga kimasu. Issho ni tabe ni ikimashoo. (-tara) 3 O-kane ga arimasu. Nihon ni ikitai to omoimasu. (sae) 4 Opera no ken ga urikire desu. Shibai o mi ni ikimashoo. (-tara) 5 Moofu o kakemasu. Attakaku narimasu yo. (-tara) 6 Shachoo no yuu toori ni shimasen. Ikemasen. (-(r)eba) 7 Nihon wa keshiki ga kirei desu. Soo omoimasu. (to) 8 Sokutatsu de okurimasen. Dooshitemo ma ni aimasen. (-(r)eba) 9 Jidoosha o tsukawainaide kudasai. Chichi wa iimashita. (yoo ni) 10 Asatte no paatii ni irasshaimasu ka, irasshaimasen ka. Kikimashita. (doo ka).

B Fill in the blanks and supply the correct forms of the words in italics:

1 Kono kusuri ( ) kaze ( ) kikimasen. 2 Hashitte *iku* ma ( ) aimasu. 3 Atarashii pureeyaa ( ) *kau* bakari desu. 4 Kasa ( ) wasurenai ( ) ni itte kudasai. 5 Tomodachi mo tsurete *iku* ( ) kamaimasen ka. 6 Itsumo fuyu ni naru ( ) sukii ( ) ikimasu. 7 Sukoshi renshuu ( ) sae ( ) o-hashi de taberu no wa kantan desu. 8 Kabuki no ken ga urikire da ( ) hayaku ieba yokatta ( ) ( ). 9 Sushi o *taberu* taberu ( ) oishii to omoimasu. 10 Tenki-yohoo ( ) ( ) ( ) ashita wa yuki ( ) furu kamo ( )

C Translate into English:
1 Dooshitemo kau nara yasumono o kawanai hoo ga ii to omoimasu.
2 Kanazawa-yuki no kisha wa nanbansen desu ka. 3 Okawari wa
ikaga desu ka. 4 Go-meiwaku desu ga kono tegami o kachoo ni
watashite kudasai. 5 Kyoo wa panfuretto o watasanakereba naranai
hi desu. 6 Kono kuuraa wa yoku kikimasen ne. 7 Mada kaeranakute
mo ii deshoo. Doozo go-yukkuri. 8 Kekkon shita bakari no toki ni
wa shujin no ryooshin to issho ni sunde imashita. 9 Kimiko san ga
iku nara watashi wa ikimasen. 10 Doozo o-kake kudasai.

D Translate into Japanese:
1 If you want another one I'll give you mine. 2 I told him to come at
3 o'clock yesterday, but he did not come. 3 How much do you think
that clock would cost? 4 I don't know what time the train leaves
tomorrow. 5 If you are not busy this afternoon please drop in to my
office. 6 Take three of each of those pamphlets on the desk. 7 We
have just built a new house so come and see it when you have the
time. 8 If I'd only had a dictionary I could have spoken to [=with;
use to] Mr Inoue in Japanese. 9 I'll give you one toy each, so don't
cry. 10 I'll have to be going now as I told my wife I'd be home early
this evening.

DÁI JUUYÓNKA

■ **BÉNRI NA HYOOGEN**

. . . o oshiete itadakemásψ ka.   O-ki no doku désψ.
. . . o goran kudasái/nasái   Kánben shψte kudasái.

O-sumai wa dóchira desψ ka.   Mooshiwake arimasén.

BUNKEI

Kore wa senséi ga kudasátta hón desψ.
Sψkiyaki no tsψkurikata o oshiete agemásψ.
Dáiku ni yoofψkudánsu o koshiraete moraimáshψta.
Sore o Nihongo de itte míte kudasai.
Káji de záisan o zénbu ushinatte shimaimáshψta.
Nihongo no áisatsu o íkψtsψka obóete oita hóo ga íi desψ.

■ **KAIWA**

1 A: Sono momo o kudasái.   B: Hái. Íkψtsu agemashóo ka.

   A: Góko kudasai.   B: Hψtótsu nihyakuen desψ kara
                                  sen'en itadakimásψ.

2 A: Sono wanpíisu o dóko   B: Imootó ni Itaria kara okψtte
       de kaimáshψta ka.   moraimáshψta.
   A: Watashi ni mo itchakú   B: Ée, mochíron. Tegami de
       tanónde   tanónde agemasψ.
       kudasaimasen ka.

3 A: Unténshusan. Soko o   B: Asoko wa ippoo-tsúukoo
       hidari e magatte   desψ kara sasetsu
       itadakemásψ ka.   dekimasén.
   A: Sore nára soko no   B: Okyakψsan, moo sψkóshi
       yakkyoku no máe de   háyaku itte itadakanai to
       orimasψ.   komarimásψ yo.

4 A: Yáa, kaminóke ga   B: Ekimáe no tokoya de katte
       mijikáku narimashψta   moraimáshψta.
       né.

LESSON FOURTEEN

USEFUL EXPRESSIONS

Would you mind telling . . .?
Please look at . . .

Where do you live?

What a pity! What a shame!
Please excuse me/bear with me,
    etc.
I'm terribly sorry.

SENTENCE PATTERNS

This is the book the teacher gave me.
I'll teach you how to make *sukiyaki*.
I got the carpenter to make me a wardrobe.
Try saying that in Japanese.
He ended up losing all his property in the fire.
You should learn a few Japanese greetings.

CONVERSATIONS

1   A: Give me some of those
        peaches, please.
    A: Five, please.

B: Yes. How many do you
    want?
B: They're ¥200 each so that'll
    be ¥1,000.

2   A: Where did you buy that
        dress?
    A: I wonder if you could
        ask her to send me
        one too.

B: My sister sent it to me from
    Italy.
B: Yes, certainly. I'll write and
    ask her.

3   A: Driver. Would you mind
        turning left here?

    A: In that case, I'll get off
        at the chemist's there.

B: I can't make a left turn
    there. It's a one-way
    street.
B: I wish you could have told
    me a bit earlier.

4   A: Hey! Your hair is
        short[er], isn't it?

B: I had it cut at the barber's by
    the station.

A: Umái tokoya désṵ né.

B: Suzuki san mo soko de katte míte morattára dóo desṵ ka.

5 A: Hiza ga itái desṵ.

B: Korobimáshṵta ka.

A: Ée. Subétte kaidan kara ochimáshṵta.

B: Isha ni míte moratta hoo ga íi desu yo.

6 A: Chótto tsṵmete itadakemasṵ ka.

B: Hái. Dóozo o-kake kudasái.

A: Dóomo shṵtsúrei shimashṵta.

B: Dóo itashimashṵte.

7 A: Kinoo Daiei-Hakubutsṵkan e itte kimashṵta.

B: Náni ga ichiban omoshírokatta desṵ ka.

A: Yahári, kódai-Ejipṵto no monó ga subarashíi desṵ né.

B: Ée. Ítsṵka Ejipṵto e itte mitái desṵ.

A: He is a good barber,
   isn't he?

B: Why don't you try getting
   your hair cut there too
   (Mr Suzuki)?

5 A: I've got a sore knee.
  A: Yes. I slipped and fell
     down the stairs.

  B: Did you fall over?
  B: You'd better get a doctor to
     have a look at it.

6 A: Would you move over a
     little, please.
  A: Thank you very much.

  B: Yes. Please sit down.

  B: That's quite all right.

7 A: I went to the British
     Museum yesterday.

  A: You're right. The
     ancient Egyptian
     things are wonderful.

  B: What did you like best?

  B: Yes. I'd like to go to Egypt
     some day.

VERBS OF GIVING AND RECEIVING

Japanese has a number of verbs for giving and receiving. Which is used depends on the relative status of the giver and receiver and whether the action is towards or away from the speaker. The verbs of in-giving (i.e. to the speaker or a third person) are *kudasáru*, (where a social superior gives the speaker or a third person) and *kureru* (where someone other than a social superior gives the speaker or a third person). *Kudasáru* and *kureru* cannot be used with a first person subject. In practice *kudasáru* often indicates a second person subject, 'you', and *kureru* a third person subject, 'he', 'they', etc.

Kore wa Suzuki san ga kudasátta yubiwa dés̩.	'This is the ring you [Mr Suzuki] gave me.'
Tomodachi ga kureta inú ni Shíro to yuu namae o ts̩kemásh̩ta.	'We called the dog our friends gave us Shiro.'

For out-giving, 'I give', 'he gives', etc., *ageru* is normally used regardless of the social position of the recipient.

Senséi ni omiyage o agemásh̩ta.	'I gave my teacher a gift (brought back from my travels).'
Kangófu wa kanja ni k̩suri o agemásh̩ta.	'The nurse gave medicine to the patient.'

There is a verb *yaru*, 'to give to an inferior', but this seems to be used mainly for actions directed towards junior members of one's own family, particularly one's own children. It is also used with non-human indirect objects.

Mus̩ko no tanjóobi ni táko o yarimásh̩ta.	'I gave my son a kite for his birthday.'
Kíngyo ni esá o yarimash̩ta.	'I fed the goldfish.'
Ajisai ni mizu o yatte kudasái.	'Please water the hydrangeas.'

Paralleling the use of the giving verbs, *kudasáru* and *kureru*, are the receiving verbs: *itadaku*, 'to receive from a social superior', and *morau*, 'to receive from someone other than a social superior.'

Itadaku is very often used when the recipient is first person, 'I' or 'we', and the giver is the second person, 'you'.

Senséi ni itadaita hón wa totemo chóohoo desu̬.	'The book I got from you [teacher] is very useful.'
Tároo ni moratta o-káshi wa amasugimásu̬.	'The cakes I got from Taro are too sweet.'

The term 'social superior' should be regarded as covering a rather arbitrary category which includes everyone outside one's immediate family, or group of close friends or workmates of the same age. *Kureru* and *morau*, however, are often used to refer to social superiors if they are not actually present at the conversation. *Kore wa Suzuki san ga kureta yubiwa désu̬*, 'This is the ring Mr Suzuki gave me', is permissible even if Mr Suzuki is regarded as a social superior, as long as Mr Suzuki or someone closely connected with him is not present.

Often there is little difference in meaning between 'giving' and 'receiving' sentences such as the following:

Senséi ga kudasátta jibikí o hóndana ni okimáshita.	'I put the dictionary my teacher gave me in the bookcase.'
Senséi ni itadaita jibikí o hóndana ni okimáshi̬ta.	

In the 'receiving' sentence the giver is marked by *ni*, though *kara* is also heard.

In purely neutral contexts, where we are not concerned with the relationships between giver and recipient, *ataeru*, 'to give', and *ukéru*, 'to receive', are used.

Chiisái kodomo ni hasamí o ataeru no wa ki̬ken désu̬.	'It is dangerous to give scissors to small children.'
Kono heyá wa yuu'utsu na inshoo o ataemásu̬.	'This room gives me a melancholy impression.'
Kono garasu wa sootoo no atsúryoku o ataete mo waremasén.	'This glass won't break even when subjected to considerable pressure.'
Atatakái kangei o ukemáshi̬ta.	'We received a warm welcome.'
Ano é kara dóo yuu inshoo o ukemáshi̬ta ka.	'What impression did you get from the picture?'

For receiving letters, parcels, etc., *uketóru* is often used.

Sokͩtatsu o táshͥka ni   'I am in receipt of your express-
   uketorimáshͥta.   delivery letter.' (formal
                                     cliché)

Ukéru is also used for 'to take [sit] an examination' or 'to undergo' a medical examination.

Tookyoo-dáigaku no nyuugaku-   'He took the Tokyo university
   shͥkén o ukemáshͥta.   entrance examination.'
Shintai-kénsa o ukemáshͥta.   'I had a medical examination.'

THE GIVING AND RECEIVING VERBS AS AUXILIARIES

After the *-te* form of a verb the giving and receiving verbs are used as auxiliaries indicating the relationship between the initiator and recipient of an action. We have met *kudasái*, the imperative of *kudasáru*, used after the *-te* form to make a polite request, 'please'. In fact *-te kudasái* means 'you [my superior] do . . . for me.'

Saitoo san wa furúi kataná o   'Mr Saito showed me an old
   mísete kudasaimashͥta.   sword.'

-te kureru indicates that the action is done for me or for somebody else by someone who is not a social superior.

Kodomo ga michi o annái shͥte   'A child showed me the way.'
   kuremáshͥta.

-te ageru indicates that the action is done for a social superior. Usually the subject of a *-te ageru* verb is 'I' or 'we'.

Tokei o shúuri ni dáshͥte   'Shall I put your watch in for
   agemashoó ka.   repair for you?'

As with the simple verb *yaru*, *-te yaru* is used mainly with actions directed towards junior members of one's own family.

Musͩko o tsuri ni tsurete itte   'I took my son fishing.'
   yarimáshͥta.

-te yatte kudasái is often used when asking someone to do something for a member of one's own family, a subordinate or a pupil.

| *Kodomo no machigái o naóshite yatte kudasái.* | 'Please correct the child's mistakes for him.' |

When the receiving verbs are used after the *-te* form, there is often, though not necessarily, a causative connotation indicating that the subject of the sentence instigated the action. The agent is followed by *ni*.

| *Dáiku ni yáne o naóshιte moraimashιta.* | 'I got the carpenter to fix the roof.' |

(Literally, 'I received a mending of the roof by the carpenter' (who is not my social superior).)

| *Abe senséi ni subarashíi é o káite itadakimashιta.* | 'I was lucky enough to have Dr Abe paint me a wonderful picture.' |

In the last example there is no feeling that 'I' caused Dr Abe to paint the picture. The sentence is very similar in meaning to *Abe senséi ga subarashíi é o káite kudasaimashιta.*

-te itadakemásι ka

A very polite request can be made with the *-te* form of the verb followed by *itadakemásι ka* or *itadakemasén ka* based on the potential verb *itadakeru*, 'to be able to receive'.

| *Shió to koshóo o tótte itadakemasι ka.* | 'Would you mind passing the salt and pepper?' |
| *Buraun san no jimúsho wa dóko ni áru ka oshiete itadakemasén ka.* | 'I wonder if you could tell me where Mr Brown's office is?' |

-te itadakitai, -te moraitai, 'I'd like you [him] to', 'I wish you would'

The receiving verbs combined with the desiderative ending *-tai* express the idea of wanting someone to do something. *-te itadakitai* would normally be used to refer to a second person or a third person present in the conversational situation and *-te moraitai* to an absent third person. In any case this construction is more assertive than *-te itadakemásι ka* and is not used in normal polite requests.

Kinoo katta yasai ga kᵤsátte   'The vegetables I bought
  imasᵤ kara torikáete itadakitai   yesterday are rotten so I'd like
  désᵤ.   you to change them for me.'
Háyaku chᵢchí ni káette kᵢte   'I wish father would come back
  moraitai desᵤ.   home quickly.'

In neutral situations, where the relationship between individuals is
not involved, -*te hoshíi* can be used instead of -*te moraitai*.

Moo sᵤkoshi suzushᵢku nátte   'I wish it would get a bit cooler,
  hoshíi desᵤ née.   don't you?'

OTHER AUXILIARIES USED AFTER THE -TE FORM

-te míru, 'try . . . -ing', 'do . . . and see'

It is very common to end a sentence in a -*te* form followed by an
auxiliary, as we have seen with the verbs of giving and receiving.
Míru, 'to see', used after the -*te* form adds a connotation of 'try
. . . doing', 'just do', 'do and see'. It makes the sentence less abrupt
and is used in Japanese more often than we use the equivalents in
English.

Kázuko san ni denwa shᵢte   'I tried giving Kazuko a call.'
  mimáshᵢta.
Tábete mite kudasái.   'Just try eating it [to see how
        you like it].'
Afurika ni itte mitái to   'I'd like to go and have a look at
  omoimásᵤ.   Africa.'

-te oku, 'do beforehand', 'set aside', 'do in preparation'

Oku, 'to put', 'to place', 'to set', after the -*te* form indicates the
action has been left done, done in preparation for something else, or
done and set aside. A few examples should make the meaning clear.

Bíiru o reizóoko ni irete   'I put some beer into the
  okimáshᵢta.   refrigerator [so it would be
        cold when you arrived].'
Sono dái no ue ni oite óite   'Please leave it on the stand
  kudasái.   [i.e., put it on the stand and
        leave it there].'

*Móo isha ni hanáshte
   okimashta kara shinpai
   shináide kudasai.*

'I've already spoken to the
doctor about it so don't
worry.'

-te kúru, 'go and do', 'keep on doing'

Kúru, 'to come', after the *-te* form of a verb conveys a number of
different meanings depending on the meaning of the preceding verb.
Often it means 'to go and do something', although the Japanese way
of putting it is 'do something and come back.' We have seen this in
the expression *itte kimas* (or *itte mairimas*), 'goodbye' (when leaving a place to which one will later return); *motte kúru*, 'to bring'; and
motte iku, 'to take'.

*Íchiba de shinsen na sakana o
   katte kimás.*

'I'll go and buy some fresh fish
at the market.'

Keisatsu ni todókete kimas.

'I'll go and report it to the
police.'

Used after certain intransitive verbs *-te kúru* indicates that something 'begins' or 'gradually becomes more and more . . .' as in *Áme
ga fútte kimashta*, 'It began to rain'.

*Sékai no jinkoo ga fúete
   kimashta.*

'The world's population has
increased.'

-te iku, 'go on doing something'

This indicates an action or state that begins at a certain point and
from there moves forward in space or time.

Kore kara rakú ni nátte ikimas.

'Things will get easier from now
on.'

*Tsugí kara tsugí e to furúi
   kenchíku ga kiete ikimás.*

'Old buildings [literally,
architecture] are disappearing
one after the other.'

-te shimau, 'do completely', 'end up doing'

Shimau, 'to finish', after the *-te* form means something is done com-
pletely or one ends up doing something.

Zénbu ippén ni tábete   'He ate it all up at once.'
 shimaimashįta.
Tabesugi de onaka o kowáshįte 'I got an upset stomach from
 shimaimashįta.   eating too much.'

This ending is particularly common in the Tokyo area, where informal speech *-te shimau* is often contracted to *-chimau* or simply *-chau*. Some speakers use it indiscriminately after almost any verb with no particular connotation of completion of finality. While you will no doubt hear this usage, be careful not to overuse it.

Sonna kotó o ittára   'If you say that sort of thing, I'll
 káetchaimasu yo.   go home!'

VERB STEM -KATA, 'WAY OF DOING'

A noun meaning the way of doing something can be formed by adding *-kata* to the verb stem: *oyogikata*, 'way of swimming'; *tabekata*, 'way of eating'; *arukikata*, 'way of walking', etc.

Nihonjín to Seiyóojin wa   'Do you think the ways of
 kangaekata ga chigau to   thinking of Japanese and
 omoimásų ka.   Europeans are different?'

-kata removes any accent from the verb root, resulting in an unaccented word. There is an alternative pronunciation, *-káta*, which behaves like *-másu*, giving the same accent pattern for accented and unaccented roots.

NOTES

O-ki no doku désų is used when expressing sympathy. The more formal form *o-ki no dokų-sama* is used in conveying condolences, when it means, 'I am very sorry to hear that . . .'.

Mooshiwake arimasén literally means 'there is no excuse', 'there is no way to explain [my behaviour]'. This is a rather formal form, but it does not convey much more than 'I'm very sorry'.

Conversation 3 Unténshusan. When words indicating an occupation are used as forms of address they are usually followed by *san*. This does not apply to titles or rank; *shachoo* can be used as a form of address without the following *san*, though many people say *shachoosan*.

VOCABULARY

kyaku	guest, customer	*hiza*	knee
o-kyakųsan	guest (honorific)	*kaminóke*	hair
		hasamí	scissors
isha	doctor	*kataná*	sword
o-ishasan	doctor (honorific)	*Daiei hakubutsųkan*	British Museum
kangófu	nurse	*Ejipųto*	Egypt
kanja	patient	*Afųrika*	Africa
keisatsų	police	*sékai*	world
kenchikųka	architect	*jinkoo*	population
kenchįku	architecture	*atsúryoku*	pressure
dáiku	carpenter	*inshoo*	impression
yáne	roof	*tabemonó*	food
dái	stand	*shió*	salt
garasu	glass	*koshóo*	pepper
tansu	cupboard	*o-káshi*	cakes
yoofųku-dánsu	wardrobe	*momo*	peach
		íchiba	market
yoofųku	(Western) clothes	*tabesugi*	over-eating
		yakkyoku	pharmacy, chemist
wanpíisu	dress		
sebiro	(man's) suit	*ajisai*	hydrangea
-chaku	counter for suits, dresses, etc	*jibikí*	dictionary
		táko	kite; octopus
zaisan	property, fortune	*kíngyo*	goldfish
		esá	feed, bait
káji	fire, conflagration	*tsuri*	fishing
		otsuri	change (money)
michi	road	*reizóoko*	refrigerator
ippoo-tsúukoo	one-way traffic	*Tookyoo-dáigaku*	Tokyo University
usetsu	right turn	*Toodai*	Tokyo University
sasetsu	left turn		
kádo	corner	*nyuugaku-shíken*	entrance exam
wá	wheel, ring		
yubiwa	ring	*nyúushi*	entrance exam
yubí	finger	*kangei (suru)*	(to) welcome

annai suru	to guide, show around	*naósu*	to repair, cure
chóohoo na	valuable, useful	*naóru*	to get better
kĮken na	dangerous	*nazukéru*	to name
rakú na	easy, comfortable	*na(mae) o tsĮkéru*	to name
shinsen na	fresh	*ageru*	(I) give (you, him)
yuu'utsu na	gloomy, depressing	*yaru*	(I) give (an inferior)
ekimáe (no)	in front of the station	*kudasáru*	(you) give (me)
		kureru	(he) gives (me)
kódai (no)	ancient	*ataeru*	to give
mijikái	short	*itadaku*	(I) receive (from you)
nagái	long	*morau*	(I, he) receive(s) (from him)
amai	sweet		
ochíru	to fall	*ukéru*	to receive
korobu	to fall over	*uketóru*	to receive (letter, etc.)
subéru	to slip		
oríru	to get down, get off	*-te shimau*	end up . . . ing, do completely
todokéru	to report, deliver	*-te míru*	to try . . . ing
torikáeru	to exchange, change	*-te oku*	do in preparation
		-te kúru	to be getting more . . .
ushinau	to lose		
kĮsáru	to rot	*-te iku*	to go on getting more . . .
magaru	to turn		
kieru	to go out, disappear	*zénbu*	all
		yáa	(exclamation) hey!
tsuméru	to pack, squeeze in	*tsugí kara tsugi e (to)*	one after the other
karu	to cut, mow		
koshiraeru	to make	*ippén ni*	at once, at the same time
wareru	to get broken, shatter	*táshĮka ni*	certainly, safely

EXERCISE 14

A Substitute the correct form of the word in brackets for the word in italics and make any other changes necessary:
1 Kore wa sensei ga *kudasatta* tokei desu. (itadaku) 2 Daiku *ni* tsukue o koshiraete moraimashita. (ga) 3 Tomodachi *ga* oshiete kuremashita. (ni) 4 *Kodomo* ni yubiwa o katte yarimashita. (obaasan) 5 Michi ga wakaranakattara untenshu ga shirabete *kuremasu*. (morau koto ga dekiru). 6 Kono sebiro o kite mite *kudasai*. (itadaku) 7 *Kobayashi sensei* ni watashite agete kudasai. (uchi no musuko) 8 Motto shizuka ni shite *kudasai*. (. . . -tai) 9 Biiru o reizooko ni irete oite *kudasaimasen* ka. (itadaku) 10 *O-tetsudai san* wa shinsen na sakana o katte kuremashita. (watashi)

B. Fill in the blanks:
1 Byooin ( ) shintaikensa o ( ) ni ikimasu. 2 Reizooko ni irete okimasen deshita ( ) tabemono wa zenbu kusatte ( ). 3 Chichi ( ) moratta zaisan ga arimasu ( ) kore kara ( ) raku deshoo. 4 Kaze o hiite iru ( ) kono kusuri o nonde ( ) kudasai. 5 Konban kyaku ga kuru kara momo ( ) futatsu zutsu katte ( ). 6 Hakubutsukan ( ) tsutomete iru Abe san ni furui katana ( ) misete ( ). 7 Moo ushinatte ( ) mono wa wasureta ( ) ga ii desu. 8 Konogoro wa futotte ( ) kara kyonen katte ( ) wanpiisu wa minna chiisa (-). 9 O-tegami ( ) tashika ( ) uketorimashita. 10 Musuko no kaminoke ( ) katte ( ) kudasai.

C Translate into English:
1 Kangofu ni hiza o mite moraimashita. 2 Toodai no nyuugaku-shiken o ukemashita ga dame deshita. 3 Sono ame wa amasugimasu kara ippen ni zenbu tabete shimawanaide kudasai. 4 Tsugi kara tsugi e iroiro na okurimono o moraimashita. 5 Tsuri no esa o takusan katte kite reizooko ni irete okimashita. 6 Uchi no mae no michi wa ippootsuukoo desu kara nishi no hoo kara haitte itadakemasu ka. 7 Suzuki san no okusan ni moo sukoshi yukkuri shabette morawanai to anmari yoku wakarimasen. 8 Kono aida koronde ashi o itaku shimashita kara isha ni mite morawanakereba narimasen. 9 Yuube mita eiga wa kodomo ni donna inshoo o ataemashita ka. 10 Hokkaidoo e ryokoo ni itta toki itoko ni ironna tokoro o annai shite moraimashita.

D Translate into Japanese:
1 Please tell my son where he has to get off the bus. 2 I'll teach you how to make *sukiyaki*. 3 Would you mind passing the pepper and salt? 4 Where do you live? 5 I had two suits made for me when I was in London last year. 6 The vase fell off the stand and broke. 7 Please correct my mistakes. 8 Don't you think these cakes are too sweet? 9 You'll have to report the traffic accident to the police, you know. 10 Could you turn right at the lights [= where the lights are], please?

DÁI JÚUGOKA

■ **BÉNRI NA HYOOGEN**

Náni mo arimasén ga
  dóozo . . .

O-kuchi ni awánai deshoo
 ga . . .

Moo íppai ikága des𝑢 ka.

O-kotoba ni amaete . . .

Kanpai!

Mata o-me ni kakarimashóo.

BUNKEI

Tabenágara hanasóo to sh𝑖te imash𝑖ta.

Tak𝑢sán tábeta no ni máda o-naka ga suite imás𝑢.

Mizu ga kírei na no de ike no soko máde miemás𝑢.

Ten'in wa iroiro na monó o misetagarimásh𝑖ta.

Íma choodo dekakéru tokoro dés𝑢.

Yukue- fúmei ni nátta n' ja nái ka to omoimas𝑢.

■ **KAIWA**

1 A: Shuumatsu ni tsuri ni
      ikóo to omótte imas𝑢.

   B: Uchi no choonán wa ítsumo
      tsuri ni ikitagarimás𝑢.

   A: Yókereba issho ni
      tsurete itte agemásu
      yo.

   B: Go-méiwaku ja nakattara
      zéhi o-negai shimás𝑢.

2 A: Nihón ni k𝑖kái o
      yush𝑢ts𝑢 shiyóo to
      sh𝑖te imás𝑢.

   B: Dákara Nihongo o benkyoo
      sh𝑖te irú n' des𝑢 ka.

   A: Sóo des𝑢. Ash𝑖ta áru
      kaisha no daihyoo to
      toríh𝑖ki no hanashí o
      surú n' desu yo.

   B: Seikoo suru yóo ni inótte
      imas𝑢.

3 A: Dantai-ryókoo de
      Háwai ni ikóo to
      omótte imas𝑢.

   B: Mukoo wa mushiatsúi des𝑢
      kara karui f𝑢kú o motte
      itta hóo ga íi desu yo.

LESSON FIFTEEN

USEFUL EXPRESSIONS

It's only a simple meal, but . . .   That's very kind of you.

You might not like it, but . . .   Cheers!

How about another glass?   Let's meet again.

SENTENCE PATTERNS

He was trying to speak while he was eating.
I ate a lot but I'm still hungry.
As the water is clean you can see to the bottom of the pond.
The shop assistant wanted to show me all sorts of things.
I'm just about to go out now.
I think he must have gone missing.

CONVERSATIONS

1   A: I'm thinking of going   B: My eldest son is always
         fishing at the   wanting to go fishing.
         weekend.

     A: If you like I can take him   B: If it is no trouble, that would
         with me.   be very nice, thank you.

2   A: I'm trying to export   B: Is that why you are studying
         machinery to Japan.   Japanese?

     A: That's right. In fact,   B: I hope you are successful.
         tomorrow I've got
         some negotiations
         with the representa-
         tive of a certain
         Japanese firm.

3   A: I'm thinking of going on   B: It's very humid over there.
         a package tour to   You'd better take light
         Hawaii.   clothing.

A: Kore kara hanzúbon o
kaóo to omotte imasu.

B: Íma depáato wa séeru desu
kara yasúi no ga mitsukaru
hazu désu.

4 A: Kono goro o-kane o
setsuyaku shiyóo to
shite imasu.

B: Démo infure de bukka ga
dóndon agaru kara taihen
deshóo.

A: Táshika ni sóo desu ga
shújin ga tabako o
yameta no daké demo
daibu tasukarimásu.

B: Sonna ni chigaimásu ka né.

5 A: Kono heyá wa semái
desu kara dókoka
chigau tokoro de
hanashimashóo yo.

B: Kissáten de koohíi demo
nominágara hanashitara
dóo desu ka.

A: Sore wa íi desu né.
Choodo nódo ga
kawáite kita tokoro
désu.

B: Eki-mae ni íi kissáten ga áru
n' ja nai ka to omoimásu.

A: I'm just going to buy some shorts.

B: They're having a sale at the department store at the moment, so you should be able to get some cheap ones.

4 A: Lately I've been trying to cut down on expenses.

B: That must be hard with prices going up so quickly with inflation.

A: That is certainly so, but even my husband's just giving up smoking is a great help.

B: I wonder if it really makes so much difference.

5 A: This room is cramped. Let's talk somewhere else.

B: What about talking at the café over a cup of coffee or something.

A: That would be fine. I've just started to feel thirsty.

B: I think there should be a good coffee shop near the station.

In Lesson Thirteen you met the quotative particle *to*. This *to* is used in a number of expressions after the plain propositive form of the verb. The propositive form has been introduced in the polite ending *-mashóo*, but the plain form is made by attaching the suffix *-(y)óo* to the verb root, dropping the initial *-y* when the verb root ends in a consonant: *tabeyóo*, 'let's eat'; *ageyóo*, 'let's give'; *kakóo*, 'let's write'; *ikóo*, 'let's go'. Note the suffix bears the accent regardless of the original accent of the verbal root. The irregular verbs *suru* and *kúru* become *shiyóo* and *koyóo* and as we have seen the propositive of the *-másu* ending, *-mashóo*, is also formed irregularly.

-(Y)ÓO TO SURU, 'TO TRY TO', 'TO BE ABOUT TO'

One use of the plain propositive is before *suru*. This means 'to try to' or 'to be about to', depending on the context. It usually indicates that the proposed or attempted action is prevented or interrupted and should not be confused with *-te míru*, which means 'to do something and see', 'to try doing something'.

Ryóoshin ni renraku shiyóo to shimashļta ga dekimasén deshļta.	'I tried to contact my parents, but I was unable to do so.'
Choodo dekakeyóo to shļte ita toki ni denpoo ga todokimáshļta.	'Just as I was about to go out a telegram arrived/was delivered.'

-(Y)ÓO TO OMOU, 'TO HAVE A MIND TO', 'TO THINK ABOUT'

The plain propositive suffix is also used before *to omóu* in sentences of the type: *Saraishuu kaigan e ikóo to omótte imasu*. 'I'm thinking of going to the seaside the week after next.' The expression is made vaguer by inserting the question particle *ka*. *Hikóoki de ikóo ka to omoimasu*. 'I think I might go by plane.'

JA (OR DEWA) NÁI KA TO OMOIMASU, 'MUST BE', 'PROBABLY IS'

This expression is used after a noun or descriptive noun.

Anokatá wa Tanaka senséi ja nái ka to omoimásu.	'That must be Dr Tanaka.'

Nihongo ga joozú ja nái ka to omoimásu̜.	'I think he must be good at Japanese.'

After a verb or adjective *n' ja nái ka to omoimásu̜* is used.

Ashļta irassharú n' ja nai ka to omoimásu̜.	'I think he must be coming tomorrow.'
Yuugata áme ga fúru n' ja nái ka to omoimásu̜.	'It will probably rain in the evening.'

N' ja nái desu̜ ka and *'n ja arimasén ka*, 'Isn't it so that?', 'Don't you think that?', are often used in questions which anticipate an affirmative answer.

Móo osói n' ja nái desu̜ ka.	'Isn't it already too late?'
Máiasa háyaku okíru n' ja arimasén ka.	'Don't you get up early every morning?'

MORE CLAUSE-FINAL PARTICLES

No ni, **'although', 'but', 'however'**

These two particles combine to express much the same idea as the clause-final particle *ga*, 'although', 'but'. *No ni*, however, contrasts the clauses with a strong emphasis on the verb preceding *no ni* and is usually preceded by a plain form of a verb or adjective (unlike *ga*, which follows *-másu̜* or *désu̜*). The plain present form of the copula, *da* becomes *na* when it occurs before *no ni*.

Ojísan ni séki o yuzuttá no ni suwaróo to shimasén deshļta.	'Although I gave up my seat to the old man, he made no attempt to sit down.'
Natsú na no ni máda séetaa ga hļtsuyoo désu̜.	'Even though it is summer you still need a jumper.'

This is the *no ni* introduced after *íi, yókatta*, etc., used in conjunction with the conditional, as in *Háyaku ieba yókatta no ni . . .*, 'You should have said so earlier.'

Where there is no concessive or contrastive link between the clauses *no ni* often means 'in order to'. In this case *no* simply acts as a nominalizing particle and *ni* is 'for'.

Kírei na ji o káku no ni íi fudé o	'In order to write beautiful

tsukatta hóo ga íi desu.	characters you should use a good writing brush.'
Bijútsukan e iku no ni tochuu de básu o norikaenákereba narimasen.	'To get to the art gallery you have to change buses on the way.'

No de, 'because'

This is a common connective used to link clauses of cause and effect or circumstance and consequence. It seems to be similar to *kara* except that it usually follows a plain form and is more widely used in formal speech and in the written language. *No de* is not usually used where the verb of the main clause is imperative, assertive or interrogative or where it implies obligation or permission. *Kara* has a wider application and is safer at this stage, though you should understand *no de* when you hear it.

Yuki ga yandá no de yamá ni sukíi ni dekakemáshita.	'As it had stopped snowing we set out for the mountains to do some skiing.'
Koko wa késhiki ga íi no de yuumei désu.	'This place is famous for its lovely scenery.'

In this last example *no* is probably a pronoun, 'the fact' or such like and *de* the instrumental particle.

THE ADJECTIVAL SUFFIX -GÁRU

-gáru is attached to the root of certain adjectives to form verbs with the meaning 'to give the appearance of', 'to look like', 'to seem to be'. It usually has a third person subject. *Hazukashíi*, 'to be shy, embarrassed [etc.]', becomes *hazukashigáru*, 'to act in a shy manner'.

Tomodachi wa hajímete no miai de hazukashigátte imashita.	'My friend was very shy at her first marriage interview.'

Hoshíi, 'to want', becomes *hoshigáru*, 'to appear to want', 'someone else wants'.

Kodomo wa amai monó o hoshigarimásu.	'Children [always] want sweet things.'

The most common use of this suffix is with the suffix -*tai*. The ending -*tagáru* means a third person 'wants to do something'. As -*tai* is subjective in feeling it is usually used with a first person subject or in questions with a second person subject. -*tagáru* is more objective and is used to refer to third persons.

Musu̧ko wa fu̧ttobóoru no shiai o mí ni ikitagátte imasu̧.	'My son wants to go and see a football match.'
Háyaku kaeritagátte imasḩta.	'She wanted to go home early.'

Compare these with the use of -*tai* with first and second person subjects in the following sentences.

Hocḩķsu̧ to jóogi to keshigomu o katte moraitai déşu.	'I want you to buy me a stapler, a ruler and a rubber.'
Súgu séki ni modoritái déşu ka.	'Do you want to go back to your seat straight away?'

TOKORO DESU, 'TO BE ON THE POINT OF'

Used after the plain present tense of a verb, *tokoro deşu* conveys the idea 'to be about to'.

Íma káeru tokoro deşu.	'I'm just about to go home now.'
Choodo deyóo to sḩte iru tokoro deşu.	'I'm just trying to get away now.'

After a plain past tense *tokoro deşu* means 'to have just . . .'

Sákki káette ķta tokoro deşu.	'I just got back a short time ago.'

In this last pattern *bákari* is perhaps more common than *tokoro*

Kono pán wa déķta bákari deşu.	'This bread has just been made.'
Oshieta bákari na no ni móo wasuremásḩta ka.	'Have you forgotten already? I've just taught you.'

-NAGARA, 'WHILE'

When two actions are being performed by the same subject at the same time, they may be joined by -*nagara*, 'while', which is attached to the verb stem: *kakinágara*, 'while writing'; *tabenágara*, 'while eating'. With accented verbs the accent moves to the first syllable of the suffix. Unaccented verbs have unaccented *-nagara* forms. *-nagara* is usually attached to the activity with secondary importance and the main activity is in the final verb.

Kaisha no hookokｕsho o yominágara asagóhan o tabemáshｌta.	'I read the company report while I was having breakfast.'
Kissáten de koohíi o nominágara shoodan o shimáshｌta.	'We discussed business in a tea room over a cup of coffee.'

If the subjects of the clauses are different 'while' is expressed by *aida*, 'interval', or *aida ni* usually after the plain present form of the verb.

Kánai ga súupaa de kaimono o shｌte iru aida ni toshókan kara hón o karite kimáshｌta.	'While my wife was shopping in the supermarket, I went and borrowed a book from the library.'

Uchi is sometimes used instead of *aida* in this construction, but it is more often used after a negative verb to convey the idea of 'before'.

Senseigáta ga irassharánai uchi ni kaigíshｌtsu no sooji o shimashóo.	'Let's clean the conference room before the teachers come.'

VOCABULARY

kao	face	*súupaa*	supermarket
kｕchi	mouth	*shokúryoo*	foodstuff, provisions
kｕchibiru	lips		
hana	nose	*koohíi*	coffee
agó	chin	*kissáten*	coffee shop, tea shop
fｕkú	clothes		
zubón	trousers	*bunboogu(ya)*	stationery (shop)
hanzúbon	shorts		
séetaa	jumper, sweater	*keshigomu*	rubber, eraser
séeru	sale	*jóogi*	ruler
ten'in	shop assistant	*inku*	ink
bukka	prices	*hó(t)chｌkisｕ*	stapler
infure	inflation	*toshókan*	library

bijútsukan	art gallery	aida	while, between
bíjutsu	art	uchi	while, inside
fudé	writing brush	mushiatsúi	humid
késhiki	scenery	hazukashíi	shy, ashamed
kaigan	coast, seaside	hazukashigaru	feel shy, ashamed
Heian-jídai	Heian Period	inóru	to pray for
kaigíshitsu	conference room	mitsukeru	to find
séki	seat	mitsukaru	to be found
shoodan	business discussions	agaru	to go up, rise
toríhiki	transaction, dealings	todóku	to reach, be delivered
daihyoo	representative	yuzuru	to pass over, give up, give way, bequeath
hookokusho	report		
nyúusu	news	suwaru	to sit down
fúttobooru	football	norikáeru	to change (buses, trains, etc.)
sákkaa	soccer		
shiai	match	yamu	to stop
miai	marriage meeting	hoshigaru	to want
choonán	eldest son	otósu	to drop, let fall
iké	pond	hirou	to pick up
soko	bottom	haku	to wear (footwear, trousers, skirt, etc.)
yuugata	evening		
máiasa	every morning		
shuumatsu	weekend	tasukáru	to be saved, be a help
saraishuu	the week after next		
dantai-ryókoo	group trip	daibu	considerably, very
setsuyaku suru	to economize	dóndon	rapidly, quickly
renraku suru	to contact	sákki	a short time ago, just now
sooji suru	to clean		
hitsuyoo na	necessary	-gáru	(verbalizing suffix)
tochuu	on the way		
yukue-fúmei	whereabouts unknown	-tagáru	to want to . . .
		-nágara	while
hajímete(no)	first	-(y)óo to suru	to try to . . .
ni tsuite(no)	about	no ni	although, in spite of the fact that
ni totte	for		
áru	a certain	no de	because

EXERCISE 15

A Combine into a single sentence using the words in brackets and make any other changes necessary:
1 Rajio no nyuusu o kikimashita. Asa-gohan o tabemashita. (-nagara) 2 O-kane o setsuyaku shimasu. Soo omotte imasu. (to) 3 Nandomo renraku suru yoo ni tanomimashita. Denwa o shite kuremasen deshita. (no ni) 4 Terebi ga kowaremashita. Kinoo shuuri ni dashimashita. (no de). 5 Ashita sakkaa no shiai ga arimasu kara ikimasu. Miyoo to omotte imasu. (ni) 6 Tabako o suimashita. Shoodan o shimashita. (-nagara) 7 Shuumatsu desu. Kaigan wa amari konde imasen. (no ni) 8 Basu de ojiisan no suwaru tokoro ga arimasen deshita. Seki o yuzutte agemashita. (no de) 9 Kami ya inku nado o kaimasu. Soo omotte imasu. (to) 10 Tanabe sensei wa kaigishitsu ni irasshaimasu. Soo omoimasu. (dewa nai ka)

B Fill in the blanks and give the correct forms of the words in italics:
1 Tochuu ( ) bijutsukan ( ) yorimashoo. 2 Yama ( ) yukue-fumei ( ) natta ( ) ( ) nai ( ) to omoimasu. 3 Tenki-yohoo ni ( ) to yuugata *suzushii* naru ( ) desu. 4 Booeki-gaisha no daihyoo ( ) shoodan o ( ) yoo ( ) denwa ga kakatte kimashita. 5 Ototoi chuumon shimashita ( ) moo sorosoro todoku ( ) da ( ) omoimasu. 6 Saraishuu wa kanai no tanjoobi ( ) no de seeru ( ) wanpiisu o katte ( )- mashita. 7 *Taberu* hanasu ( ) ( ) shitsurei desu. 8 Heya o sooji ( ) to omotte ita ( ) e o-kyaku san ga kimashita. 9 Zutto hanzubon ( ) haite ita ( ) ( ) zenzen samuku ( ) desu. 10 Bukka ni tsuite no hookokusho ( ) okutte ( ) desu.

C Translate into English:
1 Doko de norikaetara ii ka oshiete kudasai. 2 Choonan wa doobutsuen e ikitagatte imasu ga watashi wa tsuri ni ikitai desu. 3 Koko wa natsu mushiatsui desu ga umi kara no suzushii kaze de daibu tasukarimasu. 4 O-kuchi ni awanai deshoo ga, doozo. 5 Tabeta bakari na no ni mada onaka ga suite imasu ka. 6 Michiko san ga nanika amai mono o hoshigatte ita no de o-kashi o katte agemashita. 7 Toshokan kara Heian-jidai no bijutsu ni tsuite no hon o karite kimashita. 8 Nihon no kodai no rekishi ni tsuite nanimo

shirimasen kara sukoshi benkyoo shiyoo to omotte imasu. 9 Kore wa Suzuki san ni totte hajimete no dantai-ryokoo ja nai ka to omoimasu. 10 Sore dewa o-kotoba ni amaete, itadakimasu.

D Translate into Japanese:
1 He says he still doesn't understand although I explained it to him just now. 2 Would you mind picking up the ring I dropped there? 3 I don't think you need change trains. 4 I'm thinking of going to see a soccer match this weekend. 5 My eldest son wanted me to buy the suit, but it was too expensive for me. 6 She is always shy meeting people for the first time. 7 They said 'cheers' before drinking their sake. 8 Although it is a very big supermarket, I doubt whether the food here is very fresh. 9 You had better have your business discussions in the coffee shop while I am writing the report in my office. 10 These trousers were quite expensive although I bought them at a sale.

DÁI JUURÓKKA

■ **BÉNRI NA HYOOGEN**

O-kaeri désɥ ka.

... o-ari désɥ ka.

... o-mochi désɥ ka.

O-mochi shimashóo ka.

O-tétsudai shimashoo ka.

O-wakri désɥ ka.

BUNKEI

Rájio o kiitári térebi o mítari shimashɥta.

Anóhito wa piano ga joozú ni hikemásɥ.

Senséi no machigái de miná waraidashimáshɥta.

Ano ie ni dáremo sunde inai yóo desɥ.

Mukoo no shima no suna ga totemo kírei rashíi desɥ.

Sore wa yumé mitai na hanashí desɥ.

■ **KAIWA**

1 A: Ano kyookai no yóo na bíru wa nán desɥ ka.

   A: Kawatta kenchɥku désɥ né.

   B: Dékɥta bákari no gekijoo rashíi desɥ.

   B: Ée, konogoro hén na tatemono ga óoi desɥ né.

2 A: Kono jínja no mori wa suzushíi desɥ né.

   A: Ano sakura ga sakɥ kóro wa subarashíi deshoo.

   B: Ée, tori no nakigóe ga kɥkoete íi desɥ né.

   B: Ée. Sore kara áki no kooyoo mo mígoto rashíi desu yó.

3 A: Kono heyá o tsɥkurinaóshɥte moraoo to omótte imasɥ.

   A: Kabe o tóttari atarshíi tenjoo o iretári shimásɥ kara watashi ni wa muzukashisugimásɥ.

   B: Hɥto ni yatte morau to tákakɥ tsɥkimásu yó.

   B: Yókattara watashi ga tetsudátte agemashoo.

LESSON SIXTEEN

USEFUL EXPRESSIONS

Are you going home?
Have you got . . . ?
Have you got . . . ?

Shall I carry it for you?
Shall I help you?
Do you understand?

SENTENCE PATTERNS

I listened to the radio and watched television.
He can play the piano well.
Everyone burst out laughing at the teacher's mistake.
It looks as if nobody lives in that house.
It seems the sand on the island over there is very clean.
That story is like a dream.

CONVERSATIONS

1   A: What is that building like a church?

    B: It seems it's a theatre they've just built.

    A: It's strange architecture, isn't it?

    B: Yes. These days there are a lot of strange buildings around.

2   A: The grove of this shrine is cool, isn't it?

    B: Yes. It's nice being able to hear the birds singing.

    A: It must be wonderful when that cherry tree is in bloom.

    B: Yes. And apparently the coloured leaves in autumn are magnificent.

3   A: I'm thinking of having this room rebuilt.

    B: It'll be expensive if you get someone in to do it.

    A: It's too difficult for me. I've got to take out a wall and put in a new ceiling and so on.

    B: If you like, let me help you.

4 A: Anóhịto wa shótchuu
ō-sake o nóndari
tabako o sụttári shịte
yóku karada o
kowashimasén né.

B: Ée, nán demo yarisugíru to
ikemasén née.

A: Sóo desụ. Daitai
tanoshíi koto wa
karada ni warúi yoo
desụ né.

B: Zannen-nágara soo rashíi
desụ né.

5 A: O-yasumi no aida náni o
shimáshịta ka.

B: Máinichi oyóidari umá ni
nottári shimashịta.

A: Dáre demo asoko e
ikemásụ ka.

B: Ie, kúrabu no kai'in de
nákereba damé desụ.

6 A: Kanji ga yomemásụ ka.

B: Iie, hiragana daké desụ.

A: Kanban nado ga
yoménai to fúben
deshoo.

B: Hái. Tóku ni basu-nóriba o
sagasu ba'ai muzukashii
désụ.

7 A: Moyori no kooban wa
dóchira deshoo ka.

B: Asoko ni miéru takái
manshon-bíru no tonari
désụ.

A: Gáado no shịta o tóote
ikemasụ ka.

B: Iie, ano hodookyoo o
watatte ikụ to íi desụ yo.

8 A: Séngetsu kashịta hón o
yomiowarimáshịta ka.

B: Iie, kono aida yomihajímeta
bakari desụ.

A: Shinseki no hịto ni
kashịtai désụ kara
raishuu káeshịte
itadakemasén ka.

B: Hái. Wakarimáshịta. Asátte
made ni zénbu yoméru to
omoimásụ.

4 A: He is always drinking sake and smoking. It's a wonder he doesn't injure his health.

B: Yes. Overdoing anything is bad.

A: That's right. By and large, things which give us pleasure are bad for the health.

B: Unfortunately that seems to be so.

5 A: What did you do during your holidays?

B: Every day I went swimming or horse-riding or something.

A: Can anyone go there?

B: No you have to be a member of the club.

6 A: Can you read Chinese characters?

B: No, only *hiragana*.

A: It must be inconvenient if you can't read signs and things.

B: Yes. It's particularly difficult when you are looking for a bus stop.

7 A: Can you tell me where the nearest police-box is?

B: It's next to the big block of flats you can see over there.

A: Can you get there through the railway arch?

B: No. You should cross that pedestrian bridge.

8 A: Have you finished reading the book I lent you last month?

B: No, I just started reading it the other day.

A: I wonder if you could return it next week. I want to lend it to a relation.

B: Yes, certainly. I think I can read it all by the day after tomorrow.

THE POTENTIAL VERBS

Consonant-root verbs have corresponding vowel-root verbs which express potentiality; 'can do'. For example, *káku*, 'to write'; *kakéru*, 'to be able to write'. In practice you merely substitute *-eru* for the plain present-tense ending, but remember you end up with a new vowel-root verb capable of taking most of the normal verb suffixes. (The potential verbs do not normally occur before *-tai*, the request form *-te kudasái*, or the passive, causative or imperative endings, to be introduced in later lessons.) Accented verb roots have accented potential forms and unaccented verbs have unaccented potential forms: *nómu*, 'to drink'; *noméru*, 'to be able to drink'; *tobu* 'to fly'; *toberu*, 'to be able to fly'.

You have already met the potential form in the expressions, *kamo shiremasén*, 'perhaps' (whether or not I cannot know), *-te itadake-masén ka*, 'would you kindly . . .' (can I not receive?), and *ikemasén*, 'it won't do', 'stop it', etc.

In very casual speech, particularly among younger speakers, you often hear potential verbs coined from vowel-root verbs, *tabéru* becoming *taberéru*, etc. These forms are still not fully accepted and should be avoided. The passive construction (to be introduced in Lesson Seventeen) doubles up to act as the potential of the vowel-root verbs. In the meantime use the *kotó ga dekiru* construction to express the idea of potentiality with the vowel-root verbs: *tabéru kotó ga dekiru*, 'can eat', etc.

As the potential verbs describe states rather than actions, they mark their subjects with the particle *ga*.

Anóhito wa Supéingo ga hanasemásu̥.	'He can speak Spanish.'
Móo íi hanga ga yásu̥ku kaemasén.	'You can no longer buy good wood-block prints cheaply.'

Sometimes potentiality can be expressed with an intransitive verb.

Techoo ga mitsu̥karimasén.	'I can't find my pocket notebook.'
Atarashíi jidóosha wa sháko ni hairimasen.	'I can't fit my new car in the garage.'
Doroboo wa tsu̥kamarimasén deshi̥ta.	'They couldn't catch the thief.'

The verbs *miéru*, 'to be able to see', and *kikoeru*, 'to be able to hear', are formed irregularly, but both are potential verbs marking their objects with *ga*.

Koko wa hotóndo kootsuu no soo'on ga kikoemasén kara yóku nemuremásu.	'You can sleep well here as you can hardly hear the noise of the traffic at all.'
Tookú ni mieru shimá wa Izu no Óshima desu.	'The island you can see in the distance is Oshima in Izu.'

Kiku also has the regular potential form *kikeru*, which is used for 'can ask' and for 'can hear' in the general sense, opposed to *kikoeru*, which refers to sounds actually audible at the time in question.

Wakaránakattara gáido ni kikemásu yo.	'If you don't know you can ask the guide.'
Róndon de ítsu demo náma no koten-óngaku ga kikemásu yo.	'In London you can always hear live performances of classical music.'

-TÁRI

This suffix is attached to the stem of verbs and adjectives and undergoes the same contractions we saw in the *-te* form and the past tense. To produce the *-tári* form of a verb or adjective just add *-ri* to the past-tense form: *káitari*, 'writing and so on'; *ittári*, 'going and so on'; *tábetari*, 'eating and so on'.

The function of this suffix is similar to the use of *nádo* after nouns. It indicates that the actions or states mentioned are given as examples of a longer list. Often the idea is that two or more actions occur time after time or one after the other. Hence the terms 'frequentative' or 'alternative' which are often applied to this form. Usually two *-tári* forms occur in a sentence with the second *-tári* being followed by some form of the verb *suru*.

Yoaké made o-sake o nóndari sushí o tábetari shimáshita.	'We drank *saké* and ate *sushi* [and talked and played cards, etc.] until dawn.'
Tegami o káitari shorui o séiri shítari shimáshita.	'I did such things as writing letters and putting my papers in order.'

Konogoro no ténki wa áts|kattari sámukattari suru no ni yoku kaze o h|kimasén née.	'The weather lately has been hot one minute and cold the next. It's a wonder we don't catch colds.'
Anóhito wa ittári k|tari sh|te ochits|kimasén né.	'He is very restless, isn't he? Coming and going like that.' (Notice Japanese says 'going and coming'.)
Hooeichuu táttari suwattári shináide kudasai.	'Please don't keep getting up from your seat during the screening.'

Rarely are there more than two *-tári* in a sentence.

O-shaberi o sh|tari, utá o utattari, odottári shimash|ta.	'They chatted, sang songs and danced.'

Frequently there is only one *-tári*.

Uchi de hón o yóndari shimas|.	'I stay home and read books or something.'
Tamá ni wa yótte ni nottári suru kotó mo arimás| ka.	'Do you also occasionally go sailing or something?'

Sometimes *dés\|* replaces *suru*.

Ano rés|toran wa oish|kattari oish|ku nákattari dés| kara chotto o-kyak|san o tsurete ik| kotó ga dekimasen.	'Sometimes the food at that restaurant is good and sometimes it's bad so you can't really take a guest there.'

YÓO, RASHÍI, MÍTAI, 'BE LIKE', 'SEEM TO BE'

These words, very similar in meaning, can be used either attributively (before a noun) or in final predicates (at the end of the sentence). *Yóo* and its casual colloquial equivalent *mítai* behave as descriptive nouns, requiring *na* when they are used before another noun. While *yóo* must be linked to the preceding noun by *no*, *mítai* follows its noun directly. *Rashíi* follows directly on the preceding noun and, being a true adjective in form, it undergoes no change when it comes before a noun or *dés\|*, but occurs in the *-ku* form, *ráshiku*, before verbs. The following examples should make these differences clear.

o-máwarisan no yóo na hi̥to	'a man [who looks] like a policeman'
o-máwarisan mítai na hi̥to	'a man [who looks] like a policeman'
o-máwarisan rashíi hi̥to	'a man [one is given to believe is, looks or acts] like a policeman'

There is a good deal of overlapping in the meaning of these expressions. *Yóo na* and *mítai na* are virtually synonyms. Both seem to refer mainly to actual physical appearance. *Rashíi* has the added connotation of hearsay ('someone told me that', etc.). This applies, too, when they occur at the end of the sentence.

Ano puréeya wa kowárete iru yóo desu̥.	'That record-player seems to be [looks as if, or sounds as if it is] broken.'
Anóhi̥to wa máinichi gókiro hashíru rashii desu̥ yo.	'Apparently he runs five kilometres every day.'

In addition to the word *rashíi*, there is a suffix *-rashíi*, '-like', which makes adjectives from certain nouns: *otokorashíi*, 'manly'; *onnarashíi*, 'womanly, feminine'; *bakarashíi*, 'foolish'. In this case the accent of *-rashíi* dominates the accent phrase, removing any accent from the noun to which it is attached.

-SOO, 'LOOK LIKE', 'SEEM TO BE ABOUT TO'

The suffix *-soo(na)* is used after the stem of a verb or the root of an adjective in expressions such as

Áme ga furisoo désu̥.	'It looks like rain.'
Sore wa takasoo na sebiro désu̥ né.	'That is an expensive-looking suit, isn't it?'

With *yói*, 'good', and *nái*, 'not have', *-soo* is attached to the stem plus *-sa* resulting in the irregular forms *yosasoo* and *nasasoo*.

Háyaku itta hóo ga yosasoo desu̥.	'It looks as if it would be better to go quickly!'
O-kane ga nasasoo désu̥ né.	'He doesn't look as if he has any money, does he?'

-soo mo arimasen, **'to show no sign of . . . ing'**

Káre wa kaerisoo mo arimasén.	'He shows no sign of going home.'
Inú wa kono esá o tabesoo mo arimasén.	'The dog shows no sign of eating this food.'

COMPOUND VERBS

Japanese has a large number of compound verbs made up of one verb attached to the stem of another. Most of these will be acquired as separate items of vocabulary, but some of the second elements with wide application are set out below. The tendency nowadays is to place an accent on all compound verbs.

-dasu	'to begin', 'to start suddenly', 'to break out'
furidásu	'to start raining';
e.g. *Áme ga furidashimáshｊta.*	
nakidásu	'to burst into tears';
e.g. *Akanboo ga nakidashimáshｊta.*	
waraidásu	'to burst out laughing';
e.g. *Ookíi kóe de waraidashimáshｊta.*	
iidásu	'to start saying', 'speak out';
e.g. *Kyuu ni iidashimáshｊta.*	
-hajiméru	'to begin'
yomihajiméru	'to begin to read';
e.g. *'Sensoo to Heiwa' [War and Peace] o yomihajímeta bakari desｊ.*	
narihajiméru	'to begin to become';
e.g. *Kuraku narihajimemáshｊta.*	
naraihajiméru	'to begin to learn';
e.g. *Ashｊta kara Eigo o naraihajimemásｊ.*	
shihajiméru	'to begin to do';
e.g. *Setsumei shihajimemáshｊta.*	

-owaru	'to finish'
kakiowáru	'to finish writing';
e.g. *Tegami o kakiowarimashḷta.*	
tsṵkuriowáru	'to finish making';
e.g. *Móo tsṵkue o tsṵkuriowarimáshḷta.*	
-naósṵ	'to redo', 'do again'
nurinaósu	'to repaint';
e.g. *Kabe ni pénki o nurinaosánakereba narimasén.*	
yarinaósu	'to do again';
e.g. *Moo ichido saisho kara yarinaoshimashóo.*	
kangaenaósu	'to rethink';
e.g. *Sakṵsen [strategy] o kangaenaoshimásṵ.*	
-tsuzukéru	'to continue to do', 'keep on doing'
arukḷtsuzukéru	'to keep walking';
e.g. *Ashí ga ítaku naru made arukḷtsuzukemáshḷta.*	
yomitsuzukéru	'to go on reading';
e.g. *Yomitsuzúkete kudasai.*	
-sugíru	'to overdo', 'do too much', 'be too . . .' (also used with adjective root).
nomisugíru	'to drink too much';
e.g. *Uísṵkii o nomisugimáshḷta.*	
shaberisugíru	'to talk too much';
e.g. *Ano okṵsan wa shaberisugimásṵ.*	
takasugíru	'to be too expensive';
e.g. *Denshḷkeisánki wa takasugimásṵ.*	

VOCABULARY

piano	piano	*machigái*	mistake
gítaa	guitar	*karada o kowásu*	to damage one's health
yumé	dream	*hanga*	woodblock print
yumé o míru	to dream	*hiragana*	*hiragana* script
yótto	yacht	*katakána*	*katakana* script
suna	sand	*kanban*	notice board, sign
shima	island	*techoo*	notebook, pocket diary
hayashi	forest		
mori	wood, grove	*hooeichuu*	during projection (of a film)
jínja/o-miya	shrine (Shinto)		
tera/o-tera	temple (Buddhist)	*gozenchuu*	all morning, in the morning
sakura	cherry blossom		
kooyoo	autumn leaves	*ichinichijuu*	all day long
yoake	dawn, daybreak	*suutsukéesu*	suitcase
ushi	cow	*basu-nóriba*	bus terminal/stop
umá	horse		
kúrabu	club	*o-sháberi suru*	to chat, chatter
kai'in/ménbaa	member	*séiri suru*	to put in order
gáido	guide	*hén na*	strange, peculiar
akanboo/ákachan	baby	*fúben na*	inconvenient
		náma (no)	raw
nakigóe	cry	*moyori (no)*	nearest
kóe	voice	*saisho (no)*	first
o-máwarisan	policeman	*tooku (no)*	distant, in the distance
kooban	police box		
soo'on	noise	*warúi*	bad
gáado	railway arch	*mazúi*	bad, not tasty
hodookyoo	pedestrian bridge	*otokorashíi*	manly
manshon-bíru	block of flats	*onnarashíi*	feminine
mánshon	flat	*bakarashíi*	stupid
kabe	wall	*tákaku tsuku*	cost a lot, turn out expensive
tenjoo	ceiling		
sháko	garage	*tetsudáu*	to help
sensoo	war	*híku*	play (piano, guitar, etc.)
heiwa	peace		
sakusen	strategy	*kawaru*	to change

kawatta	strange, peculiar	*shótchuu/*	all the time,
sagasɥ	to look for	*shíjuu*	always,
miéru	to be visible; can		constantly
	see	*daitai*	for the most part,
wataru	to cross		approximately,
tsɥkamaru	to be caught		generally
nemuru	to sleep	*zannen-*	unfortunately
ochitsɥku	to settle down	*nágara*	
utau	to sing	*hotóndo*	most, mostly,
utá o utau	to sing		almost always,
odoru	to dance		nearly
sugósu	to pass time	*tamá ni*	occasionally, once
noboru	to climb		in a while
nuru	to paint, apply	*-eru*	(potential suffix)
-dásu	to break out	*-tári*	(alternative-
	. . . ing		frequentative
-hajiméru	to start . . . ing		suffix)
-owaru	to finish . . . ing	*-rashíi*	-like
-naósu	to redo . . . ing	*-soo*	looks as if . . .
-sugíru	to overdo . . . ing		seems to be
-tsuzukeru	to keep on		about to
	. . . ing	*yóo na*	like, as
sore kara	than, next, and	*mítai na*	like, as

EXERCISE 16

A Make into single sentences incorporating the appropriate forms
of the words in brackets, or change according to the instructions
given. In either case make any other changes the sense demands.

1 Piano o hikimashita. Zasshi o yomimashita. (-tari) 2 Yama ni
noborimasu. Umi de oyogoo to omotte imasu. (-tari) 3 Naoshimasu
ga takaku tsukimasu yo. (potential). 4 Minna de o-sake o nomimashita. Uta o utaimashita. Waraimashita. (-tari). 5 Kurabu no
kai'in ni narimasen. (potential) 6 Sakura no hana wa mada saite

imasen. (rashii) 7 Mukoo ni tatte iru hito wa omawarisan desu.
(yoo) 8 Nihongo o hanashimasu ka. (potential) 9 Yoru anmari yoku
nemuremasen. (yoo) 10 Kaette kuru no ga hayai desu. Osoi desu.
(-tari)

B Fill in the blanks and supply the correct forms of the words in
italics:
1 Ano tooku ( ) *miru* shima wa nan ( ) iimasu ka. 2 Basu wa
hayaku *kuru* osoku *kuru* ( ) no de fuben desu. 3 Akanboo no
nakigoe ( ) *suru* kootsuu no soo'on ( ) *kikoeru* ( ) zenzen
nemuremasen deshita. 4 Nakada san wa chotto hen ( ) hito
( ) yoo desu ne. 5 Kabe ( ) *nurinaosu* kirei ni naru deshoo. 6
Jibun ( ) shitari tomodachi ( ) tetsudatte morattari ( ) uchi ( )
tatenaoshimashita. 7 Tanaka san ga sunde ( ) manshon-biru o
sagasu to shimashita ga mitsukarimasen deshita. 8 Ima jimusho o
seiri *suru* denwa o *kakeru* shite isogashii yoo ( ). 9 Dokoka hanga
( ) yasuku *kau* tokoro ( ) go-zonji ( ) ka. 10 Kanai ( ) shotchuu tonari no okusan ( ) o-shaberi suru ( ) desu.

C Translate into English:
1 Konogoro no resutoran wa nedan ga takakattari, tabemono ga
mazukattari shite bakarashii desu ne. 2 Hayaku kekkon shite
ochitsukitagatte iru yoo desu. 3 Aki nara kooyoo ga kirei ni narisoo
na tokoro desu ne. 4 Sore wa amari yosasoo na sakusen de wa
arimasen. 5 Itsu made ni hon o kakiowaranakereba narimasen ka. 6
Minna de gitaa o hiitari uta o utattari shite tanoshii desu ne. 7 Ano
akachan wa ima ni mo nakidashisoo na kao o shite imasu yo. 8
Nihon de juusho o sagashite iru toki, mitsukaranakattara kooban de
kikeba oshiete kureru rashii desu. 9 Tama ni yotto ni notte dokoka
tooku no shima e itte mitai to omoimasen ka. 10 Abe san-tachi no
paatii ni shotchuu kawatta hito ga kuru mitai desu ne.

D Translate into Japanese:
1 When did you start learning English? 2 The sky has started to
cloud over from the west and it looks like rain. 3 Shall I carry your
suitcase for you? 4 I like such things as painting pictures and making
toys. 5 Let's start walking towards that little temple you can see in
the distance. 6 Shall I help you? 7 Mr Tanaka bought a big
American car, but unfortunately it won't fit into his garage. 8 I spent

all morning cleaning my room and putting my books in order. 9 We are a small trading company which imports machinery from Japan and exports meat and fish to Europe. 10 I can't read Chinese characters, but I can write *hiragana* and *katakana*.

DÁI JUUNÁNAKA

■ **BÉNRI NA HYOOGEN**

O-tómo shíte mo yoroshii désy ka.

Ókysan mo go-issho désy ka.

Haiken shíte mo íi desy ka.

Haishaku shíte mo íi desy ka.

Ossháru toori desy.

O-suki na yóo ni . . .

BUNKEI

Inú ga kodomo ni keraremáshíta.
Doroboo ni hooseki o nusumaremáshíta.
Áme ni furaremáshíta.
Shíkén ni óchíta no wa benkyoo shinákatta tamé desy.
Yukí ga fytta ba'ai ni wa yamemashóo.
Kono nikú wa katakyte náifu de kirinikúi desy.

■ **KAIWA**

1 A: Tabako wa karada ni warúi desy yo.

   B: Sore o shíte ite mo yameraremasén.

   A: Watashi wa isha ni yameru yóo ni meirei saremáshíta.

   B: Watashi wa meirei sarete mo yamerarenai to omoimásy.

2 A: Dóoshíte nikú o sonna ni kau n' desy ka.

   B: Tomodachi ni tanomáreta bun mo háitte iru n' desu yo.

   A: Omókyte mochiagerarénai deshoo.

   B: Ée. Nikúya ni jidóosha made hakonde moraimásy.

3 A: Gaikoku de pasypóoto o nusumáreta ba'ai ni wa dóo shimasy ka.

   B: Súgu Nihon no taishíkan ka ryoojíkan ni todokénakereba narimasen.

LESSON SEVENTEEN

USEFUL EXPRESSIONS

May I come with you?

May I borrow it, please?

Is your wife going/coming with you?

That's right. It's as you say.

May I have a look at it, please?

As you like . . .

SENTENCE PATTERNS

The dog was kicked by the child.
I had my jewellery stolen by a burglar.
We were caught in the rain.
My failing the examination was because I did not study.
If it snows, let's call it off.
This meat is so hard it is difficult to cut with a knife.

CONVERSATIONS

1   A: Smoking is bad for your health.

   B: I know that, but I still can't give it up.

   A: I was ordered to give it up by my doctor.

   B: I don't think I could give it up even if I were ordered to.

2   A: Why are you buying so much meat?

   B: This includes what my friend asked me to get for him.

   A: I suppose it is too heavy to lift.

   B: Yes. I'm getting the butcher to carry it to the car for me.

3   A: What do you do if your passport is stolen abroad?

   B: You have to report it immediately to the Japanese Embassy or Consulate.

A: Sore jáa. Nen no tamé, ryoken-bángoo o techoo ni káite oita hoo ga íi desu né.

B: Ée. Bangóo sae areba kantan ni shiraberaréru deshoo.

4 A: Kono uekíbachi wa dóoshi̧te warete irú n' deshoo.

B: Yuubé, kaze ni fu̧kárete dái kara óchi̧ta n' deshoo.

A: Kono tsu̧tsúji o betsu no tokoro e uekaeraréru to omoimásu̧ ka.

B: Ée, ano bara no tonari ni uete mimashóo.

5 A: Dóno kyoku ga ichiban yókatta desu̧ ka.

B: Sanbammé ni hiita kyóku ga yókatta to omoimasu̧.

A: Are we Báhha ni yotte sakkyoku sareta kyóku desu yo.

B: Dóori de subarashíi to omoimáshi̧ta.

A: Then, just in case, I should write my passport number in my notebook.

B: Yes. As long as they have the number I expect they can check easily.

4 A: I wonder why this flower pot is broken.

B: It must have been blown off its stand by the wind last night.

A: Do you think we can transplant this azalea somewhere else?

B: Yes. Let's try planting it next to that rose.

5 A: Which piece did you like best?

B: I liked the third piece he played.

A: That piece was composed by Bach.

B: No wonder I thought it was wonderful.

THE PASSIVE

The passive in Japanese is formed by adding *-(r)areru* to the verb root, the initial *r* of the suffix dropping when the verb root ends in a consonant; e.g., *kakaréru*, 'is written, will be written'; *okareru*, 'is put, will be put'; *taberaréru*, 'is eaten, will be eaten'. Accented verb roots produce accented passives, while unaccented verb roots give unaccented passives. The passive of *kúru* (which surprisingly can have a passive form in Japanese) is *koraréru*, and *suru* is *sareru*.

The agent of the passive sentence (indicated with 'by' in English) is followed by *ni*, or in more formal style sometimes by *ni yotte*, in Japanese.

Kímiko wa Tároo ni naguraremáshɪta.	'Kimiko was hit/beaten by Taro.'
Hanáyome wa shuutome ni homeraremáshɪta.	'The bride was praised by her mother-in-law.'
Mishima Yukio no shoosetsu wa máda híroku yomárete imasɪ.	'Yukio Mishima's novels are still widely read.'
Ano tóoki wa Séto no kama de yakaremáshɪta.	'That pottery was fired in a Seto kiln.'
Kono take to suzume no sumie wa zén no oboosan ni yotte kakaremáshɪta.	'This brush and ink painting of bamboo and sparrows was painted by a Zen priest.'
Kono shinamono wa takɪsán no hɪto ni aiyoo sarete kimáshɪta.	'This product has been regularly (lovingly) used by many people.'

Sometimes an English passive goes more readily into a Japanese *-te áru* form or an intransitive verb.

Shinyoojoo wa móo okɪtte arimásɪ.	'The letter of credit has already been sent.'

Perhaps the commonest use of the passive construction in Japanese is the 'adversative passive', which suggests that one has suffered or been inconvenienced by the action of another. The subject or topic in this case is usually a person, very often the speaker, but is often omitted from the sentence. The object of the underlying active sentence remains the object in the adversative passive construction.

Saifu o surárete shimattá n' desu.   'My wallet was picked from my pocket.'

Where the agent is present it is marked by *ni*.

Zubón o inú ni yogosaremásh̥ta.   'I had my trousers dirtied by the dog.'

An unusual feature of the Japanese passive is that it can be used with intransitive verbs.

Akísu ni hairaremásh̥ta.   'We were entered by a sneak-thief.'

Totsuzen kyaku ni koraremásh̥ta.   'I was put out by the sudden arrival of a guest.'

Tsúma ni shinaremásh̥ta.   'I suffered the death of my wife.'

Apart from its use as a passive the *-rareru* ending is used to form the potential of the *-ru* verbs: *taberaréru*, 'to be able to eat'; *agerareru*, 'to be able to give'. Here are some more examples.

Taberarénai kínoko ga áru kara ki o tsu̥kete kudasái.   'There are some mushrooms you cannot eat, so be careful.'

Kono hón wa kariraremasén.   'You cannot borrow this book.'

Sono sh̥tsumon ni kotaeraremasén.   'I can't answer that question.'

The potential of *iku*, 'to go', is often expressed by the passive *ikareru*, as the form *ikeru*, particularly in the negative, has taken on the added connotation of 'to be good, to be all right'.

Kyóo wa betsu no yooji ga arimásu̥ kara ikaremasén.   'I can't go because I have other business to attend to today.'

Miraréru is used as a potential form to refer to something which one may go to see, but which is not actually visible, or potentially visible, from where one is located. Some examples may clarify the difference.

Ano eigákan de Nihón no éiga ga miraremásu̥.   'You can see Japanese films at that cinema.'

Compare

Kumótte ita no de Fújisan ga miemasén desh̥ta.   'We couldn't see Mt Fuji because it was cloudy.'

in which Mt Fuji would have been visible from our position if it had not been cloudy, and a sentence like

Gaikoku de Fújisan no yóo na   'You can't see a mountain like
   yamá wa miraremasén.   Mt Fuji in any other country.'

Often the *-rareru* ending is used to form an honorific expression, showing respect to the person who is the subject of the verb to which the ending is attached. It cannot be used in the honorific sense after a first person subject.

Denwachoo o dóko ni   'Where did you put the
   okaremáshịta ka.   telephone directory?'
Kaneko senséi wa kinoo   'Dr Kaneko returned from
   Yooróppa kara   Europe yesterday.'
   kaeraremáshịta.
Heitai to shịte Nihón ni koráreta   'Apparently he came to Japan as
   kotó ga aru soo désụ.   a soldier.'
Ototói Hayashị san no otóosan   'Mr Hayashi's father died the day
   ga nakunararemáshịta.   before yesterday.'

-TAMÉ, 'SAKE'

Tamé is used in a number of constructions as follows:

1 Noun + *no tamé (ni)*, 'for the sake of', 'for the benefit of', 'on account of'.

Byooki no tamé ni kesseki   'He was absent on account of
   shimáshịta.   illness.'
Zénbu kodomotachi no tamé   'It's all for the sake of the
   désụ.   children.'
Anáta no tamé nara nán demo   'I'd do anything for you.'
   shimasu.

2 After the plain present-tense form of a verb, *tamé (ni)* sometimes replaces the more common *no ni* to convey the idea 'in order to'.

Kono kawá o wataru tamé ni fúne   'To cross this river you need a
   ga hịtsuyoo désụ.   boat.'
Sakụsen o kimeru tamé ni nágaku   'We debated for a long time to
   tóoron shimashịta.   decide our strategy.'

3 The past tense of a verb followed by *tamé (ni)* means 'because' and is equivalent to *no de*.

Kagí o nakushḷta tamé ni mádo kara hairimáshḷta.	'I got in through the window as I had lost my key.'
Ooáme ga fḷtta tamé ni koozui ni narimashḷta.	'There was a flood because of the heavy rain.'
Ressha ga okureta tamé ni kaigí ni deraremasén deshḷta.	'I was unable to appear at the conference as the train was late.'

BA'AI (sometimes pronounced BAWAI), 'CIRCUMSTANCE', 'IF', 'WHENEVER'

Like the nouns *toki*, 'time', and *koro*, 'time, period', *ba'ai* is often used to make a conditional or temporal clause.

O-kane ga tarinai ba'ai (ni wa) dóo shimasu ka.	'What do you do if you haven't got enough money?'

Often a past-tense form is used before *ba'ai* even when referring to a general statement or a specific future action.

Watashi ga mángaichi ma ni awánakatta ba'ai hḷtóri de itte kudasái.	'If by any chance I'm not there in time, go by yourself.'
Kootsuu-jíko ga okótta ba'ai kanarazu keisatsu ni renrakḷ shinakereba narimasén.	'If you have a traffic accident you must contact the police without fail.'

VOCABULARY

hooseki	jewel, jewellery	*nezumi*	rat, mouse
ishí	stone	*kawá*	river
kama	kiln	*hashí*	bridge
tóoki	pottery	*ooáme*	heavy rain
uekíbachi	flower/tree pot	*koozui*	flood
tsḷtsúji	azalea	*zén*	Zen Buddhism
kínoko	mushroom	*oboosan*	Buddhist priest
take	bamboo	*hanáyome*	(new) bride
suzume	sparrow	*shuutome*	mother-in-law

toshiyóri	old person	*kyóku*	a tune,
oyá	parent		composition
heitai	soldier	*yooji*	business, affairs,
nikúya	butcher		something
eigákan	cinema		to do
há	tooth	*meirei suru*	to order
mídori	green	*sh̩tsumon*	to question, ask
happa	leaf	*suru*	
yakyuu	baseball	*tóoron suru*	to debate
gaikoku	foreign country,	*soodan suru*	to discuss
	abroad	*aiyoo suru*	to use regularly,
pas̩̩póoto	passport		patronize
ryoken	passport	*sh̩ssek̩*	to be present,
ryoken-	passport number	*suru*	attend
bángoo		*sakkyoku*	to compose
taish̩kan	embassy	*suru*	
táishi	ambassador	*kesseki suru*	to be absent
ryoojíkan	consulate	*taisetsu na*	important
ryóoji	consul	*betsu (no)*	separate, dif-
ak̩su	sneak thief		ferent, another
saifu	wallet, purse	*oozei (no)*	a large number
shin'yóojoo	letter of credit		of (people), a
seisaku	policy		crowd
kóro	around the time,	*dóori de*	no wonder
	about when	*katai*	hard
kaerí	the way home,	*omói*	heavy
	going/coming	*mezurashíi*	rare
	home	*utsukushíi*	beautiful
ressha	train, locomotive	*kéru*	to kick
torákku	truck	*nusúmu*	to steal
mezamashi-	alarm clock	*kír-u*	to cut
dókei		*mochiagéru*	to lift up
shinamono	article, goods	*hakobu*	to carry,
kagí	key		transport
náifu	knife	*nagúru*	to hit, beat
seiseki	results, record,	*ueru*	to plant
	score	*uekáeru*	to transplant
shoosetsu	novel	*yaku*	to bake, burn
jí	letter, character	*súru*	to pick pockets

yogosu	to soil, dirty	*susumeru*	to recommend,
kotáeru	to answer (takes		advise
	ni after object)	*sore jáa/*	in that case, then
nakunaru	to pass away,	*déwa*	
	to die	*totsuzen*	suddenly
kimeru	to decide	*mángaichi*	if by any chance
nakusu	to lose	*kanarazu*	without fail
okóru	to get angry, rise	*tamé (ni)*	for the sake of, in
	up, happen		order to,
nagaréru	to flow		because
nagásu	to sweep away,	*ba'ai*	circumstance,
	sluice down,		occasion, time;
	pour away		when, if
korosu	to kill	*-nikúi*	difficult to
nureru	to get wet	*-yasúi*	easy to
kakéru	set (alarm clock)	*-me*	(ordinal suffix)
homéru	to praise	*-(r)areru*	(passive suffix)

EXERCISE 17

A Change the following sentences as indicated in brackets:
1 Oozei no hito ga Matsumoto san no shoosetsu o yomimasu. (passive) 2 Doroboo ga haitte hooseki o nusumimashita. (passive) 3 Utsukushii ishi o mitsukemashita. (potential) 4 Oya ga kodomo o shikarimashita. (passive) 5 Koozui de hashi ga nagaremashita kara moo kawa o wataremasen. (passive of *nagasu*) 6 Kono niku wa katakute watashi no yoo na ha no nai toshiyori wa tabemasen. (potential) 7 Dareka ga watashi no saifu o sutta n' desu. (passive) 8 Ooki na torakku de nimotsu o hakonde kimashita. (passive) 9 Neko wa nezumi o koroshimashita. (passive) 10. Hisho ga yamemashita kara komatte imasu. (passive)

B Fill in the blanks and give the correct forms of the words in italics:
1 Kinoo yakyuu no shiai ( ) kaeri ni ame ni *furu* daibu nure-
mashita. 2 Sono kinoko ( ) taberaremasen ( ) hirowanaide
( ). 3 Anoko ( ) seiseki ga betsu ni yoku nai ( ) ( ) kesseki
shita ( ) ga arimasen kara sensei ( ) homeraremasu. 4 Kodomo
( ) techoo ( ) nakusarete komatte imasu. 5 Mangaichi kootsuu-
jiko ni atta ( ) ni wa ( ) sureba ii deshoo ka. 6 Motto ooki ( )
yomi ( ) ji o kaite itadakemasen ka. 7 Taisetsu ( ) shiryoo ( )
sensoo ( ) yakaremashita. 8 Zen no o-boosan ( ) kaita ( )
iwarete iru mezurashii e ( ) mimashita. 9 Totsuzen kyaku ni *kuru*
( ) deraremasen deshita. 10 Kono kikai ( ) nan no ( ) ni
tachimasu ka.

C Translate into English:
1 Sore wa watashi ga inai aida ni kimerareta seisaku desu kara yoku
wakarimasen. 2 Ashita yama no ue no o-tera made irassharu to
kikimashita ga o-tomo shite mo yoroshii desu ka. 3 Watashi ga kaitai
to omotte ita tooki o saki ni hito ni kawarete zannen deshita. 4
Heitai wa itsumo ue kara meirei sareru no de iya desu. 5 Nihongo o
benkyoo suru yoo ni susumeraremashita. 6 Sensei ga motte
irassharu Chuugoku no furui kabin o haiken shite mo yoroshii desu
ka. 7 Anoko wa homerareru yori shikareru hoo ga ooi yoo desu. 8
Ooame de koozui ni natta ba'ai kono hashi wa nagasaresoo desu ne.
9 Ashita hayaku okiru tame ni mezamashi-dokei o kakemashita. 10
Go-shoochi no yoo ni kono machi wa tooki de shirarete imasu.

D Translate into Japanese:
1 May I borrow your book on Japanese history? 2 Is it difficult to do
ink painting? 3 No matter what kind of difficult question he is asked
he can usually answer it. 4 This car is very easy to drive, isn't it? 5 I
had some important business, but a friend turned up suddenly and I
couldn't attend to it. 6 Apparently the passport I dropped was
picked up and sent to the embassy. 7 Do you think we can plant the
rose next to the cherry tree? 8 It was recommended that I should
buy pottery in Korea. 9 Because of my headache I was unable to go
to [use *deru*] the meeting. 10 If by any chance we should get caught
in the rain tomorrow we could abandon the picnic and go to see a
film.

DÁI JUUHÁKKA

■ **BÉNRI NA HYOOGEN**

. . . -te sashitsμkae arimasén ka.
O-ki ni irimáshμta ka.
Dóozo go-enryo naku.

Enryo naku itadakimásμ.
Asobi ni irasshátte kudasai.
Zéhi yorasete itadakimásμ.

BUNKEI

Kodomo ni utá o oboesasemáshμta.
Kyóo wa háyaku kaerásete itadakimasμ.
Kanjóo o harawasaremáshμta.
Jikan ga kakáru shi mendóo desμ kara yamemashóo.
Káre wa yóku asobi yóku benkyoo shimásμ.
Sμki na dake nónde kudasai.

■ **KAIWA**

1 A: Dóoshμte yude-támago
       ga kirai désμ ka.

   B: Chiisái toki yóku múri ni
       tabesaseráreta kara da to
       omoimásμ.

   A: Kodomo wa nán demo
       múri ni saseru to
       óokiku natte kara
       hankoo suru sóo desμ.

   B: Sore wa sóo desu ga, áru
       téido kúnren sasenai to
       damé desμ né.

2 A: Asátte, éiga o mí ni
       ikimasμ ka.

   B: Ikμtai désμ ga chμchí wa
       ikasete kurenái n' désu yo.

   A: Dóoshμte desμ ka.

   B: Itóko no kekkón-shμki ga ári
       sore ni dénakereba
       naranai n' desμ.

3 A: Yuube Hána san ni
       kawaseta ika ga
       nioimásu yo.

   B: Daijóobu desu yo. Chótto
       namagusai daké deshoo.

   A: Kyóo wa atsúi shi
       shokúyoku ga amari
       nái desμ kara watashi
       wa tabemasén.

   B: Watashi wa ika ga dáisμki
       desμ kara hμtóri de
       tabesásete itadakimasμ.

LESSON EIGHTEEN

USEFUL EXPRESSIONS

Would it be all right if I . . .

Did you like it?/Do you like it?

Please don't stand on ceremony.

Thank you. I'd love some.

Please come and see us.

I'll certainly be dropping in.

SENTENCE PATTERNS

I made the child remember a poem.

Today I am going [to be permitted] to go home early.

I was made to pay the bill.

It takes time and it's a nuisance so let's not bother.

He plays hard and studies hard.

Drink as much as you like.

CONVERSATIONS

1 A: Why do you dislike boiled eggs?

   B: I think it is because I was often forced to eat them when I was small.

   A: Apparently if you force children to do anything, they rebel when they grow up.

   B: That's true, but you must train them to some extent.

2 A: Are you going to see the film the day after tomorrow?

   B: I'd like to, but my father won't let me.

   A: Why not?

   B: Because my cousin is getting married and I have to go to the ceremony.

3 A: The squid we got Hana to buy last night smells.

   B: It is all right! I expect it is just a bit fishy-smelling.

   A: It's hot today and I haven't much appetite, so I shan't have any.

   B: I love squid, so I hope you don't mind if I eat it by myself.

4 A: Kónban wa sukí na dake
       nómi sukí na dake
       tábete kudasai.

   B: Arígatoo gozaimasu.

   A: Nomímono wa sochira
       désu shi tabemonó wa
       achira désu.

   B: Sore déwa katte ni sasete
       itadakimásu.

5 A: Kono chikáku ni késhiki
       ga yóku shízuka
       na tokoro wa
       arimasén ka.

   B: Hakone wa ikága desu ka.

   A: Máda itta kotó ga
       arimasén ga.

   B: Asoko nára nagamé mo íi shi
       o-ki ni iru deshóo.

4 A: Tonight please eat and drink as much as you like.

B: Thank you.

A: The drinks are just there and the food is over there.

B: I'll go ahead and help myself, thank you.

5 A: Isn't there a quiet scenic spot near here?

B: What about Hakone?

A: I've never been there.

B: The scenery is nice there. I think you would like it.

THE CAUSATIVE

The causative is formed by adding *-(s)aseru* to the verbal root. With consonant root verbs the initial *-s* of the suffix drops: *tabesaséru*, 'to make eat, let eat'; *ikaseru*, 'to make go, let go'; *omowaséru*, 'to make think, suggest'. The causative of *kúru* is *kosaséru* and *suru* becomes *saseru*. Accented verb roots have accented causative forms and unaccented verbs remain unaccented in the causative. The addition of the causative suffix results in a new vowel-root verb, which in turn takes most of the usual verbal inflections: *tabesásetara*, 'if make eat'; *ikasenai*, 'not make go', etc.

The causative is used mostly with animate objects and means 'to make someone do something' or to 'let someone do something'. Sometimes a distinction between the causative and permissive connotations can be indicated by using *o* or *ni* respectively after the object.

Musúko o ikasemáshíta	'I made my son go.'
Musumé ni páatii ni ikasemáshíta.	'I let my daughter go to the party.'

This does not apply if there is another object in the sentence. In this case the person caused or permitted to do something is always followed by the particle *ni*.

O-tétsudai ni kuríininguya e wáishatsu o tori ni ikasemáshíta.	'I had the maid go and pick up my shirts from the cleaners.'

Here are some more examples of the causative.

Shúnsúke ga imootó o nakasemáshíta.	'Shunsuke made his younger sister cry.'
Oji wa yóku omoshirói hanashí o shíte watashítachi o warawasemáshíta.	'My uncle often told us amusing stories and made us laugh.'
Musumé ga mimai ni kíte yorokobásete kuremashíta.	'My daughter came to visit me when I was ill and cheered me up [caused me to be glad].'
Warawasenáide kudasai.	'Please don't make me laugh.'

Sometimes the causative is used with inanimate objects.

Chichí wa kotoshi mo mígoto na kikú o sakesemáshita.	'This year, too, father raised some splendid chrysanthemum blooms [caused to bloom].'

In casual speech the full causative forms are often replaced by contracted forms made by attaching *-(s)asu* to the verbal root (the initial *-s* dropping after a consonant). The shorter form is particularly common before the *-te*, *-ta* and *-tara* endings. The long forms *tabesáseta* and *ikaseta* become *tabesáshita* and *ikashita*.

Often the causative construction implies a command and suggests the subject of the causative verb is a superior. It follows, then, that causatives of this type should not be used to refer to persons present unless they fall within one's immediate circle of family, close friends or subordinates at work. In other cases the *-te morau* or more polite *-te itadaku* constructions should be used.

Kore wa Tanaka san ni katte itadaita hón desu yo.	'This is the book I got you to buy for me, Mr Tanaka.'

There are a number of transitive verbs in Japanese derived from causative forms. These are best learnt as separate items of vocabulary as they vary a little in form. They often have inanimate objects. Here are some examples:

awaséru	'to bring together'
kikaseru	'to tell, inform'
shiraseru	'to tell, inform'
kiseru	'to dress [someone else]'
hakaseru	'to put shoes on [someone else]'
miséru	'to show'
nekasu	'to put to bed'
nemuraseru	'to put to sleep'
nakusu	'to lose'
odorokásu	'to surprise'
tobasu	'to drive fast, throw' [literally, 'make fly']
ugokásu	'to move'
yorokobású/-éru	'to please'

-SASETE ITADAKIMÁSU

A very polite verb ending used in formal situations is made up of the *-te* form of a causative verb plus *itadaku*, 'to receive [from a social superior]'. It is often used when asking a favour and has the literal meaning, 'I receive the favour of being allowed to do something.' It is often used in a number of set routines such as the following:

O-jáma sasete itadakimásu.	'Kindly permit me to come in/ see you/visit you/trouble you [etc.]'
Chótto agarasete itadakimásu.	'I'll just step in for a moment.'
Háyaku kaerásete itadakimasu.	'I am going home early [if you don't mind].'
Chótto yasumásete itadakitai desu ga.	'I'd like to be permitted to have a short rest.'
Minásan, kore kara Ákita no min'yoo o utawasete itadakimásu.	'Ladies and gentlemen, with your kind permission I shall now sing a folk song from Akita.'

PASSIVE OF THE CAUSATIVE

The causative verbs can be followed by the passive suffix *-(r)areru*, resulting in an ending which means 'to be made to do something'. The idea of permission does not seem to be included in this ending. The full passive-causative ending is *-saserareru*, but in the conversational style the passive suffix is usually attached to the contracted causative form resulting in the ending *-sareru*, *kakaseraréru* or *kakasaréru*, 'to be caused to write'. The passive-causative of *suru* is always the long form *saserareru*, 'to be made to do'.

Ítsumo kánojo ni ichijíkan íjoo matasárete shimaimasu.	'I'm always kept waiting over an hour by her.'
Kekkón-shíki de teeburu-supíichi o saseraremáshita.	'I was made to give a speech at the wedding ceremony.'

SHI, 'AND'

Shi is used as an emphatic 'and' between clauses. It appears at the end of a clause after the plain form of a verb or adjective or, in more formal speech, after a polite form. Its function is similar to the linking use of the *-te* form, but it is much stronger, with the connotation 'and what is more', 'and also'. It often links clauses with different subjects and sometimes it seems to indicate cause or reason and is equivalent to 'because . . . and . . .'.

Raishuu no doyóobi ni wa ane mo kúru shi otootó mo kimásʉ.	'Next Saturday my elder sister is coming and my younger brother is coming too.'
Yúkɪko wa kírei da shi atamá mo íi shi kanemóchi desʉ kara kánojo to kekkon shɪtai hɪto ga óoi soo desʉ.	'Yukiko is beautiful, clever and rich, so apparently there are a lot of people who want to marry her.'
Kono ie wa hiatari mo íi shi kazetooshi mo íi desʉ.	'This house is sunny and airy.'

THE VERB STEM AS A CONNECTIVE

The stem of the verb and the *-ku* form of the adjective are sometimes used for 'and' or 'and so' between clauses. The construction is more common in the written language, but is also used in spoken Japanese. Its uses overlap somewhat with the use of the *-te* form and the clause-final particle *shi* introduced above. Where the actions of the clauses to be linked do not occur in a clear time sequence, the stem or *shi* connective forms are preferred over the *-te* form. The negative equivalent of this construction employs the suffix *-(a)zu* on the verb root.

Buráun san wa yóku tábe, yóku nomimásʉ.	'Mr Brown eats and drinks a lot.'
Konokatá wa watashi ni Nihongo o oshie, imootó ni Chuugokugo o oshiete imásʉ.	'He [this gentleman] teaches me Japanese and my sister Chinese.'
Kono shinamonó wa nedan mo tákakʉ shɪtsú mo warúi desʉ.	'This product is expensive and the quality is poor too.'
Anóhɪto wa o-sake mo nomázu tabako mo suwanai désʉ.	'He doesn't drink and he doesn't smoke either.'

NOTES

Enryo, a noun meaning 'reserve', 'restraint', 'holding back', is used with the honorific prefix *go-* in the expression *go-enryo náku* when asking a second person not to be formal. *Enryo* without the honorific prefix refers to one's own actions: *Enryo náku itadakimásụ*, 'I shall eat without reserve', is used when accepting food offered in circumstances where it would appear rude to accept without being strongly persuaded, as when receiving a second helping or another drink, etc.

Conversation 4 Katte ni, 'selfishly', is very similar in meaning and usage to *enryo náku*.

VOCABULARY

hiatari	exposure to sun	*gúramu*	gramme
kazetooshi	ventilation	*shịkí*	ceremony
kúuki	air	*kekkón-shiki*	wedding ceremony
nagame	view, prospect		
téire	care, mending	*mimai*	visit to express sympathy
furó/o-fúro	bath		
daidokoro	kitchen	*wakamono*	young man
kudámono	fruit	*otona*	adult
ika	squid	*teeburu-*	dinner speech
yude-támago	boiled egg	*sụpíichi*	
shokúyoku	appetite	*min'yoo*	folk song
nomímono	drinks, drink	*kịkái*	opportunity
sakaya	liquor merchant/ shop	*joodán*	joke
		dóoro	road
kuríininguya	dry cleaner('s)	*koosui*	perfume
kụtsúya	shoemaker('s), shoe shop	*kaori*	fragrance
		kúnren suru	to train
koméya	rice merchant/ shop	*hankoo suru*	to oppose, resist, rebel
pán'ya	baker, bakery	*keiken (suru)*	(to) experience
sakanaya	fish monger('s)	*mendoo na*	bothersome
kanjoo	bill, account	*sụkí na dake*	as much as one likes
dáasụ	a dozen		

tekítoo na	suitable	*tobasu*	to make fly, hit,
namagusái	fishy smelling		drive fast
wakái	young	*ugóku*	to move
katte ni	selfishly		(intransitive)
áru teido	to a certain extent	*ugokásu*	to move
asobu	to play, spend		(transitive)
	time at leisure,	*yorokobásu*	to please, make
	be unoccupied		happy
nióu	to smell	*erábu*	to choose
	(intransitive)	*íjoo*	from . . . and
awaséru	to bring		above, more
	together		than
kíkaseru	to tell, relate	*shibaraku (no*	for a while
hakaseru	to put shoes on	*aida)*	
	someone	*-(s)aseru*	(causative suffix)
nekasu	to put to bed	*-(s)asete*	(polite request)
odorokásu	to startle	*itadaku*	be allowed to

EXERCISE 18

A Change the following sentences as indicated in the brackets:
1 Musume ga ichiba e kudamono ya yasai o kai ni ikimashita.
(causative) 2 Kodomo ga niwa no teire o shimashita. (causative) 3
Nikuya ga niku o haitatsu shimashita. (causative) 4 Sakaya ga biiru o
ichidaasu todokemashita. (causative) 5 Ano kutsuya ga kono kaban
o naoshimashita. (causative) 6 Sanjikan han mo machimashita.
(passive of causative) 7 Ano wakamono wa wakarimashita. (causative). 8 Chichi ga okorimashita. (causative) 9 Iranai mono o
kaimashita. (passive of causative) 10 Konban shichiji goro o-jama
shimasu. (formal-causative construction)

B Fill in the blanks and give the correct forms of the words in italics:
1 Koko ( ) oishiku nai ( ) nedan ( ) takai desu ( ) hoka no
tokoro e ikimashoo. 2 Sushi o suki na ( ) tabete ( ). 3 Watashi wa
moo toshiyori desu ( ) suki ( ) yoo ni sasete ( ) imasu. 4 Anoko
( ) yoku *asobu* yoku benkyoo shimasu. 5 Byooin ( ) nani o
tabesaserareru ( ) mazukatta desu. 6 Kodomo ( ) kutsu ( )
hakasete ( ) soto e demashoo. 7 Ika ( ) namagusai desu ( ) yoku

arawasete ( ). 8 Yuube oji ga kita ( ) iroiro no omoshiroi hanashi
( ) *kikaseru*. 9 Kuruma ( ) sonna ni *tobasu* ( ) ikemasen.
10 Kaisha no shigoto mo aru ( ) kite iku sebiro ( ) kuriiningu ni
dashite aru ( ) kekkon-shiki ni denai koto ni shimashita.

C Translate into English:
1 Kodomo no toki ni wa yoku otana no mae de min'yoo o uta-
wasaremashita. 2 Shujin wa ichinichi sanjuppon mo tabako o
suimasu kara nakanaka yamesaseraremasen. 3 Koko wa nagame mo
yoku kuuki mo kirei desu kara yasumi ni totemo ii tokoro desu ne. 4
Ashita mimai ni yorasete itadakimasu. 5 O-saki ni kaerasete itadaite
mo sashitsukae arimasen ika. 6 Ono san wa omocha de kodomo o
yorokobashi joodan de otona o warawasemashita. 7 Ano bara no
koosui no kaori o kagasete kudasai. 8 Kono tatemono wa kaze-
tooshi mo waruku hiatari mo yoku arimasen ne. 9 Motte kosaseru
no ga mendoo desu kara jibun de tori ni ikoo to omotte imasu. 10
Konna ni ii mono o tsukawasete itadaku no wa hajimete desu.

D Translate into Japanese:
1 Is there any objection to my bringing my daughter to your party,
Mr Honda? 2 I've finished my work and I've put the children to bed,
so now I think I'll watch television for a while. 3 Please tell me about
your experience working for a Japanese trading company. 4 Ring
the fish shop and get them to deliver 500 grams of squid. 5 Please
borrow as many magazines as you like. 6 My son likes driving his car
fast, but it's very dangerous so I'm trying to get him to stop it. 7 I let
my younger sister choose her own birthday present. 8 My wife won't
let me into the kitchen. 9 Please don't stand on ceremony. 10 I'll
have my bath first [if you don't mind].

DÁI JUUKYÚUKA

■ BÉNRI NA HYOOGEN

O-namae wa nán to osshaimásu͏̸
ka.

Wataku͏̸shi wa koo yuu monó de
gozaimásu͏̸.

Sakↄhodo wa shↄtsúrei
itashimáshↄta.

Súmisu͏̸ to mooshimásu͏̸.

Go-shoochi no yóo ni . . .

Nochihodo mairimásu͏̸.

BUNKEI

Yuube no hoosoo o o-kↄki ni narimáshↄta ka.
Dónna hón o yónde irasshaimasu͏̸ ka.
Tachíbana senséi de irasshaimásu͏̸ ka.
Sakújitsu wa náni o nasaimáshↄta ka.
Góji ni róbii de o-machi shↄte imásu͏̸.
Máe ni o-me ni kakarimáshↄta.

■ KAIWA

1 A: Chótto o-ukagai shimásu
ga.

  A: Shachoo ga íma o-hima
déshↄtara o-me ni
kakaritái n' desu
ga . . .

  B: Hái. Nán no go-yóo deshoo
ka.

  B: Kiite mairimásu no de
shóoshoo o-machi
kudasái.

2 A: Senséi, ítsu o-kaeri ni
narimáshↄta ka.

  A: Go-ryokoo wa ikága
deshↄta ka.

  B: Shigatsú hatsu͏̸ka ni káette
kimashↄta.

  B: Hↄto ga oosúgite su͏̸kóshi
gakkári shimashↄta.

3 A: Sono kaban o o-mochi
shimashóo ka.

  A: O-nímotsu o taku͏̸sán
o-mochi desu͏̸ kara
dóreka motásete
kudasai.

  B: Íya, karui desu͏̸ kara
daijóobu desu yo.

  B: Jáa, kono kása to kámera
o mótte kudasai.

LESSON NINETEEN

USEFUL EXPRESSIONS

What is your name?	My name is Smith.
Here is my business card.	As you know . . .
Sorry I troubled you just now.	I'll come later.

SENTENCE PATTERNS

Did you hear the broadcast last night?
What sort of book are you reading?
Are you Dr Tachibana?
What did you do yesterday?
I shall be waiting in the foyer at 5 o'clock.
I have met you before.

CONVERSATIONS

1   A: Excuse me, please.   B: Yes. Can I help you?

      A: I'd like to meet the director, if he is free.   B: Wait a moment, please. I'll go and ask.

2   A: When did you get back home?   B: I came back on the twentieth of April.

      A: How was your trip?   B: I was a bit disappointed. There were too many people.

3   A: Shall I carry that bag for you?   B: No, it's light. I can manage.

      A: You have a lot of luggage. Please let me carry something.   B: Oh, well. Carry this umbrella and camera for me then.

4 A: Móshimoshi. Yánagi san irasshaimásᵤ ka.

   A: Watakᵤshi wa Kuráakᵤ to mooshimásᵤ ga.

   B: Hái. Dóchira-sama de irasshaimásᵤ ka.

   B: Yánagi wa íma té ga hanasemasén no de mata áto de o-dénwa itadakemásᵤ ka.

5 A: Konogoro wa dónna go-kenkyuu o nasátte imasᵤ ka.

   A: Kakiowarimáshᵢtara watashi ni mo zéhi yomásete kudasai.

   B: Nihón no keizai-séichoo ni kánsuru ronbun o káite imasᵤ.

   B: Ée, mochíron. Ichíbu o-okuri shimásᵤ.

6 A: Máda kottoohin o atsúmete irasshaimasᵤ ka.

   A: Goran ni iretai Chúugoku no chawan ga arimásu ga.

   B: Hái, séngetsu Kánkoku de furúi kágu o katte kimáshᵢta.

   B: Áa, sore o zéhi haiken sasete itadakitai désᵤ.

4 A: Hello. Is Mr Yanagi
      there, please?

   B: Yes. May I ask who is
      calling?

   A: My name is Clark.

   B: Mr Yanagi is occupied at the
      moment. I wonder if you
      would mind ringing back
      later?

5 A: What sort of research
      have you been doing
      lately?

   B: I'm writing a thesis on
      Japan's economic growth.

   A: Please be sure to let me
      read it when you have
      finished.

   B: Yes, of course. I'll send you
      a copy.

6 A: Are you still collecting
      antiques?

   B: Yes, last month I bought
      some old furniture from
      Korea.

   A: I have a Chinese tea-
      bowl I'd like to show
      you.

   B: Oh, I'd really like to have a
      look at that.

RESPECT LANGUAGE

You have already met a number of honorific expressions in the 'Useful expressions' section and have become well acquainted with the honorific verb *irassháru* (*irasshaimásᵤ*), which means 'a respected person goes, comes or is'.

Japanese has a well developed system of honorifics, as much a part of the language as the definite and indefinite articles and singular and plural are part of English. Custom dictates the categories of people to whom honorifics are used and you will gradually come to feel the subtleties of the system as you become more at home in Japanese society.

Respect language in Japanese falls into two main types: that which shows politeness to the person you are talking to (the addressee), known as 'the polite style', and that which conveys respect towards the person you are talking about (the referent), which comprise the 'honorifics' proper. All verbs in Japanese carry an indication of the degree of politeness to the addressee and the degree of respect shown to the referent.

The polite style

The polite style is part of a system of address which consists of the plain, polite and formal styles. In this book we have been using the polite style, characterized by *désᵤ* and the *-másᵤ* ending. We have also met one or two expressions with the formal-style verb, *gozaimásᵤ*. The polite style is used nowadays in most situations except within the family and between very close friends, workmates or students of the same age, or when adults talk to children. It is, therefore, the style with the widest application, and is the best one for a foreigner to learn first.

Although the plain style is not introduced until the next lesson, you are already familiar with the plain verb forms as they occur in subordinate clauses. As long as the final verb ends in *-másᵤ* (or *désᵤ*), the sentence is in the polite style.

The formal style, marked by the verb *gozaimásᵤ* (and a few more given below), is limited almost entirely to formal greetings, speech-making and telephone conversations, though some individuals use it indiscriminately as a mark of refinement or high social class. Other verbs used in the formal style are: *móosu*, 'to say'; *máiru*, 'to go, to come'; *itásu*, 'to do'; *oŕu*, 'to be'; and *itadaku*, used in the sense of 'to eat'. These verbs usually have the speaker, or someone closely connected with the speaker, as the subject.

Watak̸ushi wa Buráun to mooshimás̸.	'My name is Brown.'

(Notice the formal-style first person pronoun *watak̸ushi* instead of the usual polite-style *watashi*.)

Itte mairimás̸.	'Goodbye.'

(Literally, 'I'm going and coming back', said on leaving a place to which one is to return.)

Súgu itashimás̸.	'I'll do it straight away.'
Róndon ni rokunénkan súnde orimash̸ta.	'I lived in London for six years.'
Móo juubún itadakimásh̸ta.	'I've already had sufficient.'

The formal style also employs certain vocabulary items, often of Chinese origin, like *sakújits̸*, 'yesterday', and *myóonichi*, 'to-morrow', instead of the more common *kinóo* and *ash̸ta*. The noun *monó*, 'person', is often used in the formal style to refer to oneself.

Let us now turn to the honorifics proper. Honorifics are used to refer to people to whom respect should be shown. This category includes persons of little acquaintance, unless obviously much younger than the speaker, superiors at work, teachers, doctors and old people.

As honorifics appear most often in the verb, we shall look at the honorific forms of the verb first. Honorific expressions can be divided into two main groups, the *subject honorifics* and the *object honorifics*.

Subject honorifics

These are used when the person to whom respect is to be shown is the subject of the verb. The regular subject-honorific verbs are formed by the verb stem, preceded by the honorific prefix *o-* and followed by *ni náru*.

Neutral	Subject honorific
hanásu	*o-hanashi ni náru*
káku	*o-kaki ni náru*
akeru	*o-ake ni náru*
oríru	*o-ori ni náru*

Accented verb roots become unaccented in the *o- . . . ni náru* construction. Of course, when the honorifics occur in the final verb of the sentence they usually appear in the polite style: *o-hanashi ni narimásu̜, o-kaki ni narimásu̜,* etc. In fact, honorifics are particularly common when the *addressee* and the *referent* are the same person; in other words, when the subject of the honorific verb is 'you'. This reminds us of the special honorific pronouns for 'you' in most European languages.

The trend these days seems to be away from using honorifics unless the respected referent, or someone closely connected with him, is actually present at the time of speaking. However, many people, particularly women, follow the stricter use of the honorifics, using them to refer to respected persons even when they are not present.

In addition to the regular subject-honorific verbs, there are special honorific verbs which replace, or occur alongside, the regular forms. You are familiar with the verb *irassháru*, which acts as the honorific form of *iku, kúru* and *iru*, three verbs which do not take the regular subject honorific construction. *Irassháru* is also used as the honorific auxiliary after the *-te* form. It is usually sufficient to have either the main verb or the auxiliary in the honorific form, though in very formal and respectful language you may hear two honorifics occurring in the same predicate. *Káite irasshaimásu̜ ka, O-kaki ni nátte imasu̜ ka* and *O-kaki ni nátte irasshaimásu̜ ka* all mean 'Are you writing?'

De irassháru is the honorific form of *désu*.

Hattori san de irasshaimásu̜ ka.   'Are you Mr Hattori?'

The most important irregular subject honorific verbs are:

irassháru	'to go, to come, to be'
nasáru	'to do'
meshiagaru	'to eat, to drink'

| *kudasáru* | 'to give' |
| *ossháru* | 'to say' |

The five honorific verbs given above end in *-aru* and, with the exception of *meshiagaru*, form their imperatives by changing the final *-ru* to *-i*: *irasshái*, *nasái*, *kudasái* and *osshái*, but *meshiagare*. In addition to these special honorific verbs, there are some elegant, euphemistic verbs which occur in the subject honorific construction, usually replacing the expected regular form.

o-ide ni náru	'to go, to come'
o-mie ni náru	'to come on a visit'
goran ni náru	'to see'
o-agari ni náru	'to eat, to drink'
o-yasumi ni náru	'to go to bed'
o-motome ni náru	'to buy'
o-meshi ni náru	'to wear, to put on'
o-nakunari ni náru	'to die'
o-sumai ni náru	'to live'
o-ki ni mésu	'to like'
(or *o-ki ni iru*)	

Note that the last verb does not take *náru*. Of the verbs given above only 'to drink', 'to buy' and 'to live' also have regular forms: *o-nomi ni náru*, *o-kai ni náru* and *o-sumi ni náru*. The regular form *o-tabe ni náru* may occasionally be heard, but the irregular forms given above are to be preferred.

A common variant of the regular subject-honorific construction replaces the final *ni náru* with a form of the copula *da*. This form usually occurs in final verbs, so *da* appears in the polite (or formal) style: *désu̧* (or *de gozaimásu̧*). The *o-* verb stem *désu̧* construction seems to be used to describe states, or continuous or immediate future action. Here are some common expressions using this form:

Móo o-kaeri désu̧ ka.	'Are you going home already?' ('Won't you stay longer?')
O-dekake désu̧ ka.	'Are you going out?' (a common greeting).
Kotoshi no karéndaa o o-mochi désu̧ ka.	'Do you have this year's calendar?'

The subject honorific equivalent of *shítte iru*, 'to know', is *go-zónji desú*.

Koochoo-senséi o go-zónji desú ka.   'Do you know the headmaster?'

Object honorifics

The term 'object honorifics' is used to cover all cases when the respected referent is not in the subject of the verb. It applies when the respected referent is the direct object, indirect object, or is followed by any particles other than *wa* or *ga*.

The form of the regular object honorifics is *o*-verb stem *suru*: *o-kakí suru*, 'to write' (to or for a respected referent); *o-mise suru*, 'to show' (to a respected referent); *o-mochí suru*, 'to hold, carry, bring, take something' (for a respected referent). Often the subject of the *o*- . . . *suru* verb is the speaker, or someone closely connected to the speaker, and the respected referent is 'you'. The relationship between subject and object is clear even when neither is specifically mentioned in the sentence.

O-kaban o o-mochí shimású.   'I'll carry your bag for you.'

Just as there are irregular forms of the subject honorifics, so, too, does the object honorific construction have a number of irregular forms.

sashiagéru	'to give' (to a respected referent)
mooshiagéru	'to say' (to a respected referent)
o-me ni kakáru	'to meet' (to a respected referent)
o-me ni kakéru	'to show' (a respected referent)
goran ni ireru	'to show' (to a respected referent)
haiken suru	'to look' (at something belonging to a respected referent)

haishakṳ suru   'to borrow' (something
                                              belonging to a respected
                                              referent)

The regular forms *o-ai suru*, 'to meet', *o-mise suru*, 'to show', and *o-kari suru*, 'to borrow', are also used. *O-hanashi̥ suru* can be used in the sense of 'to say' (to a respected referent) in place of the verb, *yuu*, which does not occur in the object honorific construction.

Ukagau is often used in the object-honorific construction in the sense of 'to ask' or 'to visit'.

Chótto o-ukagai shimásu ga . . .   'Excuse me . . .' 'Could you tell
                                              me . . .?' (literally, 'I am just
                                              asking you, but . . .')
Nochihodo o-ukaigai shimásu̥.   'I'll come and see you later.'

In formal situations *itásu̥* sometimes replaces *suru* in the object honorific construction.

O-mochi itashimashóo ka.   'Shall I carry it for you?'

Here are some more examples of the use of the object honorifics.

Oota senséi ni o-mise shi̥ta   'Professor Oota, I've framed that
  shashin o gaku ni iremáshi̥ta.   photograph I showed you.'
Máe ni Hattori san ni o-ai shi̥ta   'I think I've met Mr Hattori
  kotó ga áru to omoimásu̥.   before.'
Kodomo ga haishakṳ shi̥ta hón o   'Tomorrow my child will return
  ashi̥ta o-kaeshi shimásu̥.   the book he borrowed from
                                              you.' (or 'Tomorrow I shall
                                              return the book my child
                                              borrowed from you.')

HONORIFICS WITH NOUNS AND ADJECTIVES

Often nouns indicating things belonging to somebody to whom respect is due have the prefix *o-* (or *go-*) attached to them. *O-* is usually used before nouns of native origin and *go-* is used with nouns borrowed from Chinese. It is not always possible to identify words borrowed from Chinese, though they are often composed of two syllables and contain the long vowels *oo* or *uu*, double consonants, or syllable-final *n*, all of which are rare in native Japanese words. Some common words although of Chinese origin take the prefix *o-*. Adjectives and most descriptive nouns referring to respected persons take the prefix *o-*, but a few descriptive nouns like *kenson na*, 'modest', *rippa na*, 'splendid', etc. take *go-*. Here are some examples.

O-		Go-	
o-hima	'spare time'	go-byooki	'illness'
o-tégami	'letter'	go-kázoku	'family'
o-tesuki	'free time'	go-kekkon	'marriage'
o-toshi	'age'	go-yóo	'business'
		go-kenkyuu	'research'
o-hanashi	'talk', 'story'	go-seikoo	'success'
o-namae	'name'	go-jibun	'yourself', etc.
o-ikutsu	'How old?'	go-kenson	'modesty'
o-génki	'good health'	go-rippa	'splendid'
o-isogashii	'busy'	go-yukkúri	'at leisure'
o-yu	'hot water'		

Sometimes the honorific prefix indicates not that the following noun is owned by a respected referent, but that it is a verbal noun, or the like, directed towards someone to whom respect is shown.

Go-annai shimashóo ka.	'Shall I show you around?'
O-henji ga osoku nátte dóomo sumimasén.	'I am sorry my answer was late.'
O-dénwa o sashiagemásu.	'I shall telephone you.'

With certain nouns *o-* and *go-* are used without reference to a respected person, merely as an indication of the polite style of speech: *o-ténki*, 'weather'; *o-cha*, 'tea'; *o-kome*, 'rice' (uncooked); *gó-han*, 'cooked rice'; *o-sake*, 'rice wine'; *o-teárai*, 'lavatory'. In a few cases the addition of the *o-* prefix changes the meaning of the original word: *tsuri*, 'fishing'; *o-tsuri*, 'change'. In the polite style *kane* usually means 'metal', but *o-kane* is 'money'.

The adjective yoroshii

Íi (or *yói*), 'good', has an honorific equivalent *yoroshii*, which means someone in a respected position approves a situation. It is usually used in questions.

Móo káette mo yoroshii désu̥ ka.   'May I go home now?'
Kore de yoroshii désu̥ ka.   'Is this all right?'

Normally the answer to these questions would be *Ée kékkoo desu̥*, 'Yes you may/Yes it is.' The reply '*Ée yoroshii désu̥*' would indicate that the speaker felt he was a superior in a position of authority, as for example when a teacher addresses his student.

ADJECTIVES IN THE FORMAL STYLE

When adjectives appear in formal-style predicates before *gozaimásu̥*, the *-k-* of the *-ku* form drops and the resulting diphthong becomes a long vowel. We have met this form in *o-hayoo gozaimásu̥* from *háyaku*, and *arígatoo gozaimasu̥* from *arigátaku*, the *-ku* form of *arigatái*, 'grateful'. Adjectives with roots ending in *-a* or *-o* have formal forms in *-oo*, those with roots in *-u* become *-uu*, and those with roots in *-shi* become *-shuu*. The formal form of *íi* is *yóo* (derived from *yóku*), 'good', and the honorific adjective *yoroshii*, 'good', has the formal form *yoroshuu*. The formal-style adjectives will be heard in greetings and other very formal situations. You will probably not find it necessary to use more than the four adjectives given above in the formal style. Some further examples are given below for reference.

Kyóo wa o-atsúu gozaimasu̥ né.   'It is hot today, isn't it?'
Yuube no éiga wa taihen   'The film last night was very
   omoshiróo gozaimash̥ta.   interesting.'
Kono séki de yoroshúu   'Is this seat all right, sir?'
   gozaimasu̥ ka.

NOTES

Watak̥shi wa koo yuu monó de gozaimásu̥, literally, 'I am this kind of person', is often said when handing over a business card.

VOCABULARY

		otótoshi	the year before last
monó	person	*ichíbu*	one copy, one part
dóchira-sama	who (honorific)	*-bu*	part, counter for copies (of more than one sheet)
dónata-sama	who (honorific)		
kéizai	economics		
seichoo	growth	*Kokuren*	the UN
keizai-séichoo	economic growth	*ni tsúite (no)*	about
ronbun	thesis, paper, article	*ni kánshḷte*	about
		ni kánsuru	about (before a noun)
kenkyuu	research		
hákase	doctor, PhD	*chooshi ga íi*	to work well, run smoothly
kyooju	professor		
koochoo-senséi	headmaster	*hoosoo (suru)*	(to) broadcast
		gakkári suru	to be disappointed
o-kosan/o-kosama	child (hon.), your child	*bḷkkúri suru*	to be surprised
		henjí (suru)	(to) answer
kottoohin	antique	*kḷtai suru*	to expect, anticipate
chawan	rice-bowl, tea-cup		
		enzetsḷ suru	to give a speech
kágu	furniture	*hanásu*	to let go, release
gaku	frame	*té ga hanasénai*	to be occupied, be tied up, busy
haizara	ashtray		
karéndaa	calendar	*atsuméru*	to collect
taipuráitaa	typewriter	*atsumáru*	to come together, gather
go-yóo	business (hon.), your business		
		o-...ni náru	(subject honorific)
keisatsḷsho	police station		
shooboosho	fire station	*o-...suru*	(object honorific)
shiyákḷsho	city hall	*o-/go-...desu*	(subject honorific)
óoba	overcoat		
uwagi	jacket, coat	*juubún*	enough, plenty
Nanbei	South America	*taigai*	generally, for the most part, usually
sakḷhodo	before		
nochḷhodo	later		
sakújitsḷ	yesterday (formal)	*taitei*	generally, in the main, mostly
myóonichi	tomorrow (formal)	*saikin*	recently

EXERCISE 19

A Change the following sentences as indicated in brackets:
1 Kyoo wa taihen samui desu. (formal) 2 Chotto kikitai koto ga arimasu ga ii desu ka. (honorific) 3 Nihon Keizai Shinbun o yomimasu ka. (honorific) 4 Kinoo kite ita ooba o doko de kaimashita ka. (honorific) 5 Sakki sono hanashi o Suzuki san kara kikimashita. (honorific) 6 Yuube no atsumari de Nakamura sensei ni aimashita. (honorific) 7 Ato de ikimasu. (formal) 8 Dare desu ka. (honorific) 9 Nanbei ni sunde ita toki ni wa taigai donna mono o tabemashita ka. (honorific) 10 Kono uwagi ga suki desu ka. (honorific)

B Fill in the blanks and supply the correct forms of the words in italics:
1 Kinoo o-mise ( ) chawan o *motomeru* ka. 2 Tsuchida sensei wa donna ( ) kenkyuu o ( ) imasu ka. 3 Sensei ni goran ni ( ) tai mono ga arimasu kara myoonichi uchi e *yorimasen* ka. 4 Nochihodo *ukagau* mo yoroshii desu ka. 5 O-ko ( ) ga nannin o-( ) desu ka. 6 Watakushi wa sensei ga *kaku* e o motte orimasu. 7 Tanabe hakase wa nanji ni o-*mieru* ( ) ka. 8 Kinoshita sensei, o-cha o ( ) masen ka. 9 Yazawa hakase wa daigaku no kyoojuu de ( ) kara *isogashii* gozaimasu. 10 O-*yasumu* ( ) mae ni o-cha o ippai ( ) desu ka.

C Translate into English:
1 Meiji-jidai no kottoohin no tenrankai o goran ni narimashita ka. 2 Shitsurei desu ga koochoo-sensei de irasshaimasu ka. 3 Sakihodo mooshiageta yoo ni hookokusho o myoonichi sashiagemasu. 4 Kono haizara o chotto haishaku shite mo yoroshii deshoo ka. 5 O-tegami o haiken itashimashita. 6 Sakihodo wa shitsurei itashimashita. 7 Abe san no o-toosan wa ototoshi o-nakunari ni natta soo desu. 8 Chotto o-ukagai shimasu ga shiyakusho wa dochira deshoo ka. 9 Senjitsu o-motome ni natta taipuraitaa wa chooshi ga ii desu ka. 10 Kitai shite irasshatta hodo hito ga konakatta no de gakkari nasatta deshoo.

D Translate into Japanese:

1 Please try on this jacket, sir. 2 What is your name? 3 As you are aware, these days prices have been going up very quickly. 4 What time do you usually go to bed? 5 Is it true that Professor Tanaka is going to give a speech at the United Nations? 6 I shall explain it to the director later. 7 Apparently the professor didn't like his student's way of thinking. 8 Please don't forget your hat. 9 My younger brother will come to see you at 6 o'clock tomorrow evening. 10 My father sends his regards.

DÁI NIJÚKKA

■ **BÉNRI NA HYOOGEN**

Shi̯kata ga arimasén.
Shiyoo ga arimasén.
Dóo shiyoo mo nái desu̯.

Komátta!
Shimátta!
Odoróita!

BUNKEI

Té o agero.
Sonna ni shabéru na.
Háyaku ikinasái.
Otóosan wa ítsu̯ káette kuru?
Onaka ga suitá wa.
Bóku mo hará ga hétte tamaranai.

■ **KAIWA**

1 A: Bóku wa nannénsei?

B: Kotoshi̯ kara yonénsei ni
narimásu̯.

A: Gakkoo de dónna
kámoku ga su̯kí?

B: Taisoo to shákai to chíri ga
su̯kí desu̯.

2 A: Áa, shimátta.

B: Dóo shi̯ta n' desu̯ ka.

A: Karita hón o kyoo káese
to iwaremáshi̯ta ga ie
ni oite kimáshi̯ta.

B: Ashi̯ta démo kamawánai
deshoo.

3 A: Ano dooro-hyóoshi̯ki ni
nán to káite arimasu̯
ka.

B: 'Tomare' to káite arimasu̯.

A: Jáa, ki̯tto mitooshi no
warúi tokoro deshoo.

B: Ée, koko de yóku jíko ga áru
soo desu̯.

4 A: Móo osoi kara háyaku
nenasái.

B: Ashi̯ta no shu̯kudai ga máda
na no.

A: Térebi o mínaide
háyaku hajimeréba
yókatta no ni.

B: Áto júppun de owarú wa.

LESSON TWENTY

USEFUL EXPRESSIONS

It can't be helped.   Oh dear!
It can't be helped.   Bother! Damn!
It's hopeless.   Oh! (exclamation of surprise)

SENTENCE PATTERNS

Hands up!
Don't talk so much!
Go quickly!
When is Daddy coming back?
I'm hungry.
I'm starving too.

CONVERSATIONS

1 A: What class are you in?   B: I'll be in fourth class this
                                           year.

   A: What subjects do you   B: I like physical training, social
       like at school?   studies and geography.

2 A: Oh, blast!   B: What's the matter?
   A: I was told to return the   B: I suppose tomorrow will do.
       books I borrowed
       today, but I've left
       them at home.

3 A: What does that street-   B: It says 'stop'.
       sign say?

   A: Ah. No doubt the   B: Yes, apparently there are
       visibility is bad here.   often accidents here.

4 A: It's late. Go to bed at   B: I still haven't done
       once.   tomorrow's homework.
   A: You should have started   B: I'll be finished in ten
       earlier instead of   minutes.
       watching television.

5   A: Ashí ga káyukute   B: Dóo shita no?
        shikata ga nái wa.

    A: Ka ni sasareta rashíi no. B: Koko wa kusá ga shigétte iru
                                       kara ironna mushi ga irú
                                       no yo.

6   A: Ano tori wa nán deshoo.   B: Are wa ugúisu da to omóu
                                       yo.

    A: Yáa, nakigóe ga chigau   B: Sóo ka naa.
        sa.

5 A: My foot is unbearably itchy.

     B: What happened?

  A: I seem to have been bitten by a mosquito.

     B: The grass is thick here so there are all sorts of insects.

6 A: I wonder what that bird is?

     B: I think it is a warbler.

  A: No. The song is different.

     B: I wonder.

THE PLAIN STYLE

In this lesson the plain style is introduced mainly to help you disentangle the various types of language you may hear Japanese using among themselves. The way Japanese talk to each other can reveal a lot about their relative social positions, and this information can be useful in a variety of ways. You must, however, be very careful about using the plain style yourself. Probably the only time it will be necessary for a foreigner to use the plain style will be in speaking to children or in remarks addressed to himself, as when thinking aloud in expressions like *Áa omoidáshɪta*, '[Now] I remember'; *Wasureta*, 'I've forgotten'; *Kírei na tokoro da náa*, 'What a beautiful place!'

Japanese use the plain style within the immediate family circle, among close friends, schoolmates and workmates of the same age. The tendency seems to be towards reciprocal use of the plain style, though in relationships such as teacher and pupil, employer and employee, senior family member and junior family member and, in more old-fashioned families, husband and wife, it is still common for the former member of each pair to use the plain style in addressing the other, while himself being addressed in the polite style.

The plain style is characterized by the use of the plain present, past, conjectural or propositive forms of the verb, adjective or copula in the final verb of the sentence. We have met these forms in non-final verbs so they do not present too much of a problem. In addition, there are some pronouns and sentence-final particles which are used more often in the plain style. In the plain style, too, differences between men's and women's speech become more apparent.

THE PLAIN-STYLE PRONOUNS

Paralleling the polite-style first- and second-person pronouns *watashi* (formal-style, *watakɪshi*) and *anáta* are the pronouns *bóku* and *kimi*. *Bóku*, 'I', is used by men as the normal plain-style first-person pronoun. It is also used in the polite-style by schoolchildren and university students. *Kimi*, 'you', is also used by men, usually to refer to fellow students, friends of the same age or children. It is also used to refer to subordinates. In addition to this set of pronouns is the pair *ore*, 'I', and *omae*, 'you', used only by males in casual conversation between close friends or when a man addresses his wife or children, etc. These pronouns are considerably rougher than *bóku* and *kimi* and should be avoided. *Kun*, a term of address like *san*, is used by men when referring to men. It is used by students and schoolboys towards their peers and by teachers when referring to their male students.

Atashi, 'I', is a feminine alternative for *watashi* and the form *washi*, 'I', is sometimes used by old men.

THE SENTENCE-FINAL PARTICLES

While sentence-final particles are by no means confined to the plain style, they are more common and varied in this style.

It is also these sentence-final particles which, by and large, differentiate men's and women's speech. So far we have met the particle *né* (or *née*), 'isn't it?', the emphatic particle *yo* and the interrogative particle *ka*. These are all you are likely to need to use in the polite style, but you will hear a number of others, the more common of which are listed below.

Ná (náa) 'isn't it?', 'aren't they?', 'isn't he?' etc.

Equivalent in meaning to *né* (*née*), it is used mainly by men and, although heard in the polite style, is more often used in plain-style speech.

Zo

This is an emphatic masculine particle like *yo*, but much stronger. 'I'm telling you!', 'You know', 'Really', 'Certainly', etc. express the idea of *zo* in English.

Ze

Another masculine particle indicating strong emphasis. This is used mainly in the plain style and is particularly popular among young men and students. It is like *zo*, but more friendly, expressing solidarity. It is often used after the propositive form, a position in which *zo* does not occur; e.g., *Bíiru o íppai nómi ni ikóo ze*, 'Let's go and have a beer.'

Sa

Sa or *sáa* is frequently used by men, especially in the Tokyo area, to assert the speaker's personal opinion.

Dáre demo sonna kotó ga dekiru sa	(I'm telling you) anyone can do that!

Wa

This particle, pronounced with high-falling intonation, is one of the markers of women's speech. Used in the plain style and, in informal conversational situations, in the polite style too, *wa* is a stylistic device lending feminine flavour to a sentence and as such does not translate easily into English. It is often combined with other particles as in *wa née*, 'don't you think . . .?', and *wa yo*, 'I'm telling you that . . .' It cannot be used with interrogative or propositive sentences.

Sono handobággu wa sŭteki dá wa.	'That handbag is lovely.'
Shízuko san mo ikú wa née.	'Shizuko is going too, isn't she?'
Móo anóhĭto wa ittá wa yo.	'He has already left.'

No

This particle is used after a final verb to soften a sentence. It is most often used by women, but is sometimes also used by men to give a gentle, friendly tone to their speech as in speaking to children or women. In statements it is pronounced with a falling intonation. In questions it replaces the interrogative particle, *ka*, and is pronounced with a high-falling intonation. This is actually the *no* of the *no desŭ* construction, which explains or elaborates and means 'the thing is . . .' or in questions 'is it so that?' In women's speech *no* is often combined with the emphatic particle *yo* or with *né* (*née*).

Ashĭta minná de éiga o mí ni iku no yo.	'We're all going to see a film tomorrow.'
O-yu o wakashĭte kara kore o iréru no né.	'You put this in after you've boiled the water, don't you?'

QUESTIONS IN THE PLAIN STYLE

It is very common in the plain style to indicate questions simply with a rising and falling intonation on the last syllable of the sentence.

Maiasa nánji ni okíru?   'What time do you get up every morning?'

The interrogative particle *ka* alone after a plain verb form is generally too abrupt, even for the plain style, and is often softened by the addition of a syllable, resulting in the form *kai*.

Ashįta gakkoo e ikų kai.   'Are you going to school tomorrow?'

When there is another interrogative word in the sentence, the sentence-final interrogative particle is replaced by *dai*.

Sore wa nán dai.   'What's that?'

Kai and *dai* are not generally used by women. Women use the *no* mentioned above in forming plain-style questions.

Dáre ga kúru no?   'Who is coming?'

The retrospective question particle *kke* is often used in the plain style after *da* or a final verb in the past tense to mean 'Am I right in thinking that . . .?', 'Was it so that . . . ?'.

Kimi Yokohama ni sunde itá kke.   'Am I right in thinking you live in Yokohama?' 'Did you say you lived in Yokohama?'

Nán da kke.   'What was it again?'

SOFT AND HARD FORMS

Even in the plain style there are some words which are considered too harsh for general use. The plain copula *da*, although used by men, is often avoided, or replaced by the polite-style form *désų* in women's speech. Contrast the masculine *sóo da yo*, 'that's right', with the feminine *sóo yo*, 'that's right'. *Daróo*, 'may be', the conjectural form of the copula, is even harder and is often replaced by the polite-style *deshóo* in the speech of both men and women, even when other verb forms are in the plain style. This distinction between the soft forms and the hard forms will also have become apparent in the above discussion of personal pronouns and sentence-final particles.

The brusque imperative

Another hard form often avoided even in the plain style is the brusque imperative. It is sometimes used in giving orders to rank subordinates or children or, with ironic intent, between close male friends of the same age.

The brusque imperative is formed by adding -e to the root of consonant-verbs: *káke*, 'write!'; *tomaré*, 'stop!' and -ro (or -yo in more formal and written contexts) to the root of vowel verbs and the *shi*- form of *suru*; *tabéro*, 'eat it', *háyaku shiró*, 'do it quickly'. The irregular verb *kúru* has the plain imperative *kói*, 'come!'; and the imperative of *kureru*, 'he gives me', etc. is *kuré*, 'give me!'

Póchi, kotchi kói.	'Come here Pochi [dog's name]!'
Sore tótte kure.	'Get that for me!'

The imperative of the honorific verbs ending in -*aru*, *kudasáru*, *irassháru*, *ossháru* and *nasáru* is formed by changing the final -*ru* to -*i*: *kudasái*, 'give me'; *irasshái*, 'come'; *osshái*, 'say'; and *nasái*, 'do'.

The brusque negative-imperative is made by placing *na* after the plain present-tense form of the verb: *míru na*, 'don't look!'; *shabéru na*, 'don't talk!'; *úso o yuú na*, 'don't lie'.

A softer imperative, but a command nevertheless, is made by attaching the suffix -*nasái* to the stem of the verb: *machinásai*, 'wait!' This form is often used when telling children what to do. Generally imperatives should be avoided except for the use of *kudasái* (which acts as the request form, 'please') and in set greetings like *o-yasumi nasái*, 'good night', etc.

In the plain style the request forms like *tábete*, *káite*, etc. (the -*te* forms with *kudasái* understood) may be used alone or followed by *choodái*.

Kore o yónde.	'Read this [for me].'
Sore o mísete choodai.	'Would you show me that, please.'

Any of the imperative or request forms may be followed by the particle *yo*.

Sonna bakágeta kotó o yuú na yo.	'Don't say such foolish things.'
Ki ni surú na yo.	'Don't worry.'
Kyoo wa sore de íi ni shiró yo.	'Leave it at that for today.'
Oshiete choodái yo.	'Please tell me.'

Probably the only time you will find it necessary to use the brusque imperatives is in reported speech when relating commands made to yourself. In this case, the brusque imperatives can occur even in polite-style sentences.

Iké to iwaremáshįta.	'I was told to go.'
Háyaku dáse to iimáshįta.	'He told me to send it quickly.'

In changing a direct request with *kudasái* into reported speech, the imperative of *kureru*, *kuré*, can be used.

Sánji ni kíte kure to tanomaremáshįta.	'I was asked to come at 3 o'clock.'

Reported commands can, of course, also be expressed with the *yóo ni* construction.

Iku yóo ni iwaremáshįta.	'I was told to go.'

PLAIN STYLE CONTRACTIONS

In rapid casual speech, particularly in the plain style, many speakers use a number of contractions and abbreviations which it may help to know, though you should avoid using them until you feel quite at home in the language.

Omission of particles

Wa and *o* are often omitted. The omission of *ga* is far less frequent.

Kore íi né.	'This is good, isn't it?'
Káki tabéru?	'Will you have an oyster?'

Hoshi kírei né.   'The stars are pretty, aren't
                                     they?' (The omission of the
                                     hard copula *da* in this
                                     sentence indicates that the
                                     speaker is female.)

Elision of vowels

In rapid speech when the *-te* form is followed by an auxiliary beginning with a vowel, one of the vowels is often omitted. When the
vowel following the *-te* form is *i*, this is the vowel which is dropped.
If the vowel after *-te* is *a* or *o*, the *e* of the *-te* form is lost.

Náni míteru.   'What are you looking at?'
Chanto techoo ni káitaru yo.   'I've got it written down
                                     [properly] in my note book.'

Kudámono o kago ni iretoite   'Leave the fruit in the basket,
   kudasái.   please.'

Assimilation of -r to -n

In the Tokyo dialect syllables beginning with *-r* are sometimes
reduced to *-n* when the next syllable begins with an *-n*. This usage
should be regarded as sub-standard and is to be avoided.

Wakánnai.   'I don't understand.'
Kimura kun shíttén no?   'Do you know Kimura?'

-tátte, 'even if'

This is an alternative of the *-te mo* ending. It is subject to the same
sound changes as the *-te* and *-ta* forms, so, in practice, *-tte* is added to
the past-tense form.

Nánji ni káettatte kamawánai   'You can go home any time.'
   yo.
Isóidatte onaji sá.   'Even if you hurry it will make
                                     no difference [it will be the
                                     same].'

-tte

In rapid speech the quotative particle *to* is often pronounced *-tte*.

Ashĭta kara Saitoo kun ga shigoto ni modórutte kiita.	'I heard Saitoo will be returning to work tomorrow.'

This form is often used alone at the end of a sentence to mean 'someone says that'. In this case some form of *yuu*, 'to say', has been omitted.

Hón o kakiowattátte.	'He says he has finished writing the book.'
Móo kekkon surútte?	'Did she say she is getting married [already]?'

This *-tte* can also combine with the past tense of the verb 'to say' to produce the form *-ttetta* (sometimes pronounced *-ttsŭ(t)ta*).

Kaisha no kaerí ni éiga ni ikúttetta.	'He was saying he is going to a film after work [on his way home from work].'

-chau, -chimau

These contracted forms of the *-te shimau* ending are very popular in Tokyo where they are often attached to verbs indiscriminately without adding anything to the meaning. As this ending is subject to the same sound changes as the *-te* form, it also appears in the forms *-jau* (*-jimau*) and *-tchau* (*-tchimau*).

Nigái kŭsuri o zenbu nónjatta.	'He drank down all the bitter medicine.'
Hébi o koroshĭchatta.	'I killed the snake.'

-cha (-ja)

The ending *-te wa* is often contracted to *-cha* in rapid, plain-style speech. It undergoes the same sound changes given above for *-chau* depending on the final consonant of the verb-root.

Sonna kotó o itcha damé yo.	'You mustn't say things like that' (woman speaking).

-kerya, -(a)nakerya, -(a)nakya

The adjectival conditional suffix *-kereba*, which also occurs with the negative adjective *nái* and the negative suffix *-(a)nái*, is often contracted. This is particularly common with the form *-nakya naranai*, 'must', 'have to'. *Naranai* is frequently omitted leaving *-nakya* alone at the end of a sentence.

Tákakerya kawanai sá.	'If it's expensive I shan't buy it.'
O-kane ga nákya komáru deshoo.	'You'll be in a fix without any money, won't you?'
Anzen-kámisori o kawanákya naranai.	'I have to buy a safety-razor.'
Moo jíki kaeránakya.	'I'll have to be going soon.'

In Lesson Fourteen we met *-kata*, a suffix which attaches to the verb stem to form a noun meaning 'way of doing something', as in *kangaekata*, 'way of thinking', etc. It is this suffix which appears in *shɪkata*, 'way of doing', and is part of the common idiomatic expression *shɪkata ga nai*. Literally this means 'there is no way of doing it' and it is often equivalent to the English, 'it can't be helped' or 'it is no use'.

Moo súgite shimatta kotó wa shɪkata ga arimasén.	'Nothing can be done about past events.'

It is often used after a verb with the *-te mo* ending.

Íkura mónku o itté mo shɪkata ga arimasén.	'It is no use, no matter how much you complain.'

Shiyoo can be used instead of *shɪkata* in these expressions. The suffix *-yoo* is similar in function to *-kata*. *Dóo shiyoo mo nái* means 'it/he [etc.] is beyond all hope', 'it's hopeless', 'nothing can be done about it'.

After the *-te* form, *shɪkata ga nái*, *shiyoo ga nái* or *tamaranai* adds the connotation 'intolerably', 'unbearably', 'over-', 'be dying to', etc.

Uréshɪkute tamaranai.	'I'm too happy for words.'
Ikitákɪte shɪkata ga nái.	'I'm dying to go.'

We can now summarize the Japanese system of reference and

address as it relates to verbs and the copula. Every Japanese sentence carries an indication of the degree of respect paid to what is referred to and the degree of politeness paid to the person addressed. In the chart here 'aux.' indicates the auxiliary verbs *iru* and *áru* and 'cop.' the copula, *da*.

Style of address	Degree of respect	Neutral	Honorific Subject honorific	Object honorific
Plain	verb.	káku	o-kaki ni náru	o-kakɪ suru
	aux.	iru	irassháru	——
	aux.	áru	——*	——
	cop.	dá	de irassháru	——
Polite	verb.	kakimásᴜ	o-kaki ni narimásᴜ	o-kaki shimásᴜ
	aux.	imásᴜ	irasshaimásᴜ	——
	aux.	arimásᴜ	——	——
	cop.	désᴜ	de irasshaimásᴜ	——
Formal	verb.	——†	——	——
	aux.	orimásᴜ	——	——
	aux.	gozaimásᴜ	——	——
	cop.	de gozaimásᴜ	——	——

O-ari ni náru is occasionally heard, but only in the sense of 'to have'.
†*Káku* has no formal form, but verbs like *máiru*, *móosu*, *itadaku* and *itásu* occur in the formal style.

VOCABULARY

		gín	silver
dooro-	road sign	*kago*	basket
hyóoshĮki		*bín*	bottle
mitooshi	visibility	*o-yu*	hot water
shĮkudai	homework	*o-yu o wakasĮ*	to boil water
toshi	age, year	*furobá*	bathroom
-nénsei	. . . year student	*sekken*	soap
kamoku	subject	*génkan*	entrance hall
taisoo	physical	*shinshĮtsu*	bedroom
	education	*zashĮki*	Japanese-style
shákai	society, social		room, parlour
	studies	*handobággu*	handbag
chíri	geography	*booshi*	hat
búngaku	literature	*kázu*	number
butsurígaku	physics	*úso*	lie
mondai	problem,	*mónku*	words, complaint
	question	*mónku o yuu*	to complain
seiji	politics	*bóku*	I
kyoosanshúgi	communism	*kimi*	you
kyoosantoo	Communist	*Shíntoo*	Shinto
	Party	*Búkkyoo*	Buddhism
seifu	government	*anzen-*	safety razor
yakunin	official, public	*kámisori*	
	servant	*gomí*	rubbish
ebi	prawn, lobster	*shóorai*	the future, in
káki	oyster		future
ka	mosquito	*hĮtobanjuu*	all night long
ugúisĮ	warbler,	*seikatsĮ suru*	to live
	nightingale	*ryúuchoo na*	fluent
kĮsa	grass	*sĮteki na*	lovely,
hoshi	star		marvellous,
shimi	stain		superb
chi	blood	*bakágeta*	stupid, foolish
hará	belly	*momoiro (no)*	pink
mimi	ear	*kayúi*	itchy
hige	beard, moustache	*ureshíi*	happy
kín	gold	*tamaranai*	intolerable,
kin-dókei	gold watch		unbearable

heru	to decrease, get empty	*tomaru*	to stop, stay
kóe ga suru	to hear a voice	*odoróku*	to be surprised
hajiméru	to begin	*tsɨ́ku*	to become attached; poke
tasɨkéru	to help, save	*úso o tsɨ́ku/ yuu*	to lie
shigéru	to grow thickly, become overgrown	*ki ga tsɨ́ku*	to realize
shinjíru	to believe	*tabun*	probably
kyóomi o mótsu	to be interested in (in = *ni*)	*kitto*	certainly, no doubt
núgu	to take off	*osóraku*	perhaps; probably
agaru	go up, step into	*dooji ni*	at the same time
omoidásu	to recall	*(moo) jíki*	soon
sɨtéru	to throw away	*hakkíri*	clearly
sásɨ	to sting	*chanto*	properly
yubí o sásɨ	to point	*-e; -ro/-yo*	(brusque imperative suffixes)
katazukéru	to put away, tidy up		
osowaru	to learn, be taught	*na*	(negative imperative particle)
káesu	to return, give back	*-nasái*	(plain imperative suffix)
ki ni suru	to worry (about = *o*)	*-te tamaranai*	be unbearably . . .
o-cha o ireru	to make tea	*na, zo, ze, sa*	(masculine sentence-final particles)
kabúru	to wear (on the head)	*no, wa*	(feminine sentence-final particles)
niáu	to suit, be becoming	*kun*	(familiar male address)
hige o sóru	to shave		

EXERCISE 20

A Change the following sentences as indicated in brackets:
1 Kimi bungaku ni kyoomi o motteru kai. (polite-honorific) 2 Kono sukiyaki no aji wa doo dai. (polite) 3 Itsuka uchi e asobi ni koi yo. (polite-honorific) 4 Boku wa daigaku de butsurigaku o senkoo shiyoo to omotteru. (polite) 5 Kawa ni gomi o suteru na. (polite) 6 Ka ga ashi o sashita. (polite-passive) 7 Hara ga hetta. (polite) 8 Furoba ni sekken ga arimasen deshita kara musume ga yakkyoku e kai ni ikimashita. (causative) 9 Zashiki ni agaru mae ni genkan de kutsu o nuganakya nannai yo. (polite) 10 Shoorai kagakusha ka seijika ni naritaitte. (polite)

B Fill in the blanks and supply the correct forms of the words in italics:
1 Jibun no apaato kara dete *iku* to meirei ( ) toki ni wa totemo bikkuri shita wa. 2 Yuube hitobanjuu mimi ( ) *itai* zenzen *nemuru* deshita. 3 Koko wa ki ( ) kusa ga hijoo ni shigette ( ) kara aruki ( ) desu. 4 Nando ( ) hakkiri setsumei shita no ni wakatte *morau* deshita. 5 Beekaa san ( ) nagaku Nihon de seikatsu ( ) koto ga arimasu ( ) kanari ryuuchoo ( ) Nihongo ga *hanasu*. 6 Seiji-mondai ( ) kyoomi o motte iru hito ( ) daredemo Hirayama sensei no hon o kai ( ) deshoo. 7 Kesa osoku okita ( ) hige o soru jikan shika ( ) asagohan mo tabe ( ) ie ( ) demashita. 8 Seifu no yakunin ( ) monku o itte ( ) shikata ga ( ) yoo desu. 9 Uso o yuu ( ) to otoosan wa itta ( ) ( ) dooshite sonna bakageta koto ( ) mada itteru no kai. 10 Yubi o kitta ( ) ( ) waishatsu ( ) chi no shimi ( ) tsukimashita.

C Translate into English:
1 Zutto ame de ie o derarenakatta kara sanpo demo shitakute tamaranai. 2 Komatta. Tomodachi ni denwa suru to yakusoku shita no ni denwa-bangoo no kaite aru techoo o uchi ni oite kimashita. 3 O-yu o wakashite o-cha o irero to iwaremashita. 4 Kookoo ichinen-sei ni natte kara kamoku no kazu ga ooku shukudai mo fuete tamarimasen. 5 Koko wa mitooshi ga warui kara abunakute shikata ga nai. 6 Moo shikata ga nai kara sono koto wa ki ni shinaide. 7 Kaki ya ebi nado ga meshiagaremasu ka. 8 Wakai toki ni wa kyoosan-shugi ni kyoomi o motte kyoosantoo ni haitte ita koto mo aru soo

desu. 9 Tasukete kure to yuu koe ga shimashita. 10 Mainichi asa to ban sanjuppun zutsu taisoo o suru kara konna ni genki na n' desu yo.

D Translate into Japanese:
1 Damn! I've lost my gold watch. 2 Quickly tidy up your toys and put them away properly in the box in your bedroom. 3 I told you not to complain about the food. 4 What did you learn at school today? 5 That pink hat you were wearing last night suits you well. 6 They were overjoyed at being able to meet again. 7 Stop! Thief! Give me back my wallet! 8 They say many Japanese believe in Buddhism and Shinto at the same time. 9 I was told to check the number of bottles in this box. 10 I can't recall exactly [= clearly], but it was probably the year after the war ended.

KEY TO THE EXERCISES

EXERCISE 1

A 1 Wakarimasen. 2 Ikimasen deshita. 3 Itsu irrashaimashita ka. 4 Kimasen. 5 Hanashimasen. 6 Shimasu. 7 Aimasu. 8 Ikimashoo. 9 Kaerimasu. 10 Shimasen deshita ka.

B 1 Kinoo irasshaimashita ka. 2 Ato de shimasu. 3 Kyoo kimashita. 4 Kinoo hanashimashita. 5 Itsu owarimashita ka. 6 Iie, wakarimasen. 7 Iie, ikimasen deshita. 8 Mada tabemasen. 9 Raishuu kaerimasu. 10 Ototoi aimashita.

C 1 Are you meeting [him] tomorrow? 2 Good morning. 3 When are you coming/going? 4 He didn't talk about it yesterday. 5 I don't understand. 6 Good evening. 7 [He] is coming today. 8 I didn't go. 9 Good day/Hello. 10 Thank you very much.

D 1 Ashita kimasu. 2 Kinoo aimasen deshita. 3 Konban wa. 4 Hanashimasen deshita. 5 Ashita irasshaimasu ka. 6 Wakarimasen deshita. 7 Jaa, ima shimasu. 8 Kinoo owarimasen deshita. 9 Ato de aimasu. 10 Mada tabemasen.

EXERCISE 2

A 1 Zasshi o yomimasen. 2 Kyoo kaimasu. 3 Tegami o dashimasen deshita. 4 Eiga e ikimasen deshita. 5 Shachoo ni agemashita. 6 Nani

276

o tabemashita ka. 7 Dare ni agemashoo ka. 8 Hon o kakimasen ka. 9 Moo wakarimasu. 10 Sukiyaki o tabemasen ka.

B 1 Kinoo zasshi mo dashimashita. 2 Senshuu ginkoo e ikimashita. 3 Shachoo ni nani o agemashita ka. 4 Kinoo shinbun o kaimashita ka. 5 Issho ni doko e ikimashoo ka. 6 Asatte dare ni aimasu ka. 7 Senshuu nani o kakimashita ka. 8 Kaisha de issho ni hanashimasu. 9 Eki de Suzuki san ni aimashita. 10 Itsu irasshaimasu ka.

C 1 I'm sorry. 2 Excuse me./Good bye. 3 We are going to Japan together this year too. 4 I didn't read the newspaper yesterday. 5 Where did you send the letter? 6 What shall I give Mr Suzuki? 7 Who did you meet in the park? 8 When did you come/go back home? 9 You don't drink whisky in the bar these days, do you? 10 What shall we buy at the shop?

D 1 Doozo. 2 Ikaga desu ka./O-genki desu ka. 3 O-kagesama de genki desu. 4 Tegami o owarimashita ka. 5 Moo kimashita ka. 6 Doko e irasshaimasu/ikimasu ka. 7 Nihon de Nihongo o sukoshi hanashimashita. 8 Wakarimasen. 9 Itsumo eki de Suzuki san ni aimashita. 10 Abe san mo irasshaimasu/kimasu ka.

EXERCISE 3

A 1 Koko wa kooen desu ka. 2 Anokata wa Suzuki san desu. 3 Sensei wa Igirisujin de wa arimasen. 4 Watashitachi wa basu de kimasu. 5 Doko de tabemashoo ka. 6 Gakusei wa tegami o enpitsu de kakimashita. 7 Kono tegami wa Doitsu kara kimasen deshita ka. 8 Gakkoo e nan de ikimashoo ka. 9 Afurika no hon o yomimashita. 10 Eigo de tegami o kakimasen deshita.

B 1 de, e/ni/kara 2 de, o 3 o 4 wa, no 5 wa, kara 6 de, ni 7 no, wa 8 wa, no 9 ni, no, o 10 ni, e/ni.

C 1 Last week I met a Japanese student at the station. 2 I went to Australia by plane. 3 Did you come from Russia? 4 I read the paper in the office. 5 She is not French. 6 Where is the lavatory? 7 Let me introduce Mr Honda. 8 Give my regards to your wife. 9 Who is he? 10 Sorry to bother you.

D 1 Chuugokujin no gakusei wa dare desu ka. 2 Kinoo jidoosha o kaimashita. 3 Buraun san wa Kanada kara Nihon e kimashita. 4 Anoko wa mainichi basu de gakkoo e ikimasu. 5 Kore o kami de tsukurimashita ka. 6 Eigo de hanashimashoo. 7 Are wa hikooki no koojoo desu ne. 8 Nihongo no sensei ni zasshi o agemashita. 9 Ashita daigaku de aimashoo. 10 Dore o agemashoo ka.

EXERCISE 4

A 1 Hikidashi no naka ni boorupen ga arimasu. 2 Heya ni isu ga takusan arimasu. 3 Kutsu-uriba wa doko ni arimasu ka. 4 Shorui wa tsukue no ue ni arimasu. 5 Esukareetaa de gokai e ikimashoo. 6 Hisho wa jimusho ni imasu. 7 Hon'ya wa yuubinkyoku no ushiro ni arimasu. Yuubinkyoku no ushiro ni hon'ya ga arimasu. 8 Rokuji han ni kaerimashita. 9 Shoowa juukunen ni umaremashita. 10 Mise wa eki no chikaku ni arimasu.

B 1 imasu. 2 no, ni, ga. 3 wa, ni. 4 no, ni, ga. 5 wa, ni. 6 ni. 7 no, no, de, o. 8 wa, ni. 9 de, ni. 10 wa, ni.

C 1 The memo is always on the table. 2 Let's go to the seventh floor in the lift. 3 I go to work every day on the underground. 4 Have you seen my dictionary? 5 Thank you for the wonderful meal. 6 What is behind the door? 7 Mr Tanaka was born in 1897. 8 Only [the] boys were in the room. 9 Do you mind?/Is it all right? 10 My friend is near the window.

D 1 Gomen nasai. 2 Takushii-noriba wa doko desu ka. 3 Tomodachi wa rainen mukoo ni ikimasu. 4 Watashi wa sen kyuuhyaku yonjuusannen [Shoowa juuhachinen] ni umaremashita. 5 Nooto wa ikura desu ka. 6 Nihongo no jisho wa nisen gohyakuen desu. 7 Terebi wa sanman gosen'en desu. 8 Yuubinkyoku no mae de kuji han ni aimasu. 9 O-somatsusama deshita. 10 Watashi no tomodachi wa Furansugo no sensei desu.

EXERCISE 5

A 1 Kono tegami o kookuubin de okuritai desu. 2 Koko wa shizuka ja arimasen. 3 Kyoo wa atsuku arimasen. 4 Watashi no tokei wa takakatta desu. 5 Kanojo wa Nihongo ga joozu ja arimasen. 6 Eiga wa yoku nakatta desu. 7 Atama ga itakatta desu. 8 Sukiyaki ga suki ja arimasen. 9 Abe san ni kikitaku nakatta desu. 10 Ano aoi waishatsu wa watashi no ja arimasen.

B 1 no, wa, ga. 2 kara, made. 3 na, o. 4 wa, ga. 5 kara, de. 6 no. 7 wa, ga, ja/dewa. 8 wa, ga. 9 o. 10 ga.

C 1 Do you eat Chinese food? 2 I came to Japan on the same ship as Mr Smith. 3 What is that tall building? 4 Give me a few of those vegetables/a little of that vegetable. 5 This is a summer shirt. 6 I'm going to Germany next winter. 7 What time did you get up this morning? 8 Last night I had a headache. 9 Keiko has beautiful eyes. 10 That girl is really tiny, isn't she?

D 1 Rainen no aki ni dokoka shizuka na tokoro e ikitai desu. 2 Tookyoo-eki kara kisha de ichijikan kakarimasu. 3 Ano otoko-nokotachi wa yoku hatarakimasu. 4 Watashi no waishatsu wa goji made ni dekimasu ka. 5 Gorufu ga o-suki desu ka. 6 Watashi wa itsumo onaji baa de nomimasu. 7 Yuubinkyoku no tonari no takai biru wa nan desu ka. 8 Watashi wa uta ga heta desu. 9 Watashi wa mainichi ookina koojoo de shichiji han kara sanji han made hatara-kimasu. 10 Motto ii tokei ga irimasu.

EXERCISE 6

A 1 sandai. 2 futari. 3 yattsu, too. 4 sansatsu. 5 roppiki. 6 roppon, yonmai. 7 sangen. 8 santsuu. 9 nannin. 10 ikutsu.

B 1 Senshuu tomodachi ni ai ni kimashita. 2 Hokkaidoo e uma o kai ni ikimashita. 3 Kesa koohii o sanbai nomimashita. 4 Ookina kami ga nanmai irimasu ka. 5 Yuube osoku made tomodachi to maajan shimashita. 6 Kanojo wa dare to kekkon shimashita ka. 7 Nihon e benkyoo ni kimashita. 8 Depaato e mikan o kai ni ikimasu. 9 Chuugoku-ryoori o tabe ni ikimashoo. 10 Tenrankai o mi ni ikitakunakatta desu.

C 1 I drove by myself from Tokyo to Osaka. 2 Three days ago I met Mr Sumimoto at an exhibition. 3 I saw five or six Japanese monkeys at the zoo. 4 I always study for about two hours at night. 5 Why don't you play mah jong? 6 I have three Japanese dictionaries. 7 Take care./Have a good trip. 8 On Thursday night a friend and I went out for dinner. 9 Today is the first of April. 10 About how long does it take to Karuizawa by car?

D 1 Irasshai. Koohii o ippai ikaga desu ka. 2 Doitsu ryoori o doko e tabe ni ikimashoo ka. 3 Suiyoobi no asa juuichiji juugofun mae ni doobutsuen no mon de aimashoo. 4 Tanaka san no shiroi santoo no uma/santoo no shiroi uma o mimashita ka. 5 Umi wa yuugata kirei desu ne. 6 Eki no soba no ano ooki na depaato de issho ni o-hiru o tabemashoo ka. 7 Sengetsu hon o nansatsu yomimashita ka. 8 Doko e ryokoo shitai desu ka. 9 Maiasa shichiji juppun ni asagohan o tabemasu. 10 Raigetsu no hatsuka ni Karuizawa e gorufu o shi ni ikimasu.

EXERCISE 7

A 1 nonde imasu. 2 kiite imasu. 3 yasete imasu. 4 okite imasu ka. 5 tabete imasu. 6 aite imasu. 7 oshiete imasu. 8 tonde imasu. 9 tsukatte imasu ka. 10 matte imashita ka.

B 1 kaite, arimasu. 2 oboete, imasu. 3 tsukarete, imasu. 4 e, itte, o. 5 ni, itte. 6 na, ni arimasu. 7 o, kashite. 8 oishikute, desu. 9 wa, futotte, ga, wa, yasete. 10 e, oyogi, ka.

C 1 Welcome back. 2 What do you teach at the university? 3 Do you know Michiko's mother? 4 I'm thirsty. Let's go and have a coffee in that coffee shop. 5 I bought this tie as a present for my father. 6 Whose is that large black dog? 7 Going somewhere? 8 My child's cat died so I've come to buy another one. 9 Do you walk from your house to the company every day? 10 I have some time now, but I'm leaving for the office at 2 so please hurry.

D 1 Nihongo o oshiete kudasai. 2 Ima doko ni sunde imasu ka. 3 Umi e oyogi ni ikimashita. 4 Kono resutoran wa yasukute oishii desu. 5 Jisho wa ano hondana ni oite arimasu. 6 Anohito wa yuube chotto/sukoshi yotte imashita. 7 Doa wa shimatte imasu ga mado wa aite imasu. 8 Ano nekutai o kaitai desu kara nisen'en kashite

kudasai. 9 Kyoo wa harete imasu kara doobutsuen e/ni ikimashoo.
10 Watashi no pen o tsukatte kudasai. Ima tsukatte imasen.

EXERCISE 8

A 1 Kinoo kissaten de atta tomodachi mo Nihongo o benkyoo shite imasu. 2 Shachoo no heya de matte iru hito wa untenshu desu. 3 Anohito wa itsumo omoshiroi hanashi o suru Suzuki san desu. 4 Tegami o kaku hima ga arimasen. 5 Yushutsu shite iru kamera wa taihen ii desu. 6 Kaigairyokoo o suru Nihonjin ga fuemashita. 7 Yuube paatii de atta onnanohito wa daigaku de Eigo o oshiete imasu. 8 Kore wa yushutsu-buchoo ga totta shashin desu. 9 Kinoo tabeta sashimi wa ikaga deshita ka. 10 Nihon ni kuru gaijin wa sugu Nihon-ryoori ni naremasu.

B 1 Nihon de Nihongo o benkyoo suru koto ni shimasu/shimashita. 2 Jidoosha o unten suru koto ga dekimasen. 3 Yooroppa no inaka ni sunda koto ga arimasu ka. 4 Sono hako o akeru koto ga dekimasen. 5 Moo matsu koto ga dekimasen. 6 Hanbai-buchoo wa rippa na uchi ni sunde iru deshoo. 7 Yama no keshiki ga kirei deshoo. 8 Otoosan wa oyogu koto ga dekimasu ka. 9 Kono subarashii jidoosha o mite urayamashikatta deshoo. 10 Konban wa koten-ongaku o kiki ni iku koto ni shimasu/shimashita.

C 1 I wonder who'll be at the conference tomorrow. 2 That's a marvellous car Mr Tanaka is driving, isn't it? 3 Have you ever been to England? 4 You can't take very good photographs with this camera. 5 I've decided to go for a drive in the country tomorrow. 6 The time I spend studying Japanese has decreased. 7 You must be terribly busy every day. 8 Imports of cars from Japan have increased extraordinarily. 9 Let's go back again [literally, one more time] to the place we went to in the spring holidays last year. 10 What's the matter?/What happened?

D 1 Uisukii o moo ippai kudasai. 2 Ano se ga hikui otokonohito wa dare desu ka. 3 Kanojo wa suki na hito to kekkon suru koto ga dekimasen deshita. 4 Ichinen ni kamera o nandai yushutsu shimasu ka. 5 Moo futsuka tomaru koto ni shimashita. 6 Sashimi o taberu koto ga dekimasu ka. 7 Kono heya wa haba ga semai desu. 8 Hontoo ni soo omoimasu ka. 9 Sono hako o akete sono naka no pen o kazoete kudasai. 10 Kinyoobi wa nanji ga o-hima desu ka.

EXERCISE 9

A 1 Asa hayaku okita hoo ga ii desu. 2 Kore wa yaku ni tasu ka mo shiremasen. 3 Sore o tabete wa ikemasen. 4 O-kane o sonna ni tsukatte wa ikemasen. 5 Ima hanashite mo kamaimasen. 6 Oishii o-okashi o/ga tabetai desu ka. 7 Kyoo no gogo ame ga furu deshoo. 8 Moo hitotsu itadaite mo ii desu ka. 9 Ano resutoran de shokuji shita hoo ga ii desu. 10 Kyoo wa atsuku naru kamo shiremasen.

B 1 de, o, mo. 2 e, mo, shiremasen. 3 iru, wa, desu. 4 ku, naru. 5 ni, yuu, ga. 6 no, o, hoo. 7 o, wa. 8 iru, kamo. 9 chuu, koto, ga. 10 shita, hoo.

C 1 Do you know Dr Suzuki? 2 Sorry to have kept you waiting so long. 3 I wonder what the weather will be like tomorrow. 4 Does it matter if I'm a bit late? 5 You can't smoke on the underground. 6 Perhaps there is an interesting exhibition on at the museum now. 7 The sky is cloudy, isn't it? 8 Perhaps Mrs Smith has already returned to London. 9 This sort of weather is unpleasant, isn't it? 10 You'd better return home quickly.

D 1 Kono chiisai kamera wa hijoo ni yaku ni tachimasu. 2 Miki san wa donna hito desu ka. 3 Mochiron sutte mo ii desu. 4 Denwa no soba no memo ni kotozuke ga kaite arimasu. 5 Shibaraku deshita ne. 6 Anohito wa shinsetsu de hansamu desu. 7 Anohito wa Supein-ryoori ga suki kamo shiremasen. 8 Donna niku o tabetai desu ka. 9 Ki de tsukutta hoo ga ii desu. 10 Ashita yuki ga furu kamo shiremasen.

EXERCISE 10

A 1 Ashita kokuritsu-gekijoo ni iku yotei desu. 2 Byooki desu kara soto e deru koto ga dekimasen. 3 Denki o tsukeru to akaruku narimasu. 4 Chuumon suru mae ni yoku kangaeta hoo ga ii desu. 5 Daredemo dekiru soo/dekisoo desu. 6 Doa ni kagi o kakete kara mon o demashita. 7 Iku mae ni denpoo o uchimasu. 8 Fuyu ga kuru to samuku narimasu. 9 Eiga ga hajimaru mae ni koohii o ippai nomimashoo. 10 Rainen sotsugyoo shite kara Furansu e iku tsumori desu. (*suru kara* also possible).

B 1 to, ga. 2 o, ni. 3 wa, na, da. 4 ni, ga. 5 o to. 6 wa, ga, kara. 7 no, wa, ga. 8 o, mae, hoo. 9 ga, kara, de. 10 ni, wa, da.

C 1 Thanks for the other day. 2 You'd better put on the light by the desk. 3 Let's have a cold beer (or something) at that little bar. 4 What do you intend to do after you graduate? 5 If you study too long your eyes get sore. 6 It's nothing much, but I hope you like it. 7 Before you go to bed lock the door and turn off the gas, please. 8 Congratulations. 9 Did you enjoy your recent trip abroad? 10 Have you ever seen *kabuki?*

D 1 Hayaku chuumon shimashoo. Onaka ga suite imasu. 2 Ashita wa betsu ni yotei ga arimasen kara shibai o mi ni ikimashoo. 3 Ano hito wa taihen tysuyoi soo desu ga amari atama ga yoku nai soo desu. 4 Rondon o deru mae ni denpoo o utte kudasai. 5 Yuube osoku made (okite ite) shigoto shite imashita kara konban wa hayaku neru tsumori desu. 6 Mazu nedan o shirabemashoo. 7 Konna taikutsu na hon o yomitaku arimasen. 8 Shoohin o uru mae ni buchoo to soodan shita hoo ga ii ka mo shiremasen. 9 Ashita kodomotachi o doobutsuen ni tsurete iku tsumori desu. 10 Migi no ano chiisana mise de o-miyage o utte iru kamo shiremasén.

EXERCISE 11

A 1 Ashita konaide kudasai. 2 Kono shiryoo wa kuwashiku nai desu. 3 Oosaka-yuki no kisha ni ma ni awanakatta soo desu. 4 Chizu o motte ikanakatta soo desu. 5 Harawanaide kudasai. 6 Otooto wa watashi hodo se ga takaku nai desu. 7 Kono kusuri o nomanakute mo ii desu ka. 8 Matanai tsumori desu. 9 Kore de wa tarinai soo desu. 10 Kono supootsu wa abunaku nai desu.

B 1 wa, yori. 2 o, koto. 3 wa, oishiku. 4 kuwashiku, shite. 5 de, tabenai, ga. 6 harawanai. to. 7 to, to, ga. 8 wa, hodo. 9 dake, tsukutte. 10 ga, nakute.

C 1 Which is more difficult, Spanish or French? 2 You have to explain difficult things like that in [great] detail. 3 Apparently he is in trouble because he hasn't got enough money. 4 There are few honest people. 5 Don't you have any medicine cheaper than this? 6 You must be tired. 7 Don't talk about it to other people. 8 Apparently no one came. 9 Sorry to have kept you waiting. 10 What sort of company do you work for?

D 1 O-sewasama deshita. 2 Kisha wa hikooki yori zutto yasui desu. 3 Sakana to tori to dochira ga o-suki desu ka. 4 Ano tatemono wa yuubinkyoku gurai ookii desu. 5 Kono shiryoo o hoka no hito ni misenaide kudasai. 6 Kinoo au koto ga dekinakute zannen deshita. 7 Dore ga ichiban kuwashii chizu desu ka. 8 Karate wa abunai supootsu ja arimasen. 9 Watashi no uchi wa eki kara nikiro gurai desu. 10 Shokudoo dewa shokuji suru mae ni harawanakeneba narimasen.

EXERCISE 12

A 1 Asatte wa otooto no tanjoobi na n' desu. 2 Kono heya wa nishi ni muite imasu kara natsu wa atsusugiru hazu desu. 3 Sono kara no kaban o motte kite kudasai. 4 Dooshite ma ni awanakatta n' desu ka. 5 Kaimono ga kirai na n' desu. 6 Ano tatemono wa keimusho da soo desu. 7 Oji wa ashita konai hazu desu. 8 Byooin no denwabangoo wa ano denwachoo ni notte iru hazu desu. 9 Futorisugi wa karada ni yoku nai n' desu. 10 kyonen katta pureeyaa wa moo kowarete imasu kara tsukau koto ga dekinai n' desu.

B 1 wa, kara, ni. 2 no, wa, ga. 3 ga, o. 4 wa, wa. 5 wa, yori. 6 no, ni. 7 wa, kara. 8 o, ga. 9 wa, ga. 10 o, ni, hoo.

C 1 I hate spiders but I don't mind snakes. 2 We should be leaving in three minutes. 3 That department store is expensive and they only deliver big things. 4 Sorry to bother you. May I come in? 5 They sell delicious beef at that shop. 6 Man can eat a greater variety of things than other animals. 7 He was formerly a lawyer, but now he is in prison. 8 After you, please. 9 I do clerical work in a small trading company. 10 Excuse me. Is there anyone here?

D 1 Koko wa fuyu taihen samui desu kara yoku kaze o hikimasu. 2 Watashi ga byooin ni anata no nimotsu o motte itta n' desu. 3 Mainen gaikoku e iku koto ga dekite urayamashii desu. 4 Anata no oneesan/imootosan wa gyuuniku ga o-suki desu ka. 5 Asatte no sanji made ni (sore o) haitatsu suru koto ga dekimasu ka. 6 Anohito wa futorisugi desu kara kenkoo ni ki o tsukenakereba narimasen. 7 Chichi wa rokujuu sugite imasu/sugi desu ga mada maiasa oyogi ni ikimasu. 8 Go-kyoodai wa nannin desu/imasu ka. 9 Hachikiro mo arukimashita kara ashi ga itai n' desu. 10 Kootsuu ga konde imasu ga sore demo rokuji made ni tsuku hazu desu.

EXERCISE 13

A 1 Terebi ga kowarete iru nara shuuri ni dashita hoo ga ii desu. 2 Jon ga kitara issho ni tabe ni ikimashoo. 3 O-kane sae areba Nihon ni ikitai to omoimasu. 4 Opera no ken ga urikire deshitara/dattara shibai o mi ni ikimashoo. 5 Moofu o kaketara attakaku narimasu yo. 6 Shachoo no yuu toori ni shinakereba ikemasen. 7 Nihon wa keshiki ga kirei da to omoimasu. 8 Sokutatsu de okuranakereba dooshitemo ma ni aimasen. 9 Jidoosha o tsukawanai yoo ni chichi ga iimashita. 10 Asatte no paatii ni irassharu ka doo ka kikimashita.

B 1 wa, ni. 2 ittara, ni. 3 o, katta. 4 o, yoo. 5 itte, mo. 6 to, ni. 7 shi, sureba. 8 to, no, ni. 9 tabereba, hodo. 10 ni, yoru, to, ga, shiremasen.

C 1 If you are going to buy one anyway I think it would be better not to buy a cheap [and nasty] one. 2 What is the track number of the train to Kanazawa? 3 How would you like another helping? 4 Sorry to trouble you, but would you mind passing this letter to the head of the section? 5 Today is the day we have to hand over the pamphlets. 6 This cooler doesn't work very well, does it? 7 Surely you needn't go home yet. Please take your time. 8 When we were just married we lived with my husband's parents. 9 If Kimiko is going I won't go. 10 Please sit down.

D 1 Hoka no ga hoshikereba watashi no o agemasu. 2 Kare ni kinoo (no) sanji ni kuru yoo ni iimashita ga kimasen deshita. 3 Ano tokei wa ikura da/ikura suru to omoimasu ka. 4 Asu kisha wa nanji ni deru ka shirimasen. 5 Kyoo no gogo isogashiku nakereba jimusho ni yotte kudusai. 6 Tsukue no ue no panfuretto o sanmai zutsu totte kudasai. 7 Atarashii uchi o tateta bakari desu kara jikan ga attara mi ni irasshatte/kite kudasai. 8 Jisho sae areba Inoue san to Nihongo de hanasu koto ga dekita no ni. 9 Omocha o hitotsu zutsu agemasu kara nakanaide (kudasai). 10 Kanai ni konban wa hayaku kaeru to iimashita kara moo sorosoro shitsurei shimasu.

EXERCISE 14

A 1 Kore wa sensei ni itadaita tokei desu. 2 Daiku ga tsukue o koshiraete kuremashita. 3 Tomodachi ni oshiete moraimashita. 4 Obaasan ni yubiwa o katte agemashita. 5 Michi ga wakaranakattara untenshu ni shirabete morau koto ga dekimasu. 6 Kono sebiro o kite mite itadakemasen ka. 7 Uchi no musuko ni watashite yatte kudasai. 8 Motto shizuka ni shite itadakitai desu. 9 Biiru o reizooko ni irete oite itadakemasen ka. 10 Watashi wa shinsen na sakana o katte kite agemashita.

B 1 e, uke. 2 kara, shimaimashita. 3 ni, kara, wa. 4 nara, mite. 5 o, okimasu/kimasu, okimashita/kimashita. 6 ni, o, moraimashita/age-mashita. 7 shimatta, hoo. 8 shimatta/kita, oita/moratta, sugimasu. 9 o/wa, ni. 10 o, yatte.

C 1 I got the nurse to have look at my knee for me. 2 I took the entrance examination for Tokyo University, but it was no good [I failed]. 3 Those candies are too sweet, so don't eat them all at once. 4 One after the other, I received all sorts of presents. 5 I went and bought a lot of bait for fishing and put it by in the refrigerator. 6 Would you mind going in from the west, because the street in front of my house is one way? 7 If I can't get Mrs Suzuki to speak a little slower I'll have difficulty understanding her. 8 The other day I fell over and hurt my leg so I'll have to get a doctor to look at it. 9 What kind of impression did the film we saw last night have on the children? 10 When I went on a trip to Hokkaidoo I was taken to all sorts of places by my cousin.

D 1 Doko de basu o oriru/orinakereba naranai/ka musuko ni oshiete yatte kudasai. 2 Sukiyaki no tsukurikata o oshiete agemasu.

3 Shio to koshoo o totte itadakemasen ka. 4 O-sumai wa dochira desu ka. 5 Kyonen Rondon ni ita toki sebiro o nichaku tsukutte moraimashita. 6 Kabin ga dai kara ochite waremashita. 7 Machigai o naoshite kudasai. 8 Kono o-kashi wa amasugiru to omoimasen ka. 9 Kootsuu jiko o/wa keisatsu ni todokenakereba naranai n' desu yo. 10 Shingoo (no tokoro) o migi ni magatte kudasaimasen ka

EXERCISE 15

A 1 Rajio no nyuusu o kikinagara asa gohan o tabemashita. 2 O-kane o setsuyaku shiyoo to omotte imasu. 3 Nandomo renraku suru yoo ni tanonda no ni denwa o shite kuremasen deshita. 4 Terebi ga kowareta no de kinoo shuuri ni dashimashita. 5 Ashita sakkaa no shiai ga arimasu kara mi ni ikoo to omotte imasu. 6 Tabako o suinagara shoodan o shimashita. 7 Shuumatsu na no ni kaigan wa amari konde imasen. 8 Basu de ojiisan no suwaru tokoro ga nakatta no de seki o yuzette agemashita. 9 Kami ya inku nado o kaoo to omotte imasu. 10 Tanabe sensei wa kaigishitsu ni irassharu no dewa nai ka to omoimasu.

B 1 de/no, ni. 2 de, ni n', ja, ka. 3 yoru, suzushiku, soo. 4 to, suru, ni. 5 kara, hazu/koro, to. 6 na, de, yari/age. 7 Tabenagara, no, wa. 8 shiyoo, tokoro. 9 o, no, ni, nakatta. 10 o, moraitai/itadakitai.

C 1 Please tell me where I should change. 2 My eldest son wants to go to the zoo, but I want to go fishing. 3 This place is humid in summer, but the cool breeze from the sea is a great help. 4 Please try some. I hope you like it. 5 Are you still hungry? You've just eaten! 6 Michiko wanted something sweet so I bought her some cakes. 7 I borrowed a book on the art of the Heian period from the library. 8 I don't know anything about the ancient history of Japan so I'm thinking of studying it up a bit. 9 I think perhaps this is Mr Suzuki's first group tour. 10 Well, if you insist, thank you very much.

D 1 Sakki setsumei shita bakari na no ni mada wakaranai to itte imasu. 2 Soko ni otoshita yubiwa o hirotte kudasaimasen ka. 3 Kisha o norikaenakute mo ii to omoimasu. 4 Kondo no shuumatsu ni sakkaa no shiai o mi ni ikoo to omotte imasu. 5 Choonan wa watashi ni sebiro o katte moraitagatta ga takasugimashita. 6 Kanojo wa itsumo hajimete hito ni au toki hazukashigarimasu. 7 O-sake o nomu mae ni kanpai to iimashita. 8 Kore wa hijoo ni ookina suupaa desu ga/na no ni, koko no shokuryoo wa amari shinsen ja nai n' ja nai ka ka to omoimasu. 9 Watashi ga jimusho de hookokusho o kaite iru aida ni anata wa kissaten de shoodan o shita hoo ga ii desu. 10 Kono zubon wa seeru de katta no ni kanari takakatta desu.

EXERCISE 16

A 1 Piano o hiitari zasshi o yondari shimashita. 2 Yama ni nobottari umi de oyoidari shiyoo to omotte imasu. 3 Naosemasu ga takaku tsukimasu yo. 4 Minna de o-sake o nondari uta o utattari warattari shimashita. 5 Kurabu no kaiin ni naremasen. 6 Sakura no hana wa mada saite inai rashii desu. 7 Mukoo ni tatte iru hito wa omawarisan no yoo desu. 8 Nihongo ga hanasemasu ka. 9 Yoru anmari yoku nemurenai yoo desu. 10 Kaette kuru no ga hayakattari osokattari desu.

B 1 ni, mieru, to. 2 kitari, kitari, suru. 3 ga, shitari, ga, kikoetari, shite. 4 na, no. 5 o, nurinaoseba. 6 de, ni, shite, o. 7 iru, sagasoo. 8 shitari, kaketari, desu. 9 o, kaeru, o, desu. 10 wa, to, soo/yoo.

C 1 It's ridiculous these days how either restaurants are too expensive or the food is bad. 2 It seems she is in a hurry to get married and settle down. 3 This place looks as if it would have very beautiful coloured leaves in autumn, doesn't it? 4 That doesn't seem to be a very good strategy. 5 When do you have to finish writing the book? 6 It's fun all playing our guitars and singing songs together, isn't it? 7 That baby looks as if it is going to burst into tears any minute. 8 It seems in Japan, when you are looking for an address and can't find it, if you ask at the police box they'll tell you where it is. 9 Don't you feel occasionally you'd like to try getting in a yacht and going off to a distant island somewhere? 10 It seems as if strange people are always coming to the Abes' parties.

D 1 Eigo o itsu naraihajimemashita ka. 2 Sora ga nishi kara kumoridashite kite ame ga furisoo desu. 3 Suutsukeesu o o-mochi shimashoo ka. 4 Watashi wa e o kaitari omocha o tsukuttari suru no ga suki desu. 5 Tooku ni mieru ano chiisana o-tera no hoo e arukihajimemashoo. 6 O-tetsudai shimashoo ka. 7 Tanakasan wa ooki na Amerika no jidoosha o kaimashita ga zannennagara shako ni hairimasen. 8 Gozenchuu heya o sooji shitari hon o seiri shitari shite sugoshimashita. 9 Watashitachi/Uchi wa Nihon kara kikai o yunyuu shitari Yooroppa e niku ya sakana o yushutsu shitari suru chiisa na booeki-gaisha desu. 10 Kanji wa yomemasen ga hiragana to katakana wa kakemasu.

EXERCISE 17

A 1 Matsumoto san no shoosetsu wa oozei no hito ni yomarete imasu. 2 Doroboo ni hairarete hooseki o nusumaremashita. 3 Utsukushii ishi ga mitsukarimashita. 4 Kodomo wa oya ni shikararemashita. 5 Koozui de hashi ga nagasaremashita kara moo kawa o wataremasen. 6 Kono niku wa katakute watashi no yoo na ha no nai toshiyori ni wa taberaremasen. 7 Saifu o surareta n' desu. 8 Ooki na torakku de nimotsu ga hakobarete kimashita. 9 Nezumi wa neko ni korosaremashita. 10 Hisho ni yamerarete komatte imasu.

B 1 no, furare. 2 wa, kara, kudasai. 3 wa, no, ni, koto, ni. 4 ni, o. 5 toki/ba'ai, doo. 6 na, yasui. 7 na, o, de. 8 ga, to, o. 9 korarete. 10 wa, yaku.

C 1 As that is a policy which was decided while I was away I don't know much about it. 2 I heard you are going to the temple on top of the mountain tomorrow. Would you mind if I joined you? 3 It was a pity the pottery I wanted to buy was bought by somebody else before me. 4 It's unpleasant being a soldier as you are always being ordered about by your superiors. 5 I was advised to study Japanese. 6 May I have a look at the old Chinese vase you have, sir? 7 It seems he is scolded more [often] than he is praised. 8 This bridge looks as if it would be washed away if the heavy rains brought on a flood. 9 I've set the alarm clock so I can get up early tomorrow. 10 As you know, this town is renowned for its pottery.

D 1 Nihon no rekishi no hon o karite mo ii desu ka. 2 Sumie o kaku no wa muzukashii desu ka. 3 Kare wa donna ni muzukashii shitsu-mon o sarete mo taitei kotaeraremasu. 4 Kono jidoosha wa taihen unten shiyasui desu ne. 5 Taisetsu na yooji ga atta n' desu ga tomodachi ni totsuzen korarete dekimasen deshita. 6 Watashi ga otoshita pasupooto wa hirowarete taishikan ni okurareta yoo desu. 7 Sakura no tonari ni bara o uerareru to omoimasu ka. 8 Kankoku de tooki o kau yoo ni susumeraremashita. 9 Zutsuu no tame kaigi ni deraremasen deshita. 10 Mangaichi asu ame ni furaretara pikunikku o yamete eiga o mi ni itte mo ii desu.

EXERCISE 18

A 1 Musume ni ichiba e kudamono ya yasai o kai ni ikasemashita. 2 Kodomo ni niwa no teire o sasemashita. 3 Nikuya ni niku o haitatsu sasemashita. 4 Sakaya ni biiru o ichidaasu todokesasemashita. 5 Ano kutsuya ni kono kaban o naosasemashita. 6 Sanjikan han mo matasaremashita. 7 Ano wakamono ni wakarasemashita. 8 Chichi o okorasemashita. 9 Iranai mono o kawasaremashita. 10 Konban shichiji goro o-jama sasete itadakimasu.

B 1 wa, shi, mo, kara. 2 dake, kudasai. 3 kara, na, moratte/itadaite. 4 wa, asobi. 5 de, tabesaserarete, mo. 6 ni, o, kara. 7 wa, kara, kudasai. 8 toki, o, kikasete kuremashita. 9 o, tobashite, wa. 10 shi, mo, kara.

C 1 When I was a child I was often made to sing folk songs in front of my parents' friends. 2 My husband smokes thirty cigarettes a day so it is exceedingly difficult to get him to give it up. 3 This is a very good spot for a holiday. The view is good and the air is clean. 4 I'll drop in tomorrow to see how you are. 5 Would there be any objection to my excusing myself/going home before you? 6 Mr Ono amused the children with the toys and made the adults laugh with his jokes. 7 Let me smell [the fragrance of] that rose perfume. 8 This building is poorly ventilated and doesn't get much sun. 9 It's a nuisance getting them to bring it so I'm thinking of going to get it myself. 10 This is the first time I have been privileged to use such a good one/thing.

D 1 Honda san no paatii ni musume o tsurete itte mo sashitsukae arimasen ka. 2 Shigoto mo owatta shi kodomo mo nekaseta kara, shibaraku (no aida) terebi o miyoo to omoimasu. 3 Nihon no booeki-gaisha ni tsutomete ita go-keiken o kikasete kudasai. 4

Sakanaya ni denwa shite ika o gohyaku guramu todokesasete kudasai. 5 O-suki na dake (takusan) zasshi o karite kudasai. 6 Musuko wa kuruma o tobasu no ga suki desu ga hijoo ni abunai no de yamesaseyoo to shite imasu. 7 Watashi wa imooto ni jibun no tanjoobi no purezento o erabasemashita. 8 Kani wa watashi o daidokoro ni hairasete kuremasen. 9 Go-enryo nasaranaide kudasai. 10 O-saki ni o-furo ni hairasete itadakimsau.

EXERCISE 19

A 1 Kyoo wa taihen samuu gozaimasu. 2 Chotto o-kiki shitai koto ga arimasu ga yoroshii desu ka. 3 Nihon Keizai Shinbun o o-yomi ni narimasu ka. 4 Kinoo o-meshi ni natte ita/irasshatta ooba o dochira de o-motome/o-kai ni narimashita ka. 5 Sakki sono hanashi o Suzuki san kara ukagaimashita/o-ukagai shimashita. 6 Yuube no atsumari de Nakamura sensei ni o-ai shimashita/o-me ni kakarimashita. 7 Nochihodo mairimasu. 8 Donata de irasshaimasu ka. 9 Nanbei ni sunde irasshatta toki ni wa donna mono o meshiagarimashita ka. 10 Kono uwagi ga o-ki ni meshimashita ka.

B 1 de, o-motome ni narimashita. 2 go-, nasatte. 3 iretai, o-yori ni narimasen ka. 4 ukagatte. 5 san, ari. 6 o-kaki ni natta. 7 mie, desu. 8 meshiagari. 9 irasshaimasu, isogashuu. 10 yasumi, ni naru, ikaga.

C 1 Did you see the exhibition of antiques of the Meiji period? 2 Excuse me, but are you the headmaster? 3 As I explained before we shall be presenting you with the report tomorrow, sir. 4 I wonder if I might borrow this ashtray for a moment? 5 I saw/read your letter. 6 Sorry I bothered you just now. 7 I hear Mr Abe's father passed away the year before last. 8 Excuse me, but I wonder if you could tell me where the town hall is? 9 Is the typewriter you bought the other day working well? 10 You must have been disappointed that not as many people came as you had expected.

D 1 Kono uwagi o o-meshi ni natte mite kudasai. 2 Onamae wa nan to osshaimasu ka. 3 Go-zonji no yoo ni/Go-shoochi no toori saikin wa bukka ga dondon agatte kimashita. 4 Taitei nanji ni o-yasumi ni narimasu ka. 5 Tanaka kyooju ga Kokuren de enzetsu suru to yuu no wa hontoo desu ka. 6 Shachoo ni nochihodo go-setsumei itashimasu. 7 Kyooju wa gakusei no kangaekata ga o-ki ni mesanakatta soo desu. 8 Booshi o o-wasure ni naranaide kudasai. 9 Otooto ga myoonichi no ban rokuji ni o-ukagai shimasu/ ukagawasete itadakimasu. 10 Chichi ga yoroshiku to mooshite orimasu.

EXERCISE 20

A 1 Anata wa bungaku ni kyoomi o motte irasshaimasu ka. 2 Kono sukiyaki no aji wa ikaga desu ka. 3 Itsuka uchi e asobi ni irasshatte kudasai. 4 Watashi wa daigaku de butsurigaku o senkoo shiyoo to omotte imasu. 5 Kawa ni gomi o sutenaide kudasai. 6 Ka ni ashi o sasaremashita. 7 O-naka ga sukimashita. 8 Furoba ni sekken ga arimasen deshita kara musume ni yakkyoku e kai ni ikasemashita. 9 Zashiki ni agaru mae ni genkan de kutsu o nuganakute wa ikemasen yo. 10 Shoorai kagakusha ka seijika ni naritai to itte imasu.

B 1 ike, sareta. 2 ga, itakute, nemuremasen. 3 ya, iru, nikui. 4 mo, moraemasen. 5 wa, shita, kara, na/ni, hanasemasu. 6 ni, nara, tai/ tagaru. 7 kara, nakute, naide, o. 8 ni, mo, nai. 9 na, no, ni, o. 10 no, de, ni, ga.

C 1 All this time I've been unable to get out of the house because of the rain, so I'm dying to go for a walk or something. 2 Blast! I promised to ring a friend, but I've left my notebook with his telephone number in it at home. 3 I was told to boil the water and make tea. 4 Since I've become a first-year high school student I've got a lot of subjects [to study] and the amount of homework has increased terribly. 5 This is a terribly dangerous spot because the visibility is poor. 6 Nothing can be done about it now so don't worry about it. 7 Can you eat oysters and prawns and so on? 8 They say when he was young he was interested in communism and that he has even been a member of the Communist Party. 9 I heard a voice crying, 'Help!' 10 I'm this fit because I exercise for thirty minutes each morning and night.

D 1 Shimatta! Kindokei o nakushite shimaimashita. 2 Hayaku omocha o katazukete shinshitsu ni aru hako ni chanto irenasai. 3 Tabemono ni tsuite monku o yuu na to itta no ni. 4 Kyoo gakkoo de nani o osowatta no. 5 Yuube kabutte irasshatta momoiro no booshi wa yoku o-niai deshita yo. 6 Mata aete ureshikute tamarimasen deshita. 7 Tomare! Doroboo da! Saifu o kaese! 8 Ooku no Nihonjin wa bukkyoo to shintoo o dooji ni shinjite iru soo desu. 9 Kono hako no bin no kazu o shiraberu yoo ni iwaremashita. 10 Hakkiri omoidasemasen ga sore wa tabun sensoo ga owatta tsugi no toshi deshita.

NUMBERS AND NUMERAL CLASSIFIERS

	1 2	3 4	5 6	7 8	9 10	100 ?
-bai times as much	ichibai nibai	sanbai yonbai	gobai rokubai	nanabai hachibai	kyuubai juubai	hyakubai nanbai
-ban number, ordinals	ichíban níban	sanban yonban	goban rokúban	nanában hachíban	kyúuban júuban	hyakúban nánban
-ban nights	hitóban futában	míban yóban	—— ——	—— ——	—— ——	 nánban
-bun part, fraction	ichibun nibun	sanbun yonbun	gobun rokubun	nanabun hachibun	kubun juubun	hyakubun nanbun
-byoo seconds	ichíbyoo níbyoo	sánbyoo yónbyoo	góbyoo rokúbyoo	nanábyoo hachíbyoo	kúbyoo júubyoo	hyakubyoo nánbyoo
-chakú suits, outfits	itchakú nichakú	sanchakú yonchakú	gochakú rokuchakú	nanachakú hatchakú	kyuuchakú jutchakú	hyakuchakú nanchakú
-dáasu dozens	ichidáasu nidáasu	sandáasu yondáasu	godáasu rokudáasu	nanadáasu hachidáasu	kyuudáasu juudáasu	hyakudáasu nándáasu
-dai vehicles, machines	ichídai nídai	sándai yóndai	gódai rokúdai	nanádai hachídai	kyúudai júudai	hyakúdai nándai
-dan grades, steps	ichídan nídan	sandan yondan	godan rokúdan	shichídan hachídan	kyúudan júudan	hyakudan nándan
-dó times	ichidó nidó	sandó yondó	godó rokudó	nanadó hachidó	kudó juudó	hyakudó nandó

	1	2	3	4	5	6	7	8	9	10	100	?
-do degrees, °C, °F	ichído	nído	sándo	yóndo	gódo	rokúdo	nanádo	hachído	kúdo	júudo	hyakúdo	nándo
-en yen	ichien	nien	san'en	yon'en	goen	rokuen	nanaen	hachien	kyuuen	juuen	hyakuen	nan'en
-fun fun	íppun	nífun	sánpun	yónpun	gófun	róppun	nanáfun	háppun	kyúufun	júppun	hyáppun	nánpun
-gatsú names of months	ichigatsú	nigatsú	sangatsú	shigatsú	gogatsú	rokugatsú	shichigatsú	hachigatsú	kugatsú	juugatsú		nangatsu
-gúramu grams	ichigúramu	nigúramu	sangúramu	yongúramu	gogúramu	roku-gúramu	nana-gúramu	hachi-gúramu	kyuu-gúramu	juu-gúramu	hyaku-gúramu	nan-gúramu
-hai cupfuls, glasses	íppai	níhai	sánbai	yónhai	góhai	róppai	nanáhai	háppai	kyúuhai	júppai	hyáppai	nánbai
-hĭki animals	ippíkí	níhĭki	sánbikĭ	yónhĭki	góhĭki	roppĭkí	nanáhĭki	happíkí	kyúuhĭki	juppĭkí	hyappikí	nánbikĭ
-hen number of times	ippén	nihén	sanbén	yonhén	gohén	roppén	nanahén	happén	kyuuhén	juppén	hyappén	nánben
-hon cylindrical objects	íppon	níhon	sánbon	yónhon	gohon	róppon	nanáhon	háppon	kyúuhon	júppon	hyáppon	nánbon
-hyakú hundreds	hyakú	nihyakú	sánbyakú	yónhyakú	gohyakú	roppyakú	nanáhyakú	happyakú	kyúuhyakú	—	—	nánbyakú
-ji o'clock	ichíji	níji	sánji	yóji	góji	rokúji	shĭchíji	hachíji	kúji	júuji		nánji
-juu tens	júu	níjuu	sánjuu	yónjuu	gojúu	rokujúu	nanájuu	hachijúu	kyúujuu	—	—	nánjuu
-ka lessons	íkka	níka	sánka	yónka	góka	rókka	nanáka	hákka	kyúuka	júkka	hyákka	nánka
-ka/-nichi days	ichinichi	fŭtsuka	mikka	yokka	itsŭka	muika	nanoka	yooka	kokonoka	tooka	hyakunichi	nannichi
-kái number of times	ikkái	nikái	sankái	yonkái	gokái	rokkái	nanakái	hakkái	kyuukái	jukkái	hyakkái	nankái
-kai storeys, floors	ikkai	nikai	sangai	yonkai	gokai	rokkai	nanakai	hakkai	kyuukai	jukkai	hyakkai	nangai

	1 2	3 4	5 6	7 8	9 10	100 ?
-ken	íkken	sánken	góken	nanáken	kyúuken	hyákken
buildings	níken	yónken	rókken	hákken	júkken	nánken
-ki	íkki	sánki	góki	nanáki	kyúuki	hyákki
aeroplanes	níki	yónki	rókki	hákki	júkki	nánki
-kiro	ich/kiro	sánkiro	gókiro	nanákiro	kyúukiro	hyákkiro
kilogram/	níkiro	yónkiro	rókkiro	hach/kiro	júkkiro	nánkiro
-metre						
-ko	íkko	sánko	góko	nanáko	kyúuko	hyákko
'a piece',	níko	yónko	rókko	hákko	júkko	nánko
boxes, fruit,						
furniture,						
etc., round						
or square						
object						
-mai	ichímai	sánmai	gomai	nanámai	kyúumai	hyakúmai
'sheets',	nímai	yónmai	rokúmai	hachímai	júumai	nánmai
flat objects,						
paper,						
plates,						
shirts, ties,						
etc.						
-mán	ichimán	sanmár	gomán	nanamán	kyuumán	hyakumán
ten-	nimán	yonmán	rokumán	hachimán	juumán	nanmán
thousands						
-nen	ichínen	sannen	gonen	shichínen	kunen	hyakunen
years	nínen	yonen	rokúnen	hachínen	júunen	nánnen
-nin/-ri	h/tóri	sannin	gonin	shichínin	kunin	hyakunin
people	f/tarí	yonin	rokúnin	hachínin	júunin	nánnin
-sai	íssai	sánsai	gósai	nanásai	kyúusai	hyakʉsai
years of	nísai	yónsai	rokʉsai	hássai	jússai	nánsai
age						
-satsu	issatsú	sánsatsʉ	gósatsʉ	nanásatsʉ	kyúusatsʉ	hyakʉsatsʉ
'volume',	nísatsʉ	yónsatsʉ	rokʉsatsʉ	hassatsú	jussatsú	nánsatsʉ
books						
-seki	issekí	sánsekʉ	gósekʉ	nanásekʉ	kyúusekʉ	hyakʉsekʉ
ships	nísekʉ	yónsekʉ	rokʉseki	hassekí	jussekí	nánseki
-sén	sén	sanzén	gosén	nanasén	kyuusén	——
thousands	nisén	yonsén	rokʉsén	hassén	——	nanzén
-soku	issokú	sánzokʉ	gósokʉ	nanásokʉ	kyúusokʉ	hyakúsoku
'pair'	nísokʉ	yónsokʉ	rokʉsokʉ	hassokú	jussokú	nánzokʉ
shoes, socks						

	1 2	3 4	5 6	7 8	9 10	100 ?
-soo vessels, boats	íssoo nísoo	sánsoo yónsoo	gósoo rokʉsoo	nanásoo hássoo	kyúusoo jússoo	hyakʉsoo nánsoo
-tén points, marks	ittén nitén	santén yontén	gotén rokʉtén	nanatén hattén	kyuutén juttén	hyakʉtén nantén
-too 'head', large animals	íttoo nítoo	sántoo yóntoo	gotoo rokʉtoo	nanátoo háttoo	kyúutoo júttoo	hyakʉtoo nántoo
-tsu miscel- laneous objects, years of age	hʲtótsʉ fʉtatsú	mittsú yottsú	itsútsʉ muttsú	nanátsʉ yattsú	kokónotsʉ tóo	—— íkʉtsu
-tsuu letters	ittsuu nitsuu	santsuu yontsuu	gotsuu rokʉtsuu	nanatsuu hattsuu	kyuutsuu juttsuu	hyakʉtsuu nántsuu
-wa birds	ichíwa níwa	sánba yónwa	gówa róppa	nanáwa hachíwa	kyúuwa júppa	hyáppa nánwa

NOTES

1 In the above table *yon-* and *nana-* have been used for 4 and 7 where possible, though in most cases *shi-* and *shĮchi-* can be used instead. With 9 the form which first sprang to mind has been chosen. *Ku-* and *kyuu-* are often not interchangeable, so use the form given here, but be prepared to hear the other as well. In the interrogative expressions it is always possible to place an accent on the first syllable instead of using the accent shown here. For 8 it is usually possible to use the full form *hachi-* instead of the forms with a double consonant.

2 *-jíkan*, 'hours duration'; *-jóo* '*tatami*, mats, unit of room size'; *-meetoru*, 'metres'; *-paasénto*, 'per cent'; *-péeji*, 'pages'; *-póndo*, 'pounds' undergo no sound changes or shift of accent; *-kágetsʉ*, 'months duration', retains its accent, but has double consonants in combination with 1, 6, 8, 10 and 100; *-sénchi*, 'centimetres' and *-shúukan*, 'weeks duration', retain their original accent, but double the consonant in 1, 8 and 10; *-doru*, 'dollars', is unaccented and follows the pattern of *-dai*.

APPENDIX 2

SUMMARY OF THE VERB, ADJECTIVE AND COPULA

VERB

Suffixes attached to the root[1]

Suffix	Accented consonant root *kák-* 'to write'	Unaccented consonant root *ka(w)-*[3] 'to buy'	Accented vowel root *tábe-* 'to eat'	Unaccented vowel root *ake-* 'to open'	Irregular *su-/shi-* 'to do'	verbs *kú-/kó-* 'to come'
Indeclinable[2]						
-(r)u present	káku	kau	táberu	akeru	suru	kúru
-(r)éba conditional	kákeba	kaéba	tabéreba	akeréba	suréba	kúreba
-(y)óo propositive/ conjectural	kakóo	kaóo	tabeyóo	akeyóo	shiyóo	kóyoo
-e brusque imperative	káke	kaé	——	——	——	(koi)
-ro/-yo brusque imperative	——	——	tabéro/ tabéyo	akeró/ akeyo	shiró/ séyo	
Declinable[4]						
-e- potential	kakéru	kaeru	(uses passive)	(uses passive)	(uses *dekíru*)	(uses passive)
-(r)are- passive	kakaréru	kawareru	taberaréru	akerareru	sareru	koraréru

298

Suffix	Accented consonant root *kák-* 'to write'	Unaccented consonant root *ka(w)-*[3] 'to buy'	Accented vowel root *tábe-* 'to eat'	Unaccented vowel root *ake-* 'to open'	Irregular *su-/shi-* 'to do'	verbs *kú-/kó-* 'to come'
-(s)ase-/ -(s)as- causative	kakaséru	kawaseru	tabesaséru	akesaseru	saseru	kosaséru
-(s)asare-/ -(s)ase- rare- passive of causative	kakasaréru	kawasareru	tabesase- raréru	akesase- raréru	sase- rareru	kosase- rareru
-(a)na- negative	kakánai	kawanai	tabénai	akenai	shinai	kónai

Suffixes attached to the stem[5]

Suffix	Accented consonant stem *káki-*	Unaccented consonant stem *kai-*	Accented vowel stem *tábe-*	Unaccented vowel stem *ake-*	Irregular *shi-*	verbs *ki-*
Indeclinable[2] (none) connective	káki	kai	tábe	ake	shi	ki
-nagara 'while'	kakinágara	kainagara	tabenágara	akenagara	shinagara	kinágara
-te[6] gerund	káite	katte	tábete	akete	shíte	kíte
-ta[6] past	káita	katta	tábeta	aketa	shíta	kíta
-tári[6] frequent- ative	káitari	kattári	tábetari	aketári	shítári	kítari
-tára condi- tional	káitara	kattára	tábetara	aketára	shítára	kítara
-nasái impera- tive	kakinasái	kainasái	tabenasái	akenasái	shinasái	kinasái
-soo (da) 'look as if some- thing will happen'	kakisóo	kaisoo	tabesóo	akesoo	shísoo	kísóo

Suffix	Accented consonant stem *káki-*	Unaccented consonant stem *kai-*	Accented vowel stem *tábe-*	Unaccented vowel stem *ake-*	Irregular *shi-*	verbs *ki-*
-*kata* 'way of . . . -ing'	kakikatá	kaikata	tabekatá	akekata	shị́kata	kị́katá
Declinable						
-*más-* polite address	kakimásụ	kaimásụ	tabemásụ	akemásụ	shimásụ	kimásụ
o- . . . *ni nár-* subject honorific	o-kaki ni náru	o-kai ni náru	o-tabe ni náru	o-ake ni náru	——	(o-ide ni náru)
o- . . . *suru* object honorific	o-kaki suru	——	——	o-ake suru (?)	——	——
-*owár-* etc.) compound verbs	kakiowáru	kaiowáru	tabeowáru	——	——	——
-*ta-* desider-ative	kakitái	kaitai	tabetái	aketai	shị́tai	kị́tái
-*yasú-* 'easy to'	kakiyasúi	kaiyasúi	tabeyasúi	akeyasúi	shiyasúi	kiyasúi
-*nikú-* 'difficult to . . .'	kakinikúi	kainikúi	tabenikúi	akenikúi	shinikúi	kinikúi

Notes

1 Suffixes with an initial consonant lose that consonant when the root ends in a consonant. Suffixes with an initial vowel lose that vowel when the root ends in a vowel.

2 The indeclinable suffixes come at the end of the verb and have no further suffixes attached to them. They may, however, be followed by clause-final or sentence-final particles.

3 The root consonant -*w* is written only before *a*.

4 The declinable suffixes occur in combination with other suffixes. Here they appear in the examples combined with the present-tense suffix, -*(r)u* for suffix verbs and -*i* for suffix adjectives.

5 The stem is formed by adding -*i* to the root of consonant-root verbs, but

verbs with final -t and -s have stems in -chi and -shi respectively. With vowel-root verbs the stem is the same as the root.

6 These suffixes fuse with the stem undergoing sound changes according to the final consonant of the root. Showing the final consonant of the root and the initial consonant of the suffix, the changes are: -kit- ——— -it-, -git- ——— -id-, -chit- ———-tt-, -rit- ——— -tt-, -(w)it- ——— -tt-, -nit-, -nd-, -mit- ——— -nd-, -bit- ——— -nd-. Stems of vowel-root verbs and consonant-root verbs in -s (stem ends in -shi) add the suffixes directly to the stem.

ADJECTIVE

Suffix	Accented root *taká-* 'high'	Unaccented root *aka-* 'red'
-i present	takái	akai
-ku adverbial	tákaku	akaku
-ku nái negative	tákaku nai	akaku nái
-kyte gerund	tákakyte	akákyte
-katta past	tákakatta	akákatta
-kattara conditional 1	tákakattara	akákattara
-kereba conditional 2	tákakereba	akákereba

The forms given here are those accepted as standard Tokyo pronunciation, but even in Tokyo there is a tendency for younger speakers to pronounce all accented forms with the accent on the final vowel of the root.

THE COPULA

	Plain	Polite
Present	dá[1]	désu̧
Past	dátta	déshi̧ta
Conditional	dáttara	déshi̧tara
Conjectural	daróo	deshóo
Gerund	de	(déshi̧te)[2]
Negative	de (wa) nái	de (wa) arimasén
	ja nái	ja arimasén

Notes

1 The formal copula *de áru*, which follows the pattern of *áru* may occur in either the plain or polite styles, but in spoken Japanese its use is largely confined to speech-making.

2 This form is used where extremely polite language is called for. *De* is usually sufficient.

APPENDIX 3

PARTICLES

PHRASE FINAL PARTICLES (CASE PARTICLES)

(The numbers in brackets refer to the lessons in which the particle is introduced.)

wa	topic, 'speaking of', 'as for'	(3, 12)
ga	subject; object of stative verb or adjective	(4, 12)
o	direct object; 'through', 'along'	(2, 10)
no	possessive, '. . . .'s'	(3)
ni	indirect object, 'to'; 'in'; agent in passive, 'by'	(2, 4, 17)
mo	'too', 'also', 'even'	(2)
e	direction to, 'to', 'towards'	(2)
de	place of action, 'in', 'at'	(2)
	instrument, 'with', 'by means of'	(3)
kara	'from'	(3)
máde	'up to', 'until'	(5)
daké	'only', 'as many as', 'as much as'	(4)
to	'with', 'and'	(4, 5)
tóka	'and (so on)'	(5)
nádo	'(and) so on', 'et cetera'	(5)
ya	'and'	(5)
ka	'or'	(5)

CLAUSE FINAL PARTICLES (CONJUNCTIONS)

ga, keredomo (keredo, kedo, etc.)	'but', 'however', 'although'	(7)
kara	'because'	(7)

to	'whenever', 'when', 'if'	(10)
nára	'if'	(13)
no ni	'although', 'in spite of the fact that'	(15)
no de	'because'	(15)
to	quotation, 'thus', 'that' (verbs of saying, thinking, knowing, believing, etc.)	(13)
máe ni	'before'	(10)
(-te) wa	'if'	(9)
(-te) mo	'even if'	(9)
(-te) kara	'after'	(10)

SENTENCE FINAL PARTICLES

ka	interrogative, '?'	(1)
né (née, ná, náa)	calling for confirmation, 'isn't it?', etc.	(2)
yo	emphatic, '!'	(2)
zo	very emphatic (masculine)	(20)
ze	very emphatic (masculine)	(20)
sa	assertive (masculine)	(20)
wa	soft (feminine)	(20)
no	soft (feminine)	(20)
kke	retrospective	(20)

APPENDIX 4

THE DEMONSTRATIVES

	Noun	Place	Direction	One of two	Adjective	Kind	of	Adverb
this	kore	koko	kochira	kotchí	kono	konna,	koo yuu	koo
that	sore	soko	sochira	sotchí	sono	sonna,	soo yuu	soo
that (over there)	are	asoko	achira	atchí	ano	anna,	aa yuu	aa
which who	dóre dáre	dóko	dóchira	dótchi	dóno	dónna,	dóo yuu	dóo
who (honorific)	dónata							ikága 'how'
what	náni							(honorific)

INTERROGATIVES AND INDEFINITES

dáre
'who'

dáreka
'someone'

dáremo
'no one'

dáredemo
'anyone at all'

náni
'what'

nánika
'something'

nánimo
'nothing'

nándemo
'anything at all'

dóko
'where'

dókoka
'somewhere'

dókomo
'nowhere'

dókodemo
'anywhere at all'

dóre
'which'

dóreka
'one'

dóremo
'none'

dóredemo
'any one at all'

íkɯtsu
'how many'

íkɯtsɯka
'a few'

íkɯtsumo
'very few'

íkɯtsudemo
'any number at all'

APPENDIX 5

THE JAPANESE SYLLABARIES

1 Hiragana[1]

あ a	い i	う u	え e	お o	や ya	ゆ yu	よ yo
か ka	き ki	く ku	け ke	こ ko	きゃ kya	きゅ kyu	きょ kyo
が ga	ぎ gi	ぐ gu	げ ge	ご go	ぎゃ gya	ぎゅ gyu	ぎょ gyo
さ sa	し shi	す su	せ se	そ so	しゃ sha	しゅ shu	しょ sho
ざ za	じ ji	ず zu	ぜ ze	ぞ zo	じゃ ja	じゅ ju	じょ jo
た ta	ち chi	つ tsu	て te	と to	ちゃ cha	ちゅ chu	ちょ cho
だ da	ぢ (ji)	づ (zu)	で de	ど do			
な na	に ni	ぬ nu	ね ne	の no	にゃ nya	にゅ nyu	にょ nyo
は ha	ひ hi	ふ fu	へ he	ほ ho	ひゃ hya	ひゅ hyu	ひょ hyo

ば	び	ぶ	べ	ぼ	びゃ	びゅ	びょ
pa	pi	pu	pe	po	pya	pyu	pyo
ば	び	ぶ	べ	ぼ	びゃ	びゅ	びょ
ba	bi	bu	be	bo	bya	byu	byo
ま	み	む	め	も	みゃ	みゅ	みょ
ma	mi	mu	me	mo	mya	myu	myo
ら	り	る	れ	ろ	りゃ	りゅ	りょ
ra	ri	ru	re	ro	rya	ryu	ryo
わ							
wa							
							ん
							n

2 Katakana[2] (basic symbols only)

ア	イ	ウ	エ	オ
a	i	u	e	o
カ	キ	ク	ケ	コ
ka	ki	ku	ke	ko
サ	シ	ス	セ	ソ
sa	shi	su	se	so
タ	チ	ツ	テ	ト
ta	chi	tsu	te	to
ナ	ニ	ヌ	ネ	ノ
na	ni	nu	ne	no
ハ	ヒ	フ	ヘ	ホ
ha	hi	fu	he	ho
マ	ミ	ム	メ	モ
ma	mi	mu	me	mo

ヤ		ユ		ヨ
ya		yu		yo

ラ	リ	ル	レ	ロ
ra	ri	ru	re	ro

ワ				
wa				

				ン
				n

NOTES

1 The 103 syllables which may occur in Japanese are given here. (*ji*) and (*zu*) occur in a small number of words, in which original *chi* or *tsu* become voiced when they occur in a compound; e.g., *hana*, 'nose', plus *chi*, 'blood', combine to form *hanaji*, 'bleeding nose'. As there is no difference in pronunciation between *ji* and (*ji*) no distinction is made in the romanization.

2 The *Katakana* chart gives only the 45 basic symbols in the usual Japanese order. The mnemonic, 'A katakana syllabary, think now how much you really want (to learn it)', should help you get the five vowels and ten consonants in the right order. *N* is the only sound in the chart which does not have an accompanying vowel. It is used for writing *n* at the end of syllables, as in sa*n* and shinbu*n*. The remaining *katakana* syllables are formed with the same diacritics used in the *hiragana* chart, or in combination with the *katakana* signs for ya, yu and yo.

The long vowels are written with two *kana* (a term encompassing both syllabaries) signs, usually simply by adding the appropriate vowel sign to the first syllable, but long *o* (*oo*) is usually written with the vowel *u* as its final element.

The first element of a double consonant (other than double *n*) is indicated by the sign for *tsu*, written smaller to show it does not have its full pronunciation. The first consonant in a double *n* sequence (-*nn*-) is the *kana* symbol for *n*.

In general *katakana* is used for writing words borrowed from foreign languages other than Chinese, *hiragana* is used for writing particles, grammatical inflections and words with difficult or uncommon Chinese characters, and Chinese characters are used for writing most nouns and the roots of verbs and adjectives.

In the charts above the combined syllables (*kya*, *kyu*, *kyo*, etc.) appear as they would in vertical writing running down the page from right to left. Both horizontal and vertical writing are common.

JAPANESE–ENGLISH VOCABULARY

Numbers after grammatical items refer to pages where the form is explained: hon. = honorific.

áa: Ah! (exclam.)
abunai: dangerous, Watch out!
achira: over there, that way
Afurika: Africa
agaru: to go up, rise, enter (Japanese house); eat (hon.)
agemásu: see *ageru*
ageru: to give, raise up
agó: chin
ái suru: to love
aida: between, interval, gap
aimásu: see *áu*
áisatsu: greeting
aiyoo suru: to use regularly, be a regular customer
aji: taste, flavour
Ájia: Asia
ajisai: hydrangea
ákachan: baby
akai: red
akanboo: baby
akarui: light, bright
akeru: to open

áki: autumn
akimásu: see *aku*
akusu: sneak thief
akú: to come open, open (intrans.)
amai: sweet
amari/anmari: very, a lot; (not) very
amasugíru: too sweet
ame: sweet, candy
áme: rain
Amerikájin: American
-(a)nai: negative suffix
-(a)naide: negative suffix, without 138, 143
-(a)nakereba narimasen: must . . . , have to . . . 169
-(a)nakute: negative suffix 138, 143
anata: you
ane: elder sister
áni: elder brother
anmari: see *amari*

anna: that kind of

annai suru: to guide, show around

ano: that (over there) 64

anóhḷto: he 38

anóhḷtotachi: they 38

anóko: he (child) 38

anokatá: he (hon.) 38

anokatágata: they (hon.) 38

anshin suru: be free from worry

anzen na: safe, secure

anzen-kámisori: safety razor

aói: blue, green

apáato: (rented) flat

arau: to wash

are: that (over there) 37

arígatoo: thank you

arimásu̥: *see áru*

áru: to be (located somewhere); to have 48, 72

áru: a certain

arukimásu̥: *see arúku*

arukitsuzukéru: to keep on walking

arúku: to walk

áru téido: to a certain extent

ása: morning

asa-góhan: breakfast

asátte: the day after tomorrow

-aseru: *see -saseru*

ashí: leg, foot

ashḷta: tomorrow

asobu: to play, have free time

asoko: over there

asu: tomorrow

ataeru: to give

atamá: head

atarashíi: new

atashi: I (feminine)

atatakái: warm

atchí: that way, over there

áto: later, afterward; remains

áto de: after

atsúryoku: pressure

attakái: warm

au: to meet, come together, fit; *ma ni áu*: to be in time (for = *ni*); to be enough

awaséru: to bring together

-(a)zu: negative suffix 237

báa: bar

ba'ai: occasion, time, if, when 225

bakágeta koto: stupid thing, ridiculous thing

bakarashíi: foolish, stupid

bákari: only, to the extent of

ban: night, evening

ban-góhan: dinner, evening meal

bangóo: number

bangumí: (radio, TV) programme

-bánsen: track number

bara: rose

basho: place

básu̥: bus

basu-nóriba: bus terminal (depot), bus station

basu̥tei: bus stop

báta/bátaa: butter

bengóshi: lawyer, solicitor

benkyoo suru: to study

bénri na: convenient, useful

betsu na/no: separate, different, another

betsu ni: in particular

bíiru: beer
bíjutsu: art
bijutsukan: art gallery
bín: bottle
bínboo na: poor
bíru: building
bóku: I 262
booeki-gáisha: trading company
boosan: Buddhist priest
booshi: hat, cap
-bu: copy (of document)
-bu: section (of company, etc.)
bukka: prices
búkkyoo: Buddhism
bún: share, part
bunbóoguya: stationer('s)
búngaku: literature
bunpoo: grammar
buta: pig
butsurigaku: physics
byooin: hospital
byooki: illness, disease
byooki no: sick, ill

cha: tea (*see o-cha*)
-chaku: suit, outfit (numeral, classifier)
chanto: properly
-chau: *see -te shimau*
chawan: rice bowl, tea-cup
chi: blood
chíchí: father
chigau: to differ, to be wrong, no
chiisái: small
chíisa na: small
chíizu: cheese
chíkái: near
chíkaku: vicinity, near

chíkará: strength
chíkatetsu: underground railway
-chimau: *see -te shimau* 185
chíri: geography
chízu: map
choodai: please, give me
choodó: exactly, just
chóohoo na: useful, precious
choonán: eldest son
chooshi ga íi: to run well, go smoothly
chótto: a little
-chuu: in the course of
Chúugoku: China
chuumon: to order
chuunen: middle-age

dái: stand, dais
dái: is it? 265
daibu: considerably, very
daidokoro: kitchen
Daiei-hakubutsukan: British Museum
daigaku: university
daigákusei: university student
daihyoo: representative
daijóobu: all right, OK
dáiku: carpenter
dáisuki na: to love, be very fond of
daitai: approximately, for the most part
dákara: so, therefore
daké: only, extent 230
damé: no good, stop it!
dantai-ryókoo: group travel, tour
dáre: who
dáredemo: anyone (at all)

dáreka: someone
dáremo: no one
dashimásʉ: see *dásʉ*
dásʉ: to put out, take out
de: in, at 27
de: 'agent', by means of, with 39
de gozaimásʉ: is (formal) 246
de irassháru: is (hon.) 248
déguchi: exit
dekakeru: to go out
dekimásʉ: see *dekíru*
dekíru: to be done, be ready, be made, be possible
dekiru daké: as much as possible
demásʉ: see *déru*
démo: even
dénki: electricity, light
denpóo: telegram
dénsha: electric train
denshʉkeisánki: computer
denwa: telephone
denwa-bángoo: telephone number
denwachoo: telephone directory
depáato: department store
déru: to go out, come out, appear
deshóo: probably is 100
désʉ: is 36
désʉ kara: therefore, and so
dóa: door
dóchira: which one, where (hon.)
dóchira-sama: who (hon.)
Dóitsu: Germany
dóko: where 32
dónata: who (hon.)
dónata-sama: who (hon.)
dóndon: rapidly, quickly

dónna: what kind of
dóno: which
dono kurai/gurai: how long, how far, how much
dóo: how
dóo itashimashʉte: don't mention it
dóo shimashʉta ka: what happened? What's the matter?
doo shiyoo mo nái: hopeless, impossible
dóo yuu: what kind of
dóo yuu fuu na: what kind of
dóo yuu fuu ni: how, in what way
doobutsʉ: animal
doobutsúen: zoo
dóomo: Thanks! Sorry! very
dóori de: no wonder! That's the reason!
dóoro: road
dooro-hyóoshʉki: road sign
dóose: anyway
dóoshʉte: why, how
dooshʉtémo: no matter what, without fail
dóozo: please
dóozo yoroshʉku: how do you do? Please do what you can for me
doráibu: drive (*suru*), to drive
dóre: which one
doroboo: robber, thief
dótchi: which one
doyóobi: Saturday

é: picture
e: to, toward 27

-e: brusque imperative suffix 266

-eba: see -réba

ebi: prawn, lobster

ée: yes

éeto: let me see

éiga: film, movie

eigákan: cinema

eigo: English

éki: station

én: yen 77

enpĺtsu: pencil

enryo: reserve, holding back

erábĺ: to choose

erebéetaa: lift, elevator

-eru: potential suffix 208

esá: feed, bait

esĺkaréetaa: escalator

fóoku: fork

fúben na: inconvenient

fudé: writing brush

fuéru: to increase

Fújisan: Mt Fuji

fĺku: to wipe

fĺku: to blow

fĺkuzatsu na: complicated

-fun: minutes

funábin: sea mail

fúne: ship, boat

Furansĺ: France

furidásĺ: to start raining

furó: bath

furobá: bathroom

fúru: to fall (rain and snow)

furúi: old

fĺtarí: two (people)

fĺtatsú: two

fĺtorimásĺ: see fĺtóru

fĺtorisugi: too fat

fĺtóru: to get fat

fĺtsĺka: two days, 2nd (of the month)

fĺtsĺkayoi: hangover

fĺtsuu: usual

fĺttobóoru: football

fuyú: winter

ga: subject particle 48, 155

ga: but (clause final particle) 96

gáado: railway arch

gáido: guide

gaijin: foreigner

gaikoku: foreign country, abroad

gaikokújin: foreigner

gakkári suru: to be disappointed

gakkoo: school

gaku: frame

gakĺsei: student

ganbáru: to persevere, stick to a task

ganbátte kudasai: keep at it! Give it all you've got!

garasĺ: glass

-gáru: suffix 198

gásĺ: gas, cooker

-gata: plural suffix (hon.) 38

-gatsú: suffix for naming months

gekijoo: theatre

génkan: entrance hall

génki na: healthy, fit, well

getsuyóobi: Monday

gín: silver

ginkoo: bank

gítaa: guitar

go: five

go . . . désu̜: subject honorific construction 250

go-busata shι̜te imásu̜: I have not been in touch, I have been neglectful

gochisoosama déshita: thank you for the wonderful meal

go-enryo náku, go-enryo nasaránaide kudasai: please don't stand on ceremony, don't just be polite

gógatsu: May

gógo: afternoon

góhan: cooked rice, a meal

go-issho: together, with you (hon.)

go-kúroosama deshι̜ta: thanks for your help

go-kyoodai: brothers and sisters (hon.)

go-méiwaku desu̜ ga: sorry to bother you, but . . .

gomen kudasái: excuse me, anyone home!

gomen nasái: I'm sorry

gomí: rubbish

gomibáko: rubbish bin, dustbin

Góoshuu: Australia

goran kudasái/nasái: please look (hon.)

goran ni ireru: to show (to a respected person – object (hon.)) 250

goran ni náru: to look, see (hon.) 249

górufu: golf

go-shinpai náku: please don't worry

go-shínsetsu ni: (thank you) for your kindness

go-shoochi no yóo ni: as you know

go-shóokai shimásu̜: let me introduce

goshújin: husband (hon.) your husband

go-yóo: business, something to do (hon.)

go-yukkúri: at leisure, slowly (hon.)

gozaimásu̜: is, are (formal) 246, 253

gózen: morning

gozenchuu: all morning, throughout the morning

go-zónji desu̜ ka: do you know?

gurai: about, as . . . as

gúramu: gram (weight)

gyuuniku: beef

gyuunyuu: milk

ha: tooth

haba: width

haba ga hirói: wide

haba ga semái: narrow

hachí: eight

háha: mother

hái: yes

-hai: cupfuls, glassfuls

haiken shι̜temo ii desu̜ ka: may I have a look? (to respected person)

haiken suru: to look at (object hon.)

hairimásu̜: see *háiru*

háiru: to enter, go in, fit

haishaku̜ suru: to borrow (from a respected person)

haitatsu̜ suru: to deliver

haizara: ashtray
hajimaru: to start, begin (intrans.)
hajimemáshḷte: how do you do?
hajimemásↆ: *see hajimeru*
hajimeru: to begin
hajímete no: first
hákase: doctor, PhD.
hakaseru: to put shoes or socks on someone
hakkíri: clearly
hako: box
hakobu: to carry
haku: to wear (shoes, socks, skirt, trousers, etc.)
hakubutsↆkan: museum
hán: half past, -and a half
hana: nose
haná: flower
hanashí: story, talking
hanashimásↆ: *see hanásↆ*
hanásↆ: to speak
hanásↆ: to let go
hanáyome: (new) bride
hanbai-búchoo: sales manager, head of the sales section
hanbún: half
handobággu: handbag
hanga: woodblock-print
hánsamu na: handsome
hanzúbon: shorts
happa: leaf
hará: belly
haráu: to pay
haremásↆ: *see haréru*
haréru: to fine up
háru: spring
haru-yásumi: spring holiday
hasamí: scissors

hashirimásↆ: *see hashíru*
hashíru: to run
hátachi: twenty years old
hatarakimásↆ: *see hataraku*
hataraku: to work
hatsↆka: twenty day
hayái: fast, early, quick
hayashi: forest
hazu: should be, is expected to be 155
hazukashigáru: to act shyly, be shy
hazukashíi: ashamed, shy, embarrassed
Heisei: year period 1989–
hi: day; sun
hí: fire
hiatari: exposure to the sun
hiatari ga íi: to be sunny
hidari: left
hidarigawa: left-hand side
higashí: east
hige: beard, moustache
hige o sóru: to shave
hijoo ni: extremely, very
hḷkidashi: drawer
hḷkóoki: aeroplane
hḷku: to pull; look up (in a dictionary), etc.
hḷku: to catch (a cold)
hḷku: to play (piano, guitar, etc.)
hḷkúi: low, short
hima: spare time
hiraganá: *hiragana* syllabary
hirói: broad, wide, vast
hirú: midday, lunchtime
hirugóhan: lunch
hirumá: daytime

hísho: secretary
hĮto: person, someone else
hitobanjuu: all night
hitogomi: crowd of people
hĮtóri: one person
hĮtóri de: alone, by oneself
hĮtori mo + negative: no one,
   nobody
hĮtótsu̧: one
hĮtsuyoo na: necessary
hiza: knee
hochĮkĮsu̧: (*hotchĮkĮsu̧*): stapler
hodo: extent 146; *V-(r)éba*
   V-(r)u hodo: the more . . .
   the more . . . 170
hodookyoo: pedestrian bridge
hoka: other, another
homéru: to praise
hón: book
-hón: numeral classifier for
   cylindrical objects
hóndana: book shelf, bookcase
hontóo/hontó: true
hón'ya: book shop
hóo: direction, side 120, 145
hoochoo: kitchen knife
hooeichuu: during the film,
   during projection
hookoku̧sho: report
hóomu: railway platform
hooseki: jewel, jewellery
hoosoo: broadcast
hoosoo suru: to broadcast
hoshi: star
hoshigáru: to want, appear to
   want
hoshíi: to want
hosói: thin, fine, narrow
hóteru: hotel

hotóndo: almost (all), nearly
hyakkáten: department store
hyakú: hundred
hyoogen: expression

ichí: one
íchiba: market
ichíban: first, no. 1, most
ichíbu: one part; one copy
ichigó: strawberry
ichinichijuu: all day
ie: house
ie: no
igai to: unexpectedly,
   surprisingly
Igirisu: England
Igirisújin: Englishman
íi: good
iidásu: begin to say; come out
   with a remark, utter
iie: no
iimásu̧: *see yuu*
ika: squid, cuttlefish
ikága: how (hon.)
ikága desu̧ ka: how are you?
iké: pond
ikemasén: stop it! Don't do that!
ikimásu̧: *see iku*
iku: to go
íkura: how much
íku̧tsu: how many
íma: now
imásu̧: *see iru*
ími: meaning
imootó: younger sister
inaká: countryside
Índo: India
Indonéshia: Indonesia
infure: inflation

inku/inki: ink
inóru: to pray
inshoo: impression
inú: dog
ippai: full
íppai: one glassful, cupful
ippén ni: at once, at a time
irasshái: welcome!
irasshaimáse: welcome (hon.)
irasshaimásᵻ: see *irassháru*
irassháru: to come, go, be (hon.)
iremásᵻ: see *ireru*
ireru: to put in
iriguchi: entrance
irimásᵻ: see *ir-u*
iró: colour
iru: to be
ir-u: to need
isha: doctor
ishí: stone
ishookénmei: for all one is worth, desperately
isogashíi: busy
isogimásᵻ: see *isógu*
isógu: to hurry
issho-ni: together
isu: chair
itadaku: to receive (object hon.)
itái: painful, sore, to hurt
Itaria/Itarii: Italy
itasᵻ: to do (object hon.)
íto: thread
itóko: cousin
ítsu: when
itsᵻka: five days, 5th of the month
ítsuka: sometime, one day
iu: see *yuu*

iyá na: unpleasant, disagreeable

jáa: well then, in that case
jama: hindrance, nuisance
jí: o'clock, hour
jí: character, letter
jibikí: dictionary
jibun de: by oneself
jidai: period
jidóosha: car
jikan: time; hour
jíki: soon
jíko: accident
jiko-génba: scene of an accident
jimúsho: office
-jin: person; suffix of nationality
jínja: shrine
jinkoo: population
jishin: earthquake
jísho: dictionary
jitsú wa: actually, in fact
joodán: joke
jóogi: ruler
joozú na: to be skilful; to be good at
júu: ten
-juu: suffix, all through
juubún: sufficient, enough, plenty
júudoo: judo
júusho: address
júusu: (orange) juice

ka: interrogative particle 18
ka: or 66
-ka: lesson
ka: mosquito
kaban: bag, brief case
kabe: wall

kabuki: *Kabuki* (traditional theatre)
kabúru: to wear (a hat); put on (the head)
kachimásu: *see kátsu*
kachoo: head of a department
kádo: corner
kaerimásu: *see káer-u*
káer-u: to return home, go back
káesu: to return, give back
kágaku: science, chemistry
kagamí: mirror
káge: shade, shadow
-kágetsu: months
kagí: key
kago: basket; cage
kagu: to smell
kágu: furniture
kaídan: stairs, steps
kaigai-ryókoo: overseas trip, trip abroad
kaigan: coast, seaside
kaigí: conference (also *káigi*)
kaigichuu: in conference
kaigíshitsu: conference room
kai'in: member
kaimásu: *see kau*
kaimono: shopping
kaisha: company
káji: fire
kakarimásu: *see kakáru*
kakáru: to take, cost; be hanging; *denwa ga kakáru*: to be rung up; *byooki ni kakáru*: to catch a disease
kakéru: to hang; put over; apply; *denwa o kakéru*: to ring up
kakimásu: *see káku*

kakiowáru: to finish writing
káku: to write
kamá: kiln
kamaimasén: it doesn't matter
kámera: camera
kamí: paper
kaminóke: hair
kamoku: subject, course
kámo shiremasen: perhaps
-kan: suffix indicating duration 79
Kánada: Canada
kánai: wife; my wife
kanarazu: certainly, surely, without fail
kánari: fairly
kanashii: sad
kanban: signboard, sign
kánben shite kudasái: please forgive me; please excuse me
kanemochí: rich person
kangáeru: to think, consider
kangei: welcome, ovation
kangei suru: to welcome
kangófu: nurse
kanja: patient
kanji: Chinese characters
kanjóo: bill, account
Kánkoku: (South) Korea
kánojo: she
kanpai: a toast, cheers
kánsuru: about, concerning
kantan na: simple, easy, brief
kao: face
kaori: smell, fragrance
kara: because 96
kara: from 39
kara (-te): *see -te kara*
kará: empty

karada: body; health
karada o kowásu: to harm one's health
káre: he
karimásu: see *karu* and *kariru*
kariru: to borrow
karu: to mow, cut
karui: light; not heavy
kása: umbrella
kashimásu: see *kasu*
kasu: to lend
kata: person (hon.)
-*kata*: way of doing
katai: hard
katakána: a form of Japanese syllabary
kataná: sword
katazukéru: to tidy up, put away
kátsu: to win
kau: to buy
kawá: river
kawaíi: cute, appealing
kawáku: to dry up
kawaru: to change
kawatta: strange, peculiar
kayúi: itchy
kaze: wind; a cold
kazoéru: to count
kázoku: family
kázu: number, figure
keiken: experience
keikoo: tendency
keimusho: prison, gaol
keisatsu: the police
kéizai: economy, economics
keizai-séichoo: economic growth
kekkon: marriage
kekkon suru: to marry
kekkón-shiki: wedding ceremony

kékkoo desu: it's fine; it's all right; no thank you; I've had enough
kékkoo na: fine, wonderful
kemùri: smoke
-*ken*: numeral classifier for buildings
kén: ticket
kenbutsu: sightseeing
kenchíku: architecture
kenchikúka: architect
kenkoo: health
kenkoo na: healthy
kenkyuu: research, study
kenson na: modest, humble
kéredomo: but, however
késa: this morning
késhíki: scenery
kesu: to put out, extinguish
kí: tree
ki ga tsúku: to notice, realize
ki ni iru: to like, be pleased
ki ni suru: to worry
ki o tsúkéru: to be careful
kiéru: to go out, disappear
kikái: machine
kíkai: opportunity
kikaseru: to tell, relate
kikimásu: see *kíku*
kíkoeru: to be audible; can hear
kíku: to hear, listen; ask
kíku: chrysanthemum
kíku: to work, be effective
kimásu: see *kúru*
kimeru: to decide, fix, settle
kimi: you 262
kimochi: feeling; mood
kimono: kimono, Japanese garment

kín: gold
kindókei: gold watch
kin'en: no smoking
kíngyo: goldfish
kinoko: mushroom
kinoo: yesterday
kin'yóobi: Friday
kirai na: to dislike
kírei na: beautiful; clean
kirimásu̦: see *kír-u*
kíro: kilometre, kilogram
kiru: to wear
kír-u: to cut
ki̦sha: train
ki̦ssáten: tea shop, coffee shop
ki̦ta: north
ki̦tai suru: to expect, anticipate
ki̦tanái: dirty, filthy
ki̦tte: (postage) stamp
ki̦tto: surely, certainly
kke: retrospective question particle 265
ko: child
-ko: numeral classifier for miscellaneous objects
kochira: this one, this way
kochira kóso: me too; the pleasure is mine
kódai: ancient times
kodai-Ejip̦to: ancient Egypt
kodomo: child
kóe: voice
kóe ga suru: to hear a voice
koko: here 38
kokonoká: nine days; 9th of the month
kokónotș: nine
kokóro: heart; feelings; mind
kokuban: blackboard

kokuritș: national
kokuritsu-gékijoo: National Theatre
kok̦sai (teki): international
komáru: to be in trouble; become distressed; be at a loss
koméya: rice merchant; rice shop
kómu: to get crowded
kónban: this evening
konban wa: good evening
kóndo: this time; next time
kóngetsu: this month
konna: this kind of 121
konnichi wa: hello!; good day
kono: this 64
kono aida/konaida: recently, the other day
konogoro: these days
konóh̦to: he; this person
konokata: he; this person (hon.)
konshuu: this week
koo: like this
koo yuu: this kind of
koo yuu fúu na: this kind of
koo yuu fúu ni: like this
kooban: police-box
koochoo-senséi: headmaster
kooen: park
koohíi: coffee
koojoo: factory
kookoku: advertisement; announcement
kookuubin: airmail
koori: ice
koosui: perfume
kootsuu: traffic
kootsuu-jíko: traffic accident

kooyoo: autumn leaves
koozui: flood
kore: this 37
kore kara: now, from now on
koro: time; about when; about
korobu: to fall over
korosɨ: to kill
koshiraeru: to make; manufacture
koshoo (suru): (to) break down, malfunction
koshóo: pepper
kóso: emphatic particle, the very one
kotáeru: to answer
kotchí: here; this way; this one
koten-óngaku: classical music
kotó: thing; fact
kotó ga aru: to have done; to have experienced 109
kotó ga dekíru: to be able 106
kotó ni suru: to decide to 107
kotoba: words; language
kotoshi: this year
kotozuke: message
kottoohin: antique
kowái: to be frightened; frightening
kowaréru: to get broken
kowásu: to break
kozútsumi: parcel
ku: nine
-ku: adverb suffix 60
-ku nai: negative suffix 61
kuchi: mouth
kudámono: fruit
kudasái: please give me
kudasáru: to give 180
kúmo: spider

kúmo: cloud
kumóru: to cloud over; become cloudy
kun: familiar term of address for men and boys
kuni: country; one's native place
kúrabu: club
kurai: dark
kurasɨ: to live
kureru: to give 180
kuríininguya: dry cleaner('s)
kurói: black
kúru: to come
kuruma: cart; car
kɨsá: grass
kɨsái: smelly
kɨsaru: to rot; go bad
kɨshami: sneeze
kɨsuri: medicine; medication
kɨsuriya: chemist('s)
kɨtabiréru: to get tired; exhausted
kɨtsú: shoes
kɨtsu-úriba: shoe department/counter
kɨtsúya: shoemaker('s)
kúuki: air
kúuraa: cooler; air-conditioner
kuwashíi: detailed; to be well versed in
kyaku: guest; customer
kyakuma: guest room
kyakushɨtsu: sitting room
kyóku: tune
kyónen: last year
kyoo: today
kyoodai: brothers and sisters
kyooiku: education
kyóoju: professor

kyookai: church
kyóomi: interest
kyóomi o mótsu: to be interested in (in = *ni*)
kyoosanshúgi: communism
kyoosantoo: Communist Party
kyoosoo: competition; race
kyóri: distance
kyúu: nine
kyuukyúusha: ambulance
kyúuryoo: salary

ma ni áu: to be in time (for = *ni*)
máa máa: so so; not bad
máajan: mahjong
machí: town; district
machigaeru: to mistake
machigai: mistake, error
machigau: to be wrong; make a mistake
machimásu̦: *see mátsu̦*
máda: still, (not) yet
máde: as far as, until
máde ni: by, before
mádo: window
máe: front; *no máe ni*: in front of
magaru: to turn; go around
mai-: (prefix) each; every
-mai: numeral classifier for flat objects
máiasa: every morning
mainen: every year
máinichi: every day
máiru: to go, come (formal) 247
maitoshi: every year
man: ten thousand
mángaichi: just in case
mánshon: flat; apartment

mánzoku suru: to be satisfied
-masén: polite negative ending 18
-masén deshl̦ta: polite past negative ending 18
-máshl̦ta: polite past ending 18
-mashóo: polite propositive ending, let's 18
massúgu: straight ahead
mata: again; further
mata dóozo: please come again
mátchi: matches
mátșu: pine
mátșu: to wait
mázu: first; (not) at all
mé: eye
-me: ordinal suffix 227
méetoru: metre
mégane: spectacles, glasses
Méiji: the Meiji period (1868–1912)
meirei suru: to order
méiwaku: trouble, nuisance
mekata: weight
mémo: memo; memo pad
ménbaa: member
mendóo na: bothersome; difficult
meshiagaru: to eat (hon.)
mezurashíi: rare; unusual
miai: marriage meeting
michi: road
mídori: green
miéru: to be able to see; be visible
miéru: to come on a visit (hon.)
migaku: to polish; shine; clean
migi: right
migigawa: right-hand side

mígoto na: splendid, wonderful

mijikái: short

míkan: mandarin orange

mikka: three days; 3rd of the month

mimai: inquiry after a sick person

mimásu̱: see *míru*

mimí: ear

miná: all, everyone

minami: south

minásan: everyone; all of you; ladies and gentlemen (hon.)

minato: harbour, port

minna: all, everyone

minshushúgi: democracy

min'yoo: folk song

miokuru: to see off; send off

míru: to see

míruku: (condensed) milk

misé: shop

misemásu̱: see *miséru*

miséru: to show

mítai na: like, as 210

mitooshi: visibility; view

mitsu̱karu: to be found; be able to find

mitsu̱keru: to find

mittsu̱: three

miyage: souvenir; gift

mizu: water

mizuúmi: lake

mo: also, too; even

mo . . . mo . . .: both . . . and . . .

mochiagéru: to lift up

mochíron: of course

mokuyóobi: Thursday

momo: peach

momoiro: pink

món: gate

mondai: problem, question

mónku: words; phrases

mónku o yuu: to complain

monó: person (formal)

monó: thing

moo: more

móo: already

moo jíki: soon, right away

mooshiagéru: to say (object hon.) 250

mooshiwake arimasén: I'm terribly sorry; there's no excuse

móosu: to say; be called (formal)

morau: to receive, be given

mori: wood; grove

móshi: if

móshi moshi: hello (telephone)

motoméru: to seek; to buy (hon.) 249

mótsu: to have; hold

motte iku: to take

motte kúru: to bring

mótto: more

móttomo: most

moyori no: nearest

muda na: useless; a waste

muiká: six days; 6th of the month

mukashi: the past; long ago; formerly

mukau: to face; go towards

mukoo: opposite; over there; abroad

murá: village

murásaki: purple

múri na: unreasonable, fruitless, useless

mushi: insect
mushiatsúi: humid, sultry
musubu: to tie, link, join
musɯko: son
musumé: daughter
muzukashii: difficult
myóonichi: tomorrow (formal)

'*n desɯ*: the fact is 154
na: name
na: negative imperative particle 266
ná: sentence-final particle; isn't it 263
náa: same as *ná* above
nádo: et cetera, and so on
nagamé: view, outlook
-*nágara*: verbal suffix; while
nagaréru: to flow
nagásɯ: to wash away
nagúru: to beat, thrash
nái: to be not; to have not
-*nai*: see -anai
-*naide*: see -anaide
náifu: knife
náka: inside, middle
nakanáka: very, considerably
nakidásɯ: to burst out crying
nakigóe: cry; song (of bird, etc.)
naku: to cry
nakunaru: to die, pass away
nakɯsu: to lose
náma: raw; live (entertainment)
namae: name
namagusái: fishy (of smell or taste)
námida: tear
na no de: because it is 198
na no ni: although it is 169

nán: what
nána: seven
nanátsɯ: seven
nando mo: any number of times; very often
náni: what
nánika: something
nanimo: nothing 52
nankai mo: any number of times; very often
nanoka: seven days, 7th of the month
naóru: to be cured; get better; be fixed
naósɯ: to mend; cure
-*naósu*: to re . . . .
nára: if
naraihajiméru: to begin to learn
naráu: to learn
naréru: to become accustomed (to = *ni*)
narihajiméru: to start to become
narimásɯ: see *náru*
náru: to become
-*nasái*: imperative ending
nasáru: to do (hon.)
natsú: summer
natsu-yásumi: summer vacation
náze: why
né: sentence-final particle; isn't it, etc.
nedan: price
née: sentence-final particle; isn't it, etc.
nekasɯ: to put to bed
néko: cat
nékɯtai: tie
nemuraseru: to put to sleep
nemuru: to sleep

-*nen*: years

neru: to go to bed; lie down; sleep

netsú: heat; temperature; fever

nezumi: rat, mouse

ni: two

ni: indirect object particle 27

ni kánshⱼte: about, concerning

ni kánsuru (*no*) concerning, about (adjective)

ni tótte: for 201

ni tsúite(*no*): about, concerning 201

ni yoru to: according to

ni yotte: by (agent of passive) 222; in accordance with

niáu: to suit, become

-*nichi*: -days

nichiyóobi: Sunday

nigái: bitter

nigatsú: February

nigéru: to run away, escape

Nihón: Japan

Nihongo: Japanese (language)

Nihonjín: Japanese (person)

Nihonsei: Japanese (manufacture), made in Japan

nikú; meat

-*nikúi*: to be difficult to 218

nikúya: butcher, butcher's shop

nímotsⱼ: luggage; parcels

ningen: human being; person

ningyoo: doll

niói: smell, odour

nióu: to smell

Nippón: Japan (more formal pronunciation), *see Nihón*

niru: to take after; come to resemble

nishi: west

nite iru: to resemble, look like

niwa: garden

no: possessive particle 39

no: the fact; the one (nominalizing particle) 64

no: feminine sentence-final particle 265

no de: because 198

no desⱼ: *see 'n desⱼ* 154

no ni: although 265

noboru: to climb, go up

nochihodo: later, afterwards (formal)

nódo: throat

nódo ga kawakimáshⱼta: (I'm) thirsty

nokóru: to remain

nokósⱼ: to leave behind

nomimasⱼ: *see nómu*

nomímono: drink, beverage

nomisugíru: to drink too much

nómu: to drink

nóoto: exercise book, notebook

noriba: boarding place; (taxi) rank; (bus) station

norikáeru: to change (trains, buses, etc.)

norimásⱼ: *see noru*

noru: to get on; ride (*ni* after object); appear (in newspaper, etc.)

noseru: to put on, place on; give a ride to

núgu: to take off (clothes)

nureru: to get wet

nurinaósⱼ: to repaint

nuru: to paint; apply; rub on

nusúmu: to steal

núu: to sew

nyuugaku-shiken: entrance
examination

nyuuin suru: to go to hospital

nyúushi: entrance examination
(abbreviation)

nyúusu: news

o: object particle 27

o: along, through *etc.* 133

o-: hon. prefix 252

o-agari kudasái/nasái: please
come in; please eat

o-ari dés ka: have you got . . .?

oba: aunt

obáasan: grandmother, old
woman (hon.)

obasan: aunt (hon.)

oboemás: see *obóeru*

obóeru: to remember; learn

o-boosan: Buddhist priest

o-cha: tea

o-cha o ireru: to make tea

ochíru: to fall; fail
(examination)

ochitsuku: to settle down; be
calm

o-daiji ni: take care of yourself

o-dekake dés ka: are you
going out?

odoróita: Oh! Ah! You
frightened me! (exclamation
of surprise)

odorokás: to surprise

odoróku: to be surprised

odoru: to dance

o-fúro: bath

o-génki dés ka: how are you?
Are you well?

o-hayoo gozaimás: good
morning

o-hima: spare time (hon.)

o-híru: midday; lunch

o-ide ni náru: to come; go (hon.)

o-ikutsu: how old; how many
(hon.)

oishii: delicious, tasty

o-isogashíi: busy (hon.)

o-itokosan: cousin (hon.)

o-jama shimáshita: goodbye;
sorry to have bothered you

o-jama shimás: hello; may I
come in? Sorry to bother you

oji: uncle

ojíisan: grandfather, old man
(hon.)

ojisan: uncle; middle-aged man
(hon.)

ojóosan: miss; young lady;
daughter (hon.)

okáasan: mother (hon.)

o-kaeri dés ka: are you leaving?
Are you going home?

o-kaeri nasái: welcome back;
hello

o-kagesama de: yes, thank you;
fortunately; thanks to you

o-kake kudasái: please sit down

o-kane: money

o-káshi: cakes

okashíi: funny, strange

okáwari wa ikága dés ka:
would you like another
helping?

o-ki ni iru: to like, be pleased
(hon.) 248

o-ki ni meshimáshita ka: did you
like it? Were you satisfied?

o-ki ni mésu: to like, be pleased (hon.) 248

o-ki no doku désu: what a pity, I am sorry to hear that

o-kiki shimásu: excuse my asking; would you mind telling me

okimásu: see *óku* and *okíru*

okíru: to get up

okóru: to happen

okóru: to get angry, be offended

oku: to place, put

óku: (one) hundred million

o-kuchi ni awánai deshoo ga: I hope you like it (of food), it might not be to your liking but . . .

okureru: to be late (for = *ni*)

okurimásu: see *okuru*

okurimono: present

okuru: to send

ókusan: wife (hon.)

ókusan mo go-issho désu ka: will your wife be coming with you? Is your wife with you?

o-kyakusan: guest; customer; audience

o-machidoosama déshita: sorry to have kept you waiting

o-mae: you (very familiar; used by men only)

o-mátase shimashita: sorry to keep you waiting

o-máwarisan: policeman

o-me ni kakáru: to meet (object hon.) 250

o-míyage: souvenir; gift

omócha: toy

o-mochi désu ka: have you got . . .? 249

o-mochi shimashóo ka: shall I carry it for you?

omói: heavy

omoidásu: to recall, remember

omoshirói: interesting; amusing

omoté: front, outside

omóu: to think

onaji: same

onaka: stomach, abdomen

onaka ga sukimásu: to get hungry

onaka o kowásu: to get an upset stomach

o-namae: name (hon.)

o-namae wa nán to osshaimásu ka: what is your name? (hon.)

o-néesan: elder sister (hon.)

o-negai shimásu: please; I'd be obliged if you would do it for me

óngaku: music

o- . . . ni náru: hon. verb 248

o-níisan: elder brother (hon.)

onná: woman

onnagata: actor of female roles in Kabuki

onnanohító: woman

onnánoko: girl

onnarashíi: feminine

onsen: hot spring

óoame: heavy rain

óoba: overcoat

óoi: many, numerous

óoki na: big, large

ookíi: big, large

ookisa: size

Oosaka: Osaka

oosugimásu: to be too many, too numerous

Oosｻtoráriya: Australia

oozei: a large number (of people)

ópera: opera

ore: I (vulgar, masculine) 262

orénji: orange

origami: paper folding

oríru: to get off; go down; come down

óru: to be (formal) 247

óru: to bend; to fold; to break; to weave

o-sake: rice wine, sake

o-sakｉ: in fronf; first (hon.)

o-saki ni dóomo: excuse my going first; goodbye

o-saki ni dóozo: please go first; after you

o-séwa ni naru: to be looked after

o-séwa suru: to take care of

o-sewasamá deshｊta: thank you for your help

o-sháberi (o) suru: to chatter, talk, gossip, chat

oshiemásｻ: see *oshiéru*

oshiéru: to teach

osoi: late (adjective)

osoku: late (adverb)

o-sómatsｻsama deshｊta: sorry it was such a simple meal

osóraku: probably

osóre irimasｻ: excuse me, I'm sorry

osowaru: to learn, be taught

ossháru: to speak, say (hon.)

ossháru tóori desｻ: it is as you say

o-sumai: house, dwelling (hon.)

o-sumai ni náru: to live, dwell (hon.) 249

o-sumai wa dóchira desｻ ka: where do you live?

o-taku: house (hon.); you

o-teárai: lavatory, toilet

o-tésuu desu ga: sorry to trouble you, but . . .

o-tétsudai(san): maid, household help

o-tétsudai shimashóo ka: shall I help you?

otokonohitó: man

otokónoko: boy

otokorashíi: manly

otómo: company

otómo shｊte mo yoroshii désｻ ka: may I accompany you?

otona: adult

otonashíi: gentle; mild; meek; obedient

otóosan: father

otootó: younger brother

otósｻ: to drop, let fall

otótoshi: the year before last

otsｻkarésama deshｊta: you must be tired

otsuri: change

o-uchi: house (hon.)

o-wakari désｻ ka: do you understand?

owaru: to finish

oyá: parent

o-yasumi: holiday; rest (hon.)

o-yasami nasái: good night!

o-yasumi ni náru: to go to bed, sleep (hon.) 249

oyogimásｻ: see *oyógu*

oyógu: to swim
o-yu: hot water

páatii: party
pán: bread
pánfuretto: pamphlet
pán'ya: baker, bakery
pasu̧póoto: passport
pén: pen
pénki: paint
piano: piano
píkunikku: picnic
puréeyaa: record player
purézento: present

ráigetsu̧: next month
rainen: next year
raishuu: next week
rájio: radio
rakú na: easy, comfortable
-(r)areru̧: passive ending 222
-rashíi: -like 210
-(r)éba: conditional suffix 170
reizóoko: refrigerator
rekóodo: record
renraku suru: to contact
renshuu suru: to practise
ressha: locomotive, train
résu̧toran: restaurant
ringo: apple
rippa na: splendid, fine
-ro: imperative suffix 266
róbii: lobby, foyer
roku: six
ronbun: thesis
Róshia: Russia
Roshiago: Russian (language)
ryoken: passport
ryoken-bángoo: passport
   number

ryokoo suru: to travel
ryoohóo (tomo): both
ryóoji: consul
ryoojíkan: consulate
ryóori: cooking; food
ryóori suru: to cook
ryóoshin: parents
ryúuchoo na: fluent

sá: sentence-final particle 273
sabishíi: lonely
sado: tea ceremony
sae: even
sáe . . . -reba: if only 170
sagasu: to look for
saifu: wallet, purse
saikin: recently
saisho: first
sakana: fish
sakanaya: fish shop, fish monger
sakaya: *sake* merchant, *sake*
   liquor shop
saki: first, beforehand
saki̧hodo: just now; a while ago
sákkaa: soccer
sákki: just now, a while ago
sakkyoku̧ suru: to compose
   (music)
saku: to bloom
sakújitsu: yesterday (formal)
sakura: cherry blossom
saku̧sen: strategy
samúi: cold
samurai: warrior
san: three
-san: form of address, Mr Mrs
   Miss
sanpoo suru: to go for a walk
saraishuu: the week after next

-(s)aseru: causative ending 234

-(s)asete itadaku: formal request form 236

sasetsu: left hand turn

sashiagéru: to give (object hon.)

sashimi: raw fish

sásu: to sting; poke; indicate

satóo: sugar

sawaru: to touch (*ni* after object)

sayonará/sayoonará: goodbye

sé: stature, height

se ga hĩkúi: to be short

se ga takái: to be tall

sebiro: suit

séeru: sale

séetaa: sweater, pullover

seichoo: growth

seichoo suru: to grow

séifu: government

seiji: politics

seikatsĩ: life; existence

seikatsĩ suru: to live

seikoo suru: to succeed

seiri suru: to put in order

seisaku: policy

seiseki: results, record

sékai: world

séki: seat; place

sekken: soap

semái: narrow

sén: thousand

séngetsu: last month

senjitsú: the other day

senjitsu wa dóomo: thank you for the other day

senpúuki: (electric) fan

senséi: teacher; Dr, Mr (title of respect)

senshuu: last week

sensoo: war

-seru: *see -saseru*

setsumei suru: to explain

setsuyaku suru: to economize, save

shaberisugíru: to talk too much

shabéru: to talk, chat

shachoo: company director, president

shákai: society

sháko: garage

shashin: photograph

shi: four

shi: and 236

shiai: match; game

shibai: play (theatre)

shibáraku: for a while

shibáraku desĩ né: it has been a long time, hasn't it?

shĩchi: seven

shigéru: to grow thickly, be dense

shigoto: work, job

shigoto suru: to work, do a job

shihajiméru: to start to do

shíjuu: all the time, from start to finish

shĩka (+ neg. verb): only

shikaru: to scold

shĩkáshĩ: but, however

shĩkata: way of doing

shĩkata ga nái: it can't be helped; nothing can be done about it

shĩkén: examination

shimá: island

shimáru: to close, become closed

shimásu: see suru
shimátta: damn! blast!
shimau: to finish; put away
shiméru: to close, shut
shimi: stain
shinamono: article, goods
shinbun: newspaper
shingoo: signal; traffic lights
shinimásu: see shinu
shinjíru: to believe
Shinkánsen: 'new trunk line'; 'bullet train'
shinpai suru: to worry
shinseki: relation, relative
shinsen na: fresh
shínsetsu na: kind
shinshítsu: bedroom
shintai-kénsa: medical examination
shinu: to die
shin'yóojoo: letter of credit
shió: salt
shirabéru: to investigate, check; look up
shirimásu: see shiru
shirói: white
shiru: to get to know
shíryoo: materials, records
shíta: bottom, lower part; under
shítsu: quality
shítsumon suru: to ask, question
shítsúrei shimasu: goodbye; excuse me
shiyákusho: town hall, city hall
shiyoo: way of doing
shiyoo ga nái: it's no good, it can't be helped
shízuka na: quiet, peaceful
shokúyoku: appetite

shoochi: see go-shoochi
shoochi suru: to consent, assent, agree to
shoodan: business discussions
shóohin: product
shoojíki na: honest, frank
shookai suru: to introduce
shóorai: future
shoosetsu: novel
shóoshoo: a little
Shóowa: year period 1926–1989
shorui: papers, documents
shótchuu: all the time
shújin: husband, master
shúkudai: homework
shúppatsu: departure
shúppatsu suru: to leave, depart
shúrui: type, kind
shússeki: attendance
shússeki suru: to be present; attend
shuumatsu: weekend
shúuri suru: to repair
shuutome: mother-in-law
sóba: near
sóbo: grandmother
sófu: grandfather
soko: there (by you) 38
soko: bottom, base
sokútatsu: express delivery
sonna: that kind of 121
sono: that (adjective) 64
sóo: so, that way
sóo desu (after verb): they say; I hear; apparently 132; (after verb stem) it looks like . . .
sóo desu ka: is that so?
soodan: discussion
soodan suru: to discuss

sooji suru: to clean
soo'on: noise
sóra: sky
sore: that (by you) 37
sore déwa: in that case; then
sore jáa: in that case; then
sore kara: next; after that
Sóren: the Soviet Union
sórosoro: soon
sóru: to shave
sóshịte: and
sotchí: that one, that way
sóto: outside
sotsugyoo/suru: to graduate (from = *o*)
subarashíi: wonderful
subéru: to slip
subete: every
sugi: after, past
sugíru: to exceed, go past
-sugíru: to be too
sugóku: terribly, awfully
sugósụ: to spend, pass (time)
súgu: immediately, straight away
suiei: swimming
suiyóobi: Wednesday
sụkíi: skiing
sụkimásụ: *see sụku*
sụkí na: to like, be fond of
sụkína dake: as much as you like
sụkiyaki: beef broiled in soy sauce
sụkóshi: a little
sụku: to become empty
sụkunái: few, not many
sumai: *see o-sumai*
sumáu: to live, dwell
sumie: ink painting; brush and ink painting

sumimasén (ga): I'm sorry but . . . Excuse me, but . . .
sumimásụ: *see súmu*
súmu: to live, dwell
suna: sand
Sụpéin: Spain
sụpóotsu: sport
suru: to do
súru: to pick a pocket, steal
sushí: vinegared rice with raw fish, etc.
susumeru: to recommend
sụtándo: standard lamp
sụtéeki: steak
sụteki na: lovely, wonderful
sụtéru: to throw away
suu: to suck, smoke
súupaa: supermarket
suutsụkéesụ: suitcase
suwaru: to sit down
suzume: sparrow
suzushíi: cool

-ta: past-tense suffix 106
-ta bákari desụ: to have just . . . 166
ta hóo ga íi desụ: to be better to . . . 120
tabako: cigarette
tabemásụ: *see tabéru*
tabemonó: food
tabéru: to eat
tabesugi: overeating
tábun: probably
-tachi: plural suffix 38
táda: only
tadáima: I'm here! just now
-tagáru: to want to . . . 199
-tai: to want to 62

taihéiyoo: Pacific Ocean

taihen: very; terrible, awful

taik⊎tsu na: boring

taik⊎tsu suru: to get bored

táipu o útsu: to type

taipuráitaa: typewriter

táiriku: continent

taiséiyoo: Atlantic Ocean

taisetsu na: valuable; important

táishi: ambassador

taishĮkan: embassy

Taishoo: year period 1912–1926

taisoo: exercise, physical training

táiyoo: sun

takái: high; expensive

tákak⊎ ts⊎ku: to work out expensive; cost a lot

takasugíru: to be too expensive

take: bamboo

táko: kite; octopus

tak⊎sán: a lot

ták⊎shii: taxi

tak⊎shii-nóriba: taxi-rank

tamá ni: occasionally; from time to time

tamágo: egg

tamé: for the sake of 224

tanjóobi: birthday

tanómu: to ask; request

tanoshíi: enjoyable

tanoshími ni shĮte imas⊎: I'm looking forward to it

tansu: cupboard; chest of drawers

-tara: if 168

-tári: frequentative/alternative suffix 209

tariru: to be enough; suffice

táshĮka ni: certainly; no doubt

tas⊎káru: to be saved; to be a help

tas⊎kéru: to help; save, rescue

tatémono: building

táts⊎: to stand

táts⊎: to leave

(yakú ni) táts⊎: to be useful

tatta: only

té: hand

té ga hanasenai: to be occupied; be busy

té ni háiru: to be obtained, get; come by

-te: suffix for gerund, '-te form' 90

-te agemás⊎: see -te ageru

-te ageru: to do (for a respected person) 182

-te arimás⊎: see -te áru

-te áru: to have been done 93

-te iku: to go on getting more . . . 185

-te imás⊎: see -te iru

-te iru: is/are . . . ing 92

-te itadakemasén ka: would you mind . . . ing; please . . . 183

-te itadaku: to have something done (by a respected person) 183

-te kara: after 130

-te kudasái: please 180

-te kudasáru: (a respected person) does something for someone 182

-te kúru: to go and . . .; to start to . . .; become more and more . . . 185

-*te míru*: to try . . . ing; do and
  see 184

-*te mo íi desy ka*: may (I)?; is it
  all right? 120

-*te morau*: to have someone do
  something for one 183

-*te oku*: to leave done; to do in
  preparation; do and set aside
  184

-*te sashitsykae arimasén ka*: is
  there any objection to . . .?
  may I . . . 230

-*te shıkata ga nái*: to be
  intolerably . . .; be dying
  to . . . 260

-*te tamaranai*: to be dying
  to . . . 258

-*te wa ikemasén*: must not . . .
  120

-*te yaru*: to do something for a
  social inferior 182

techoo: notebook; pocket-book

teeburu: table

tegami: letter

téido: extent

téire: care; looking after

téire suru: to care for; look after
  (garden, car, etc.)

teiryuujo: (bus) stop

tekıtoo na: suitable

ten'in: shop assistant

ténisy: tennis

tenjoo: ceiling

ténki: weather

tenki-yóhoo: weather report;
  forecast

tenpura: fish and vegetables
  deep fried in batter

tenránkai: exhibition

térebi: television

tetsy: iron

tetsudái: helper; maid. *see*
  o-tétsudai(san)

tetsudau: to help

to: with; and 65

to: quotative particle 172

to: clause-final particle; when,
  whenever 131

tobasy: to make fly; drive fast;
  hit

tobimásy: *see tobu*

tobu: to fly

tochuu (de): (on) the way

todokéru: to report; deliver

todóku: to reach; be delivered

tóka: and, and so on 66

tokei: watch, clock

toki: time; when

tokoro: place

tokoya: barber, barber's shop

tóku ni: especially, particularly

tomaru: to stop; stay

tomodachi: friend

tonari: next door; neighbouring

tóo: ten

Toodai: Tokyo University
  (abbreviation)

tooi: distant; far

tooká: ten days, 10th of the
  month

tooki: pottery

tookú ni: in the distance

Tookyoo: Tokyo

Tookyoo-dáigaku: Tokyo
  University

tóori: way; road; *yuu tóori*: as
  one says

tóoron suru: to debate

tóoru: to pass; go through
torákku: truck
tori: bird; chicken (food)
torikáeru: to change, exchange
tóru: to take
to shịte: as 96
toshiyóri: old person
toshókan: library
totemo: very
totsuzen: suddenly
tottemo: very
tsugí: next, following
tsugí kara tsugí e: one after the other
tsuitachí: 1st day of the month
tsụkamaru: to be caught
tsụkaremásụ: see *tsụkaréru*
tsụkaréru: to get tired
tsụkau: to use
tsụkéru: to put on, attach
tsụkí: moon
tsụkimásụ: see *tsụku*
tsụku: to arrive; to stick, to be attached
tsụku, tákaku tsụku: to be expensive, work out expensive
tsụkue: desk
tsụkurikatá: way of making
tsụkurinaósụ: to remake
tsụkuriowáru: to finish making
tsukúru: to make
tsúma: wife
tsumaránai: uninteresting; trifling
tsuméru: to pack in; bunch together
tsumetai: cold
tsumori: intention 132

tsurete iku: to take (a person)
tsuri: fishing
tsụtoméru: to work (for = *ni*) to strive
tsutsúji: azalea
-tsuu: numerical classifier for letters
tsuyói: strong
tsuzukéru: to keep on . . . ing; to continue to
tte: quotative particle 269

uchi: house
uchi: while 200
uchi no: our, my
uekáeru: to transplant
uekịbachi: flower pot; plant pot
ueru: to plant
ugokásu: to move (transitive)
ugóku: to move (intransitive)
ugúisu: warbler, Japanese nightingale
uísụkii: whisky
ukagaimásụ: see *ukagau*
ukagau: to ask; visit (object hon.)
ukéru: to receive
ukétoru: to receive (a letter etc.)
umá: horse
umái: to be good at; skilful, tasty
úmi: sea
umibé: seaside
unten suru: to drive
unténshu: driver
urayamashíi: to envy, be enviable
ureshíi: happy
urikire: sold out

uru: to sell
urusái: noisy, bothersome
usetsu: right-hand turn
ushi: cow; bull
ushinau: to lose
ushiro: back; behind
úso: lie
usui: thin
utá: song, poem
utá o utau: to sing (a song)
utau: to sing
útsu: to hit; send (a telegram)
utsᵤkushíi: beautiful

wa: topic particle 37, 155
wa: feminine sentence final
  particle 264
wá: wheel; hoop, ring
waishatsᵤ: shirt
wakarimásᵤ: *see wakáru*
wakáru: to understand
wakasᵤ: to boil (water)
wanpíisu: dress; one-piece
waraidásᵤ: to burst out laughing
warau: to laugh
wareru: to break
warúi: bad
washi: I (used by old men)
wasureru: to forget
watakᵤshi: I (formal)
wataru: to cross
watashi: I 38
watasᵤ: to cross
wázawaza: deliberately,
  expressly

ya: and 66
yáa: oh! hey! hi!
yahári: as expected, to be sure

yakkyoku: pharmacy, chemist
  (shop)
yaku: to burn, grill, roast
yakú: role
yakú ni tátsᵤ: to be useful
yakunin: government official
yakᵤsha: actor
yakᵤsoku: promise, appointment
yakᵤsokᵤ suru: to promise
yakyúu: baseball
yamá: mountain
yaméru: to give up; stop; retire;
  abandon
yamu: to stop
yáne: roof
yarimásᵤ: *see yaru*
yarinaósu: to redo
yaru: to do; give (to an inferior);
  send (on an errand)
yasai: vegetable
yasemásᵤ: *see yaseru*
yaseru: to get thin
yasúi: cheap
-yasúi: to be easy to 227
yasumi: holiday; rest, break
yasumimásu: *see yasúmu*
yasumono: cheap (and nasty)
  thing
yasúmu: to rest; to go to bed,
  sleep (euphemistic hon.)
yattsú: eight
-yo: sentence-final particle;
  emphatic 28
-yo: imperative suffix 267
yoaké: dawn, daybreak
yogosu: to soil, dirty
yoimásᵤ: *see yóu*
yókatta: it was good, good; I'm
  glad

yokka: four days, 4th of the month
yoko: side; beside
yóku: well; often
yomihajiméru: to start to read
yomimásu: see *yómu*
yomitsuzukéru: to keep on reading
yómu: to read
yon: four
yóo: like, as
yóo: business, things to do
yóo ni: so that; indirect command 172
-(y)óo to suru: to try to 196
yoofuku: western clothes
yoofuku-dánsu: wardrobe
yooji: business, things to do
yooka: eight days, 8th of the month
yóokoso: welcome
Yooróppa: Europe
yori: than 144
yorokobásu: to delight, make happy
yorokóbu: to be pleased
yorokónde: with pleasure
yoroshii: good (hon.)
yoroshii désu ka: is it all right? Do you mind?
yoroshíku: well, suitably; give my regards; please do what you can for me
yoru: to call at, drop in (at = *ni*)
yoru, ni yoru to: according to
yóru: night; at night
yosó: elsewhere, another place
yotei: plan 132

yotte (ni yotte): by (agent of passive)
yótto: yacht
yottsú: four
yóu: to get drunk
yowái: weak
yu: hot water (see *o-yu*)
yubí: finger
yubí o sásu: to point
yubiwa: ring
yude-támago: boiled egg
yukí: snow
-yuki: bound for . . . , to . . .
yukkúri: slowly
yukue-fúmei: whereabouts unknown
yumé: dream
yumé o míru: to dream
yunyuu suru: to import
yushutsu suru: to export
yuu: to say (most forms based on *iu*)
yuube: last night
yuubínkyoku: post office
yuugata: evening
yuugóhan: dinner, evening meal
yuumei na: famous
yuu'utsu na: gloomy, depressing
yuzuru: to hand over, give up, bequeath

záisan: fortune, property
zannén deshíta: what a pity! What a shame!
zannen-nágara: unfortunately
zashíkí: Japanese-style sitting room
zasshi: magazine

ze: emphatic sentence final
  particle 263
zéhi: certainly, without fail
Zén: Zen (Buddhist sect)
zénbu: all
zenzen: (not) at all
zo: emphatic sentence-final
  particle 263
-zu: negative suffix *see -(a)zu*
  237
zubón: trousers
zútsu: each
zutsuu: headache
zutto: all the way, all the time

GRAMMAR INDEX

SP (Sentence Pattern) refers to the page where there is an example of the grammar in a sentence patterns section. The last column gives the page where the grammar is explained in the main text.